The Anointed

New York's White-Shoe Law Firms— How They Started, How They Grew, and How They Ran the Country

Jeremiah D. Lambert and Geoffrey S. Stewart

Guilford, Connecticut

An imprint of The Rowman & Littlefield Publishing Group, Inc.
4501 Forbes Blvd., Ste. 200
Lanham, MD 20706
www.rowman.com

Distributed by NATIONAL BOOK NETWORK

British Library Cataloguing in Publication Information Available

Library of Congress Cataloging-in-Publication Data available

Names: Lambert, Jeremiah D., 1934– author. | Stewart, Geoffrey S., author.
Title: The anointed : New York's white-shoe law firms : how they started, how they grew, and how they ran the country / Jeremiah D. Lambert and Geoffrey S. Stewart.
Description: Guilford, Connecticut : Lyons Press, 2020. | Includes bibliographical references and index. | Summary: "The story of how and why such powerhouse Wall Street law firms as Cravath, Swaine & Moore, Davis Polk & Wardwell, and Sullivan & Cromwell grew from nineteenth-century entrepreneurial origins into icons of institutional law practice, and how, as white-shoe bastions with the social standards of an exclusive gentleman's club, they promoted the values of an East Coast elite"— Provided by publisher.
Identifiers: LCCN 2020013519 (print) | LCCN 2020013520 (ebook) | ISBN 9781493056330 (hardback) | ISBN 9781493056347 (epub)
Subjects: LCSH: Law—United States—History—20th century. | Law firms—New York (State)—New York—History—20th century. | Davis, Polk & Wardwell—History—20th century. | Sullivan & Cromwell—History—20th century. | Cravath, Swaine & Moore—History—20th century.
Classification: LCC KF371 .L36 2020 (print) | LCC KF371 (ebook) | DDC 338.7/61340097471—dc23
LC record available at https://lccn.loc.gov/2020013519
LC ebook record available at https://lccn.loc.gov/2020013520

The paper used in this publication meets the minimum requirements of American National Standard for Information Sciences—Permanence of Paper for Printed Library Materials, ANSI/NISO Z39.48-1992.

To Sanda Lambert, for her support, insight, love.

Jeremiah D. Lambert

Contents

Introduction

At mid-century and before, three Wall Street law firms, clustered in offices in lower Manhattan, set the tone for and dominated the corporate bar in New York and far beyond. The authors, in earlier incarnations, were associates at two such firms, Cravath, Swaine & Moore and Davis Polk & Wardwell. Informed by their personal experience, this is the story of how and why these firms and their peer, Sullivan & Cromwell, grew from nineteenth-century entrepreneurial origins into icons of institutional law practice; how, as white-shoe bastions with the social standards of an exclusive gentlemen's club, they promoted the values of an East Coast elite; and how they adapted to a radically changed legal world, surviving existential changes in American society and the legal profession. The history recounted here is more than a chronicle of a tiny law firm elite. It instead reflects, within a narrow but critical set of institutions, major developments in the nation's social and economic life.

It is no accident that these firms are found in New York, the largest city in the world's largest economy and also the nation's largest port, principal banking center, and epicenter of industry. At the dawn of the twentieth century, linked by canals, railroads, telegraph and telephone lines, transatlantic steamships and undersea cables, New York became the economic nerve center of the United States. It also wielded formidable political power, staffing the highest levels of the Departments of Justice, State, Treasury, and War and supplying virtually every President or Vice President of the United States between the Civil War and the First World War.

Boston, Chicago, and Philadelphia rivaled New York but could not displace it. Unlike its urban competitors New York was Dutch in origin, a city of traders and adventurers, thought to be crass, immoral and focused on the main chance. It became the channel for the rivers of European capital needed to build the nation's railroads, mines, and factories. It was also home to giant industrial trusts, monopolies in oil, steel, copper, lead, rubber, telephony, and tobacco financed by New York banks. J. P. Morgan, Andrew Carnegie, John D. Rockefeller, William Clark, Marcellus Hartley and other moguls lived near each other in Manhattan and had country homes close by. With fortunes to be made, they found it easy to navigate political corruption and accommodate the moral ambiguities of the Gilded Age.

Almost without exception, each of these men—and there were no women—was a white Anglo-Saxon Protestant. Despite the flood of Catholics from Ireland, Italy, and elsewhere in Europe, none was to be found in the upper ranks of industry, banking, and society at large. Equally absent were Jews, even those of educated German origin, who created a parallel power structure in banking and other sectors of the economy but were not part of the New York establishment and faced pervasive, vitriolic anti-Semitism. It goes without saying that no Blacks, Asians, or other people of color were part of this world.

Successful lawyers typically adopt the protective coloration of their clients. And so it was that the upper echelon of the organized bar proved a faithful reflection of the men who owned the nation's banks, steel mills, railroads and industrial enterprises. Leading lawyers often lived within blocks of their clients, worked near them in lower Manhattan, belonged to the same clubs, and, if sufficiently prominent, attended the same social functions. The lineage of many firms, ostensibly competitors, could be traced to a single nineteenth century lawyer, Walter S. Carter. Cravath, Swaine & Moore; Sullivan & Cromwell; and Davis Polk & Wardwell, among others, were collectively a WASP citadel, small in size by today's standards but enormously influential. They employed each other's sons, served similar clients, and operated with a gentlemen's set of unwritten rules. Yet theirs was not a genteel enterprise. Beneath the gentlemanly veneer, establishment lawyers assembled monopolies; fought off social legislation; co-opted political machines; litigated patent cases that defined ownership of the future; marketed the debt of foreign countries; and, in one instance, fomented a political revolution. In a few cases otherwise upstanding members of the bar were even called upon to fix juries, water stock, conceal assets, bribe judges, and alter documents. It was, in short, a ruffians' game, if one played by gentlemen.

Early on the New York bar had within it the outlines of the large law firms that dominate the practice in the city today. The 1889 edition of the Trow Directory of New York City shows former (and future) President Grover Cleveland, Francis Lynde Stetson, Charles W. Bangs, Charles Edward Tracy, and Francis S. Bangs practicing together in the firm of Bangs, Stetson, Tracy & MacVeigh (today's Davis Polk & Wardwell) at 45 William Street. On a different floor of the same building were Thomas G. Shearman, John W. Sterling, and John A. Garver, in the firm already known as Shearman & Sterling. Two minutes away, at 3 Broad Street, the redoubtable William Nelson Cromwell was practicing law with William J. Curtis and Algernon S. Sullivan at Sullivan & Cromwell.[1] According to Hubbell's Legal Directory for Lawyers and Business Men, by 1892, the great Paul D. Cravath—the creator of the modern law firm—was around the corner at 120 Broadway, in partnership with John W. Houston, having just parted ways with future Supreme Court Chief Justice and Presidential candidate Charles Evans Hughes. That address also housed the venerable firm of Lord, Day & Lord, consisting of five partners, each named either Day or Lord. At 10 Wall Street was the firm of Simpson, Thacher & Barnum, and a few doors down were the lawyers who were to become Cadwalader, Wickersham & Taft. Four blocks away was the firm Root & Clark, where Elihu Root—a future Secretary of State, Secretary of War, and Nobel Laureate—partnered with Samuel B. Clarke and Joseph Kunzmann.[2]

Some years later John W. Davis, the Dulles brothers, and John J. McCloy, partners in Davis Polk, Sullivan & Cromwell, and Cravath, respectively, also worked at the intersection of law and major political office. Even more than banking or industry, law was the doorway to elevated public service. "[I]n a divinely ordained system of free enterprise," wrote one of Louis Auchincloss' literary characters, "corporation lawyers were the high priests of the Deity."[3] It is no surprise, given the abilities of these men, that the law firms they founded or led would survive and define the character of American legal practice until well after mid-century. Yet the story of how this happened is not an obvious one, nor necessarily admirable. Instead it reflects the sharp distinctions of class, ethnicity, and wealth in the broader society. These markers changed slowly and grudgingly. Old-line law firms had to adapt or disband.

Wall Street law firms typically recruited ambitious, well-credentialed young men (seldom, if ever, women) from Harvard, Yale, Columbia, and a handful of other law schools. The demographics of an entering associate class tilted heavily toward products of eastern prep schools and elite colleges with the right family lineage, religion, and social background. As late as the 1960s more than two-thirds of Davis Polk partners were listed in the Social Register. The white-shoe[4] label suggested gentility and visions of summer associates wearing white bucks and straw boaters to tony law offices; it also meant the likely exclusion of anyone who was not a WASP male—especially Jews, who in the 1950s and 1960s still struggled to get hired by establishment firms.

The white-shoe ethos also shaped the practice conducted by Wall Street law firms. By the middle of the twentieth century, they came to disfavor litigation, bankruptcy, and real estate law as the province of lesser practitioners and unbecoming practice areas for elite counsel. In his history of the Cravath firm, published in 1948, Robert T. Swaine declared: "Big Business of today is less litigious than were the rugged individualist merchants and manufacturers of the old days; the modern corporate client expects its business so to be handled as to keep it out of the courts."[5] Swaine favored instead the "solicitor working out at his desk a complicated reorganization or security issue"—the staple of big-time corporate law. To Paul Cravath great lawyering took place in the conference room, not the court room. Litigation implied a failed transaction, not a strategic tool exercised by corporate clients. The snobbish preference of old-line WASP firms to avoid the taint of grittier practice areas eventually created openings for newcomers and disfavored Jewish law firms.

Small as they were by present-day standards, white-shoe Wall Street firms developed institutional and specialized practices, built around anchor corporate and banking clients. Each of Chase Manhattan, Morgan Guaranty, Marine Midland, Chemical Bank, Goldman Sachs, Morgan Stanley and Kuhn Loeb had a primary Wall Street law firm that handled its affairs. The resulting relationships were inviolate and long-lasting. Soliciting business from another firm's mainstream client was almost unthinkable. Although the firms were nominally competitors, they resembled a legal cartel, often housed in the same office buildings (15 Broad Street and later One Chase Manhattan Plaza, each in New York's downtown financial district), drawing on the same pool of associate lawyers, and paying them roughly equal salaries. From the early 1960s to the 1990s, Cravath and Davis Polk were just an elevator ride apart at One Chase. Sullivan & Cromwell was nearby at 48 Wall Street.

Each firm had a compact tier of partners, supported by a much larger group of associate lawyers, "youthful barristers . . . coming out of the law schools and plunging into the hoppers and mills of Lex."[6] Firms followed an up-or-out policy, pioneered by Cravath, in which many were called but few were chosen, usually after an apprenticeship of eight or ten years. Associates were culled from the best law school graduates, who then competed with each other for a few coveted partner slots, working long hours in pursuit of an elusive holy grail. Those who left or were gently pushed out often took corporate counsel jobs or became partners in other law firms. Many emigres became successful, even rich and famous.

As old-line religious and ethnic prejudices faded in the nation at large, white-shoe dominance of the legal world began to erode. In the 1960s once-disregarded Jewish law firms hired talented Ivy League law school graduates unable to crack the Wall Street citadel and moved into practice areas then ignored or underserved. By 1980 those firms, described by one observer as an "incredible success story," accounted for four of the ten largest firms in New York. Law firms in other cities also enjoyed explosive growth; Houston alone became home to three of the country's ten largest firms. Skadden Arps, founded in 1948, grew rich and powerful advising corporations engaged in proxy contests and takeover battles, work originally disdained by the likes of Sullivan & Cromwell and Simpson Thacher but a signature specialty of Joe Flom, Skadden's dynamo M&A—mergers and acquisitions—partner. Successful midtown law firms, including Paul, Weiss, Rifkind, Wharton & Garrison and Kaye, Scholer, Fierman, Hays & Handler, also threatened white-shoe hegemony and eventually induced a migration of Wall Street firms out of the financial district to less conventional and more convenient midtown venues.

Wall Street firms (including the anointed three) changed more than geographical locus. Starting in the 1960s they began to view their starchy social reputation as a liability. Their associate ranks became more heterogeneous as they recruited talented Jews, women, Blacks, and other minorities, previously ignored. Women associates, once a rarity, represented a formerly unexploited vein of legal smarts (even for Cravath, originally a male bastion and now, *mirabile dictu*, headed by a woman) although the road to partnership remains steep and winding for women, who make up less than 20 percent of Wall Street firms' partnership ranks. Overall, however, firms now prize diversity and have largely shed their commitment to WASP demographics.

But not every Wall Street firm navigated the treacherous waters of changing social, professional, and business dynamics. Lord Day & Lord, founded in the early nineteenth century and an arch example of old-line values, could not make the transition to the new, more cutthroat commercial world and disbanded in 1994. "The coin of the realm ceased being loyalty, predictability and continuity," said a senior partner, "and became money, money and money."[7]

Since the 1960s what once was a profession has become a global industry. Accounting metrics have replaced collegiality as law firms have metastasized. Formerly compact Wall Street law firms, often with one or two offices, now include thousands of lawyers, with multiple specialties and branch offices in every corner of the world. Aggressive players acquire entire firms, consolidate with other large firms to gain market share, and routinely discard less productive partners, once tenured until retirement. In today's legal business the bottom line rules. "Many so-called partners are little more than associates with bigger salaries," wrote James B. Stewart. "How much money lawyers make has gone from a taboo to an obsession."[8] Despite the transformation, the reputation, prominence, and influence of Wall Street firms persist. They still handle the most complex deals and bet-your-company litigation and remain committed to an intense work ethic and exacting legal standards. "*Plus ca change, plus c'est la meme chose.*"

A NOTE ABOUT CURRENCIES, EXCHANGE RATES, AND COMPARATIVE VALUES

Except where otherwise stated, all sums of money are given in their original amounts, and not today's equivalent values.

Estimating how much a dollar from the later 19th or early 20th century would be worth today is an inexact and difficult exercise because of the profound changes in economic conditions. However, as a general matter, between 1870 and 1914, the U.S. dollar was worth 25 to 30 times what it is today. Inflation caused by World War I reduced this difference to about 15 during the 1920s, after which the currency deflation of the Depression era raised the multiple as high as 20.

At all relevant times except during the World War I years, the British pound was worth about five U.S. dollars. Thus, £10 in 1890 would be worth something like $1,500 in today's U.S. currency.

1

The Past Remembered

In the waning days of 1959 one of the authors reported for his first day of work at Cravath, Swaine & Moore, then housed at 15 Broad Street, opposite the New York Stock Exchange. He entered an all-male sanctuary as hushed as a library save for the intermittent bong of the auto-call summoning a lawyer not at his desk to the phone. Walls clad in mahogany complemented the sober beige décor. It was a man's world: no women lawyers, secretaries, or stenographers compromised its Spartan and visible seriousness of purpose. Even the messengers who carried documents from one office to another were aging men in gray office jackets. A midnight shift of male stenos would type after-hours work, if needed, for early delivery to a partner's desk the following morning. The firm's lawyers, he was to learn, wore hats outside the office and dressed, typically, in three-piece suits. Vests added a sense of mainstream propriety to lawyers intently seeking an edge. Associates occupied two-man offices, the more senior nearer the window. One's name appeared on the isinglass office door, painted there by an elderly retainer. The author was one of twelve associates in the class of 1959, all men, but by the standards of the day quite diverse. Thus began his plunge into the law firm shaped and dominated by Paul Cravath, universally regarded as the founder of modern institutional law practice since the early years of the twentieth century. His firm, Cravath, Swaine & Moore, occupied the epicenter of the high-end corporate legal world.

Although almost twenty years had passed since his death, the "lidless eye of Paul D. Cravath"[1] continued to survey his most signal creation, which he had ruled like an absolute czar.[2] His presence was palpable, even to a newcomer. Many then senior partners, who had worked alongside him, embodied his intense, uncompromising ways. Donald Swatland, head of the firm's corporate practice, best reflected its ethos. Driven, with a fierce aquiline visage and intellect to match, Swatland intimidated most of his partners. A product of Princeton and Harvard Law School, where he was president of the *Law Review*, Swatland had served as a brigadier general during World War II, responsible for procurement of airplanes and equipment for the Army Air Forces at Wright Field in Ohio.[3] His corner office on the twenty-eighth floor contained a solid wall of corporate bound volumes, evidence of a prolific deal-making career. Long before computer-aided recall, Swatland was a deep fount of often arcane knowledge and equipped with a near-photographic memory enabling him to retrieve documents from a massive record at will. To a young associate he seemed Olympian and untouchable, a link to the past.

For one whose firm came to be called "distinctly the counsel for the predatory rich,"[4] Paul Cravath did not trace his origins to the eastern establishment. His father, Erastus Milo Cravath, was a Congregationalist minister and passionate supporter of Black education who became the founding president of Fisk University in Tennessee. Cravath himself later served as chairman of Fisk's board. Although concerned with the "broad problems of Negro education and race relations," Cravath did not during his lifetime hire a Black lawyer to work in his firm. After graduating from Oberlin College in 1882, he set his sights on Minneapolis, not New York. To earn tuition money for law school he worked as a salesman for an oil company and then, changing course, entered Columbia Law School.[5]

Described as "robust and humorless,"[6] Cravath was a handsome man of great stature, six-foot-four, with a massive head and piercing blue-grey eyes behind a pair of gold-rimmed pince nez.[7] One observer discerned a "ruddy, impatient face and a faintly pompous manner which testifies openly to his contempt for inferiors."[8] An extrovert with unbounded determination and self-confidence, he thrived on hard work. At Columbia, he excelled, graduating in 1886 and winning a prize tutorship that enabled him to join his classmate, Charles Evans Hughes, at Walter S. Carter's firm, a coveted perch. " . . . [T]he office arrangements even of the best firms were very simple," Hughes recalled. "Large retinues of law clerks, secretaries and various helpers were unknown."[9] Carter, Hughes & Cravath, which maintained offices on Broadway, became the influential progenitor of other major New York law firms. Hughes went on to become a two-term governor of New York, Secretary of State and Chief Justice of the United States Supreme Court. Carter established the practice, later systematically developed by Cravath, of hiring annually one or two of the best graduates of Columbia or Harvard and training them for several years before encouraging their departure to practice for themselves. Enlarging on Carter's example, Cravath was to become the preeminent architect of institutional law practice just as the wealthy clients he represented structured and developed corporate enterprise.[10] A perfectionist with an "uncanny sense" for solving complicated business and legal problems, Cravath "had an aptitude for business that developed almost into genius."[11] His domain was the conference room. He avoided litigation, but was supremely competent at finding solutions to problems of business complexity. His driving personality and ruthless conviction made him a fearsome board room adversary, intolerant of mediocrity and of opposition generally.[12]

EARLY DAYS

Although he later created the paradigmatic Wall Street law firm, Cravath got his start in an entrepreneurial three-man office as counsel for George Westinghouse, then engaged in a titanic struggle with Thomas Edison to determine the contours of the commercial electric power industry. Cravath's distant uncle, who worked at a Westinghouse subsidiary in Ohio, had recommended him as counsel for the company. Westinghouse, surprisingly, took a chance on the young lawyer, then twenty-six, and became a bulwark of his early legal career. Westinghouse was a risk taker, very much in control of his own destiny. He was also a pragmatic engineer. "He did not appeal to me, even then, as being a wizard," a colleague later recalled, "but he seemed to be a plain human being with lots of initiative, with nerve to attempt difficult things, and money enough to see them through to success or failure." Edison by contrast was an inventor of novelties and an eccentric genius who had developed the multiplex telegraph, stock ticker, phonograph, and an incandescent lightbulb. Edison was also the arch promoter of central station generating plants using direct current (DC) to serve nearby customers. As counsel for Westinghouse, Cravath faced a wily and fearsome adversary.[13]

The war between Edison and Westinghouse pitted Cravath's client against a virtual icon of technology. Cravath found himself in the midst of uncharted commercial and legal territory. Famous as the inventor of a revolutionary air brake for railroads, Westinghouse had seized on alternating current (AC) as an alternative to DC, acquired patent rights to an AC system, and became Edison's bitter rival. Each sought to raise financial backing and acquire patent protection for a system that preemptively would serve the consuming public. Edison briefly employed Nikola Tesla, a brilliant Serbian electrical engineer who had developed an AC induction motor, but then attacked AC as too dangerous for domestic use and campaigned publicly against it. Edison vowed that his company would never sell an AC system. "My personal desire," he said, "would be to prohibit entirely the use of alternating currents." Tesla, unsurprisingly, quit working for Edison and made common cause with Westinghouse, who bought the rights to Tesla's AC patents and hired him as a consultant. Edison lodged multiple lawsuits against Westinghouse, who looked to Cravath for protection against a blizzard of litigation.[14]

In the years following 1888, barely two years out of law school, Cravath became Westinghouse's principal defender. Edison was the nominal enemy, who sought to crush Westinghouse with patent infringement lawsuits and a vicious public campaign to discredit AC. But the real adversary with whom Cravath ultimately had to deal was J. P. Morgan, the ubiquitous and dominant Wall Street banker. The Edison Electric Light Company, controlled by Morgan, financed a campaign by Edison to legally constrict AC power. Edison claimed AC current was unsafe and used it to electrocute stray dogs and cats. He convinced New York to adopt AC current for use in executions, with hideous result, and sought legislation limiting the size of electric systems and outlawing AC power in residential dwellings, AC's best market. Morgan openly supported this ill-conceived political effort in order to constrain AC technology; used the Baring Brothers bank panic to gain control of Edison General Electric; and launched allegations of fraud against Westinghouse, causing its major bank lenders to withdraw short-term loans and pushing it close to bankruptcy. Far more was at stake than Cravath could manage through conventional lawyering. Defending his client against infringement suits was just the beginning. With J. P. Morgan's support, Edison had launched a wide-ranging public campaign against AC. Cravath had to fashion a solution against insuperable odds.[15]

It helped his cause that Westinghouse's AC seemed to be winning the technical battle against DC and that Edison had lost control of his own company, which was merged into General Electric without his consent. But Westinghouse now had to go head to head against the newly formed General Electric, a formidable competitor. Both companies submitted bids to provide power for the Chicago World's Fair in 1893. The competition was intense. Westinghouse's low-ball offer won the contract, marking an important turning point in the AC-DC struggle. Everything that moved or was illuminated at the fair ran on Westinghouse's polyphase system. In the year following the fair more than half of all new electrical devices in the United States were driven by AC. But Westinghouse had achieved only a short-lived pyrrhic victory. Fierce, unremitting competition and the Panic of 1893 took their toll on both companies. Each courted bankruptcy. Cravath recognized that continued corporate warfare was simply unsustainable as the Panic enveloped both companies. General Electric lost 75 percent of its value, and only Morgan's personal purchase of its local utility stocks saved it from receivership. Westinghouse tried to take advantage of its rival's financial plight by reducing prices by half, but General Electric matched the price reductions to maintain its market share. By mid-1895 both companies were barely profitable and entangled in proliferating patent suits. Cravath and the companies' bankers pressed for a negotiated settlement.

In 1896 General Electric and Westinghouse entered into a patent and cross-licensing agreement and thereafter a price agreement on bulbs. The patent agreement commenced a long period of coexistence under a Board of Patent Control. "Prices and quotas . . . were controlled by the Board," recalled Robert T. Swaine in his 1948 history of the Cravath firm. "Cravath for Westinghouse . . . gave almost daily attention to the details of its management. Active campaigns were carried on against alleged infringers."[16] The licensing agreement protected the parties from the rest of the industry, including several firms that had been infringing on their patents and undercutting their prices. The companies made their devices compatible and established industry standards. Since other producers had to use their patents, General Electric and Westinghouse were able to limit market entry and assure themselves profits, even on equipment they did not produce. By the turn of the century they had absorbed their only full-line competitors. Ever the pragmatic businessman, Cravath favored combination over competition.[17]

Although reconciled with General Electric, Westinghouse was not yet out of the woods. It had narrowly escaped receivership in 1893 when creditors finally agreed to accept company stock to settle their claims. Another financial panic in 1907 precipitated a further crisis for Westinghouse, whose bond indentures required pledged collateral to be not less than 25 percent of total indebtedness. When the Panic of 1907 reduced the collateral value below the minimum percentage, Pittsburgh banks, which held most of the debt, became agitated. George Westinghouse telephoned Cravath, who could not prevent court appointment of receivers for the Westinghouse companies. A readjustment committee worked out a complex refinancing plan that involved the issuance of new stock. Cravath personally subscribed for shares worth $225,000. The plan became effective in November 1908, and a new board of directors took office a few days later with George Westinghouse still president and the designation of a chairman, an office required by the New York banks.

A year later a committee of the board chose Robert Mather as chairman and amended the company bylaws to make him chief executive officer. Cravath described Mather, who had been chairman of the Rock Island Company, as "a man of very high character and considerable ability, a close student, but with little elasticity." Westinghouse clashed with Mather and submitted a lengthy statement to the board attacking his competence. The board was not convinced, refuted Westinghouse's charges, and requested his resignation as president. Westinghouse campaigned unsuccessfully to regain control. His quarrel with the board broke his bond with Cravath, who advised him "[m]y obligation is to the Westinghouse Company and I think you have gone back on the arrangement you have agreed to. I think my duty is to the Board of Directors and to the Company and to the plan of reorganization to which you assented and which I was instrumental in carrying out." Cravath's decision to represent the Westinghouse company rather than its founder was self-serving and clearly in his interest. He continued as counsel for Westinghouse for many years, eventually serving as chairman of its board himself. Sadly, however, he no longer had a personal relationship with Westinghouse, who ceased to be an important factor in company affairs, suffered declining mental capacity, and died in 1914. "I have no doubt," said Cravath, "chagrin over his defeat had much to do with hastening the break-up of his powers and his death."[18]

CRAVATH AND GUTHRIE

While the Westinghouse story unfolded, Cravath was himself the principal in several intervening partnerships. In 1899 Cravath joined Seward, Guthrie & Steele, an old-line firm which had consummated, among others, the Denver & Rio Grande railroad reorganization and to which Cravath, Swaine & Moore today traces its lineage.[19] Cravath developed great admiration for William D. Guthrie, a driving, effective perfectionist and dominant partner in the firm. Guthrie had entered the firm as a lowly messenger but attended Columbia Law School, was admitted to the bar in 1880, and became a partner three years later. Thereafter he rapidly achieved professional eminence as a legal perfectionist, tireless in the demands he made on himself and on others with whom he worked. Guthrie handled most of the firm's railroad litigation, leaving creative reorganization matters to his overworked colleague, Victor Morawetz, a brilliant legal theoretician and author of an early classic text, *The Law of Corporations*, who left the Seward firm in 1896 to become J. P. Morgan's handpicked general counsel of the Atchison, Topeka & Santa Fe Railway. Guthrie was a shrewd negotiator but could also be contentious and difficult. "His caustic tongue," wrote Robert T. Swaine, "brought frequent clashes with his colleagues at the bar, with his partners and even with his clients." He worked at a rapid pace, under great pressure. When dictating, he walked up and down the room, paying no attention to the stenographer. One unfortunate scribe, sent in to take Guthrie's dictation, could not cope with the torrent of words and sat mute, not daring to interrupt.

After some time Guthrie asked: "Aren't you taking this down?"

"No," was the reply.

"Did you think I was talking for your edification?" Guthrie exploded. "You're fired."

Guthrie defended property rights with equal messianic zeal, notably in successful litigation against the income tax and graduated inheritance tax in the United States Supreme Court, where he made the opening argument in *Pollock v. Farmers Loan & Trust Co.* in 1895.[20]

Guthrie reciprocated respect for Cravath. Unlike Guthrie, a scintillating and contentious litigator, Cravath had no liking for courtroom forensics. His forum was the conference room. The most important business Cravath brought to the Seward firm involved five Westinghouse companies, not least Westinghouse Electric & Manufacturing. In addition to work for these companies, Cravath negotiated with railroads and utilities that purchased Westinghouse equipment. This gave rise to "a lucrative practice . . . when the purchasers proved slow to pay, but also led to retainers by many Westinghouse customers in connection with their own corporate and financial problems." Cravath built his corporate practice on several key clients, Westinghouse perhaps the most important among them.[21]

To service his growing corporate clientele, Cravath turned to the new firm for the help he needed and brought with him talented associates. However, Cravath encountered a shambolic workplace. In his history of the firm Swaine noted the disarray. "There was no real filing system," he wrote. "When the papers in a matter were not voluminous they were folded up indiscriminately, tied with red tape, and put into wooden filing cabinets in alphabetical order. When the package grew too thick for such handling, the papers went into cardboard boxes about four inches deep and large enough for the papers to lie flat—and the boxes stood like books on shelves." Not surprisingly, Seward, Guthrie & Steele encountered difficulty attracting competent young corporate lawyers. " . . . [W]e have found it almost impossible," Guthrie wrote, "to secure men who can attend to the details of these corporate matters capably and accurately." The firm's hiring practices were casual. It was staffed by friends of the partners, random colleagues, and clients, most of whom stayed only a few months, were not paid, and were encouraged to seek their own clients. Associate lawyers and clerical staff worked in discomfort in cramped quarters without windows. Cravath focused his organizational genius on this dysfunctional workplace.[22]

In 1900 Charles Steele, a name partner in the firm, withdrew to join J. P. Morgan & Co. In a prior incarnation Steele had served as general counsel of the New York, Lake Erie & Western Railroad Company and brought the Erie business with him to the Seward firm, commending himself to Morgan partner Charles H. Coster, who retained Steele to assist with the Erie reorganization. When Coster died prematurely in 1900, J. P. Morgan invited Steele, during Coster's funeral, to become a partner in J. P. Morgan & Co. Steele became Morgan's close friend, enjoyed a long and lucrative career, and served on the corporate boards of the International Mercantile Marine Co., U.S. Steel Corporation, Southern Railroad Company, International Harvester Company, Cerro de Pasco, and the Atchison, Topeka & Santa Fe Railroad.[23]

Steele's departure closely followed Cravath's arrival at the firm and precipitated further changes. Guthrie and Cravath invited Edward C. Henderson to join the firm as Steele's successor. Like Cravath, a Columbia Law graduate, Henderson had worked on railroad finance and had ties to the investment banking firm of J. & W. Seligman & Co. A modest and self-effacing intellectual, he was at his best in analyzing complex business transactions and drafting corporate documents. The new partnership of Guthrie, Cravath & Henderson commenced business on the first day of 1901. Guthrie continued his practice as a litigator; Cravath and Henderson, neither an advocate by instinct, served as corporate strategists, draftsmen, and office practitioners. They were all young men. Guthrie was 41, Cravath 39, and Henderson 43. Their firm actively pursued corporate and reorganization matters; acquired Bethlehem Steel and International Harvester as clients; handled security issuances for Kuhn, Loeb and other underwriters; and acted for E. H. Harriman in the creation of Northern Securities Company.[24]

To attack the disorder he found in Guthrie's firm, Cravath set about reorganizing the legal staff with legendary irascibility and temper. He had "unfailing confidence in his own judgment and demanded that everything be done his way."[25] He found an ally in Henderson, who admired Cravath's administrative skill and trained many of the young lawyers who worked at the firm. Henderson's tenure marked the beginning of the Cravath system and the invention of the modern law firm. Cravath recruited new lawyers, only of the right social background, who had graduated from college and law school with high marks. Of the thirty-three associate lawyers at the Guthrie firm, only Joseph P. Cotton, Russell C. Leffingwell, and Hoyt A. Moore became partners. Cravath preferred men, like himself, with forceful personalities and rugged physiques, believing that corporate law practice required maximum effort from high-strung, tense, and driving personalities. Cronies, who usually stayed only a short time and offered little real assistance, were discarded. Also discarded was the practice of allowing young lawyers to occupy desk room while seeking to build their own book of business. Cravath insisted that all lawyers should be paid and that firm business should be their only business. Because he expected efficient—and exclusive—service, he paid top salaries and encouraged associates to maintain anonymity.[26]

One of his partners, Carl de Gersdorff, said Cravath ultimately "transformed the firm into a cohesive team containing men . . . with training and experience designed to give them a comprehensive view of the problems of the office as well as specialists highly trained through concentration in particular fields. . . ." Supported by an efficient cadre of talented young lawyers, Cravath enjoyed a phenomenal rise. George Westinghouse and Jacob Schiff of Kuhn Loeb & Co., both clients, "were impressed by his dramatic personality and ice-clear mind. . . ." With such deep-pocket backers he was able to avoid the long understudy years that typically burden young lawyers.[27]

It is an irony that general adoption of the Cravath system largely foreclosed the kind of career Cravath and his colleagues had experienced. He and Hughes were only in their mid-twenties when they were made partners in Carter's firm in 1888 and were able to move easily elsewhere, carrying their book of business with them. The Cravath system, once generally adopted, favored anonymous organization men, indentured to the firm that had recruited them out of law school, moving only if the firm did not advance them to partnership.[28] This led Adolf Berle, a professor at Columbia Law School, many years later to blame institutional law firms for a "terrible waste of many of the ablest and best trained young minds American legal education produces. . . . [T]he young men vanish into these firms. . . . In later mid-career they might even emerge as senior partners. . . . After which they honorably die, leaving as their entire life-product modest fortunes, memberships in highly respectable clubs, and a certain amount of good, unspectacular work as trustees of suburban hospitals and community funds."[29] Cravath himself had retrospective doubts about his creation. At a dinner in 1934, marking thirty-five years of membership in the firm, Cravath wondered "whether the system of a large, highly organized and intensely regimented . . . law office has been a good thing for the bar. . . . My own experience in a highly diversified practice as a member of the humble firm of Cravath & Houston was . . . a better preparation for my professional career than I could have had if I had spent the same amount of time as a cog in the machinery of a big law office."[30]

Whatever his retrospective doubts, Cravath suffered no hesitation in imposing his thumbprint on the Guthrie firm. A clash between two dominant personalities was inevitable. Once described by Upton Sinclair as "rich, smooth, hard and ignorant," Guthrie drove himself ceaselessly and became ever more inconsiderate and intolerant. His no-smoking edict drew him into conflict with Henderson, who often went into the library with a lighted cigar. Guthrie posted a "No Smoking" sign in the library. Henderson saw the sign and blew a contemptuous puff of smoke at it as he returned to his office. Guthrie demanded to know who had been violating his orders. Emerging from his office wreathed in smoke, Henderson calmly asked, "What's the matter, Mr. Guthrie?" "Don't you see that sign?" "Yes," came the reply, "but I don't believe it." While he felt free to bully Henderson, Guthrie envied Cravath's capacity for work and his growing reputation in corporate finance but was never really in sympathy with the Cravath system. The two founders became rivals both in and outside the office. Guthrie's eighty-room French chateau on Long Island, Meudon, eclipsed Veraton, Cravath's slightly more modest Long Island estate. At work Guthrie relied on his own group of older associates and took no advantage of the bright young men Cravath recruited to the office. As he and Cravath continued to fray each other's nerves, Henderson was enlisted as mediator. Guthrie carried on in splendid isolation and more than once threatened to resign. Finally, in April 1906, Guthrie withdrew from the firm, leaving Cravath as the lead partner of Cravath, Henderson & de Gersdorff, now free to build a firm of his own design that was to shape and influence institutional corporate law practice throughout the United States. The "Cravath system," nominally meritocratic, also reflected the dominant social characteristics of the establishment clientele it served. " . . . [T]he new procedure," wrote one observer, "helped make Wall Street law firms into overwhelmingly white, Protestant, upper- or middle-class, Republican and male bastions." It also drew corporate clients eager to benefit from an aggregation of talent seldom found elsewhere in the nation's bar.[31]

Guthrie's resignation did not, unfortunately for Cravath, end the contest for primacy between two towering egos. In 1908 Cravath, among other directors, was sued for fraud arising from an intercompany transaction several years earlier between Metropolitan Securities Company and New York City Railway, its wholly owned subsidiary. Plaintiffs in the $3 million suit were New York City Railway's receivers. The suit attracted lurid newspaper stories of looting and self-enrichment. Cravath hired Frank Stetson, J. P. Morgan's counsel of choice, to represent him in the lawsuit, an indication of the case's gravity. The suit alleged that Cravath and other Metropolitan directors had caused New York City Railway to borrow $6 million and then forced it to retire the loan for $9 million only months later, yielding a profit for Metropolitan of $3 million and, for no consideration, depriving New York City Railway's creditors of assets worth $3 million to satisfy their claims. The receivers argued that, when the loan repayment took place, New York City Railway was insolvent, making the transaction a fraudulent transfer. Thus, Metropolitan and its directors would have to disgorge the ill-gotten $3 million, even if Cravath and the other Metropolitan directors were unaware of the Railway's insolvency. Counsel for the receivers was Joseph Hodges Choate, onetime Ambassador to the Court of St. James and a legend of the New York bar. Choate said his clients were widows and orphans and called the case "the greatest financial enormity ever committed in New York." His purple advocacy touched a nerve and led to a settlement. Cravath contributed $100,000 to the settlement (a small fraction of the fees his firm had earned in the underlying transaction), but the case did not end there. Guthrie later sided with Cravath's accusers, who filed an ethics complaint with the bar association's grievance committee. Guthrie attacked Cravath in letters to the committee and filed copies in the Bar Association library. Although the committee took no action against Cravath, he regarded Guthrie's "treachery" as "beyond forgiveness." In his history of the firm, Swaine called the break between Guthrie and Cravath "a tragedy in the lives of the two men."[32]

2

An Ancient Rivalry

Sullivan & Cromwell and Cravath, Swaine & Moore have been called the "Harvard and Yale of the barrister set,"[1] often fierce rivals for large-scale deals and opposing counsel in major litigation. Their partners, although usually discreet, are not above casual boasting and sniping in aid of their mutual fixation on top-dog status. Occasionally, they vent to the press as one S & C partner did in an interview some years ago with *The American Lawyer*, a much-read trade periodical. "We produce the best written work of any law firm in America," he said. "Better than anything I've ever seen from Cravath." One may question the wisdom and accuracy of this declaration, but the rivalrous history of the two firms is undeniable and has roots that go back to the nineteenth century.

In 1861 Algernon Sydney Sullivan, S & C's eponymous founder and one of the best known trial lawyers in New York, was working out of a one-man office on William Street in Manhattan. A brilliant and convincing orator, he was a tall, handsome man with a winning manner and presence. No client ever sought Sullivan's help, it was said, without receiving service, guidance, and encouragement. Using his wife's Dixie connections, Sullivan represented Southern business interests in New York, but the outbreak of the Civil War virtually destroyed his practice. When the crew of the CSS *Savannah*, a Confederate privateer disguised as a Northern vessel in an unsuccessful attempt to capture the USS *Perry*, faced trial for piracy in New York, Sullivan took the case together with renowned criminal defense lawyer James T. Brady and Daniel Lord, dean of the New York bar.

Bitterly contested, the case presented a novel question of law. Was the Civil War a conflict in which commissioned private vessels were legitimate privateers or was it a criminal conspiracy in which the so-called privateers were really pirates? Even before trial, Secretary of State William Seward, formerly a name partner in Cravath's predecessor firms and an ardent abolitionist, signed an order to imprison Sullivan alleging

Sullivan's seditious contact with the enemy. (He had corresponded with Confederate officials in Virginia on behalf of his clients.) Finally released on an oath of loyalty from the dungeons of Fort Lafayette in New York harbor only days before trial, Sullivan exhorted the jury to remember that their fathers had been revolutionaries too and that they had "judged for themselves what Government they would have."

In the end, the defense prevailed. The jury deadlocked, and the government's case collapsed. Late in the fall, President Lincoln and Secretary Seward abandoned the piracy prosecutions altogether. The privateers were treated as prisoners of war and released in a prisoner exchange between North and South. Sullivan went on to found Sullivan & Cromwell. In the words of one S & C partner quoted in *The American Lawyer*, "[a] Cravath guy throws the firm's founder into jail simply for defending his client. Good feud material, no?"[2]

SULLIVAN & CROMWELL, SULLIVAN'S GIFT TO CROMWELL

After the war, Sullivan entered New York City politics, fighting the Tweed ring as a reform Democrat and eventually becoming assistant district attorney in 1870. He was active in party work but preserved his personal independence. Sullivan also ran a successful law firm, Sullivan, Kobbe & Fowler, where William Nelson Cromwell worked as a bookkeeper. Impressed by Cromwell's talents and ambition, Sullivan sent him to Columbia Law School in the last class that accepted students without an undergraduate degree. When his partners Fowler and Kobbe moved elsewhere, Sullivan, esteemed for "great generosity in act and in judgment,"[3] invited Cromwell as a junior partner to create the firm Sullivan & Cromwell in 1879. Sullivan was fifty-three and Cromwell twenty-five, only three years out of law school.[4]

A poor, supremely ambitious boy from Brooklyn who once played the organ in the Church of the Pilgrims, Cromwell might have stepped out of the pages of a Horatio Alger story. His father, a Union soldier, had been killed at the Battle of Vicksburg in the Civil War when William was only nine. He was described by a contemporary as a "nervous little man of iron," with bright blue eyes, flowing locks, and Edwardian dress. A picture of the annual firm dinner in 1914 at Cromwell's home shows him among his partners in formal attire with cascading silver hair and a prominent white mustache that gave him a striking resemblance to Mark Twain. "A successful man," he said, "never forgets his work. He gets up in the morning with it, he works all day with it, he takes it home with him, he lives with it." He devoted sixteen hours a day to business without a vacation in thirty years. Unlike his partner Sullivan, he had no interest in high-visibility trial work and shunned publicity. He was, instead, by instinct and training, a new breed: a corporation lawyer, conversant with the intricacies of railroad receiverships and business consolidations. His great genius lay in organization and anticipation, in rehearsing every move in advance. He planned with great precision, took copious notes, and checked even the most insignificant detail. Nothing was left to chance. "Accidents don't happen," he would admonish young associates, "they are permitted to happen by fools who take no thought of misadventure." He was also uniquely persuasive, with "a salesman's rapid tongue, a wizardry with figures, and . . . an intellect that works like a flash of lightning. . . ."[5] An adroit legal tactician, Cromwell also became a consummate influence peddler and lobbyist—an elder statesman with the covert moves of a blackjack dealer. An incensed congressman once called him the most dangerous man the country has produced since Aaron Burr. In declining health after the Confederate piracy case, Sullivan left much of the firm's work to Cromwell, who fought his battles behind the scenes and seldom appeared in court. As Sullivan's protégé and then on his own after Sullivan's death in 1887, he set about recasting law and politics for his own benefit and that of the firm's clients.[6]

Peers at the Nineteenth-Century New York Bar

Sullivan & Cromwell was not alone in providing legal, managerial, and financial advice to aggressive corporate clients such as Henry Villard, E. H. Harriman and J. P. Morgan. Its closest Wall Street competitors also disdained trial work, preferring the office to the courtroom. Business clientele demanded something other than traditional trial lawyer-politician-statesman-orator figures. Instead, they placed a premium on hard-headed business counselors and draftsmen of precise legal documents, wills, and trust agreements, who rarely appeared in court themselves. Cravath represented Kuhn, Loeb, a premier railroad financier; Francis Lynde Stetson of Bangs and Stetson (the precursor to Davis Polk) was J. P. Morgan's primary counsel; Anderson, Adams and Young (later Milbank Tweed) became known as the Rockefeller firm; Elihu Root advised big sugar; and Joseph Choate represented Standard Oil and American Tobacco. Beginning in the 1870s, as counsel to such robber barons, these lawyers became expert in bankruptcy and business reorganization, offering tactical and legal advice to companies seeking to cope with the bare-knuckle economics of the time, including, notably, major railroads, many of which were chronically in financial straits.[7]

"The big law firm, and with it the modern career of corporate lawyer," wrote one observer recently, "was born of the Big Deals, Big Cases, and increasingly the Big State of the industrial era."[8] Consolidation of railroads, oil, steel, and other industries entailed highly skilled and specialized legal work. At a time before uniform federal bankruptcy law, Cromwell was among an elite cadre of Wall Street counsel that perfected application of the railroad equity receivership, a precursor to Chapter 11 reorganization. The most successful business lawyers—Cromwell and a few others—were also brokers, fixers, and indispensable financial intermediaries between the great European and American merchant and investment banking houses and expanding business combines.[9]

For all the complex matters they handled, these firms were tiny. By 1900, twenty-one years after its formation, Sullivan & Cromwell had fourteen lawyers, five of whom were partners. Associates worked four to a room in dark bullpen offices at

45-47 Wall Street. Alfred Jaretski Sr., who joined the firm as an associate in 1884 out of Columbia Law School, had just become managing partner, relieving Cromwell of an administrative burden.[10] Following the Cravath example, Sullivan & Cromwell worked its recruits mercilessly. Just as Paul Cravath ruled over his firm, Cromwell dominated his. He "prowled the halls . . . night and day, supervising associates. He poked a finger into their chests and grilled them about their work. When they were not at their desks, he made sure they were in the office by checking the hat-rack."[11] William Curtis, Cromwell's partner, suffered a nervous breakdown, browbeaten, overworked, and underpaid.[12]

Despite earning huge fees, Cromwell was a penny-pincher, running the firm like a skinflint and persevering in a workaholic lifestyle. "To the end of his life," wrote Arthur Dean, "he carefully picked up paper clips or rubber bands off the floor, turned out electric lights and was saving and frugal in his habits." He arose at five and traveled to the office by carriage or limousine. At eight he was ready to commence the day's work. For an hour he might dictate to his clerks, outline a brief, and read his correspondence. Later in the day he received clients and attended board meetings. Evening found him at home "where work [was] ever at his elbow." Although often away in Europe, he kept his large corner office at the firm. Associates were consigned to the library or bullpens on the lower floors.[13] The flow of big-ticket legal cases continued unabated.

3

"Morgan's Attorney General"

For years, Davis Polk was called, half-seriously, the "Tiffany of Law Firms." The name reflected the firm's polished culture, blue-chip clients, and quiet prestige. Like other lawyers in the great downtown law firms, those at Davis Polk were enablers of their clients' great wealth. More so than those in equivalent law firms, however, Davis Polk partners saw themselves as the social equals, if not moral superiors, of their powerful clients.

Davis Polk published annually a small booklet listing the biographical details of its partners and associates. It disclosed where these men—and, after 1964, women—came from, how they were educated, when they joined the firm or became partners, and the countless vestry offices, college trusteeships, and foundation directorships they held. These matters were nobody else's business—the flyleaf noted that the directory was privately printed and "Not for General Distribution." The outside cover was a shade of medium robin's egg hue long known as Tiffany blue.

The law firm that became Davis Polk rose to prominence because of a lawyer named Francis Lynde Stetson. It was Stetson's skill as a lawyer that commended him to the banker J. P. Morgan, and it was upon his relationship with the Morgan empire that Stetson's law firm rose to prominence. Although Stetson created an extraordinary personal law practice, he had no interest in building an enduring institution. By the time he retired from practicing law, Stetson's law firm was struggling, and it was only by good luck and the talents of an unlikely pair of partners that it survived.

ANTECEDENTS

To understand the role of Stetson's law firm, and by implication that of Davis Polk, it is necessary to delve into the annals of 19th century law firm history and railroad finance. Most law firms are syncretic. Those in New York typically arose from combinations of other law firms, and their descendants vie to claim the longest pedigree. Davis Polk is no exception. The longest branch of its genealogy reaches back to a lawyer named Charles Edward Tracy, born in Utica, New York, in 1810. While still in his thirties, Tracy transplanted his family and law practice to New York City, where he specialized in the nascent fields of bankruptcy and corporate law. He became a leader of the bar. According to his obituary, Tracy's success arose from his talent for "protecting large corporate interests."

Tracy and his wife Louisa had six children. One was his son, Charles Jr., who later became a partner in his father's law firm. Five were daughters of rare intelligence and form. They came to be known in New York society as "the beautiful Tracy girls." The Tracys lived in the New York neighborhood now known as Gramercy Park. They were devout Episcopalians and worshiped at the nearby parish of St. George's Church.

In 1862, John Pierpont Morgan returned to New York after a period of mourning for his first wife, Amelia Sturges. Pierpont moved into a small house in Manhattan that he shared with his cousin, Jim Goodwin. An avid Episcopalian himself, Pierpont joined the congregation of St. George's.

As a neighbor and fellow parishioner, it was inevitable that Pierpont would come to know the Tracys. He became a frequent visitor to their house and soon found himself in love with the third of their daughters, Frances Louisa. He and Fanny, as she was known, married in May 1865. He was 28, she 23.

THE MORGAN DYNASTY

Seldom has a financial titan so dominated the American economy as did J. P. Morgan during the nineteenth century's Gilded Age. Even today, the nation's economy bears his imprint. Morgan imported much of the European capital that built America's railroads, averted at least two financial panics, assembled many of the great monopolies of the day, and, by the time of his death, dictated the terms upon which Wall Street operated. After Pierpont's death, his son and lookalike John Pierpont Morgan Jr. led the Morgan empire until his own death in 1943. For the better part of a century, the Morgans were the embodiment of Wall Street's economic power and political clout. Generations of Americans concluded that there was only one J. P. Morgan, eternal and all-powerful.

The Morgans were New Englanders. Pierpont's father, Junius Spencer Morgan, was born in Hartford and made a success of the dry goods business there and in Boston. In 1854, Junius accepted the invitation of the American banker George Peabody to join his London investment bank that financed trade between Britain and the United States. When Peabody retired in 1864, Junius took over the bank, which he renamed J.S. Morgan & Company.

Pierpont was a unique figure of the age. In some respects, he was more European than American. Transplanted to London as a teenager, he was educated in a Swiss boarding school and a German university. Later in life, Pierpont maintained a mansion in London and spent months each year at Aix-les-Bains in France. He had preternatural abilities. Morgan had an enormous appetite for detail, and an unfailing memory. He knew every aspect of his business, examined the cash balance daily and personally audited the books each New Year's Day. He may have been a mathematical prodigy. It was said that, as a teenager, he could calculate cube roots in his head, and he declined the suggestion of one of his professors at Gottingen that he become a mathematician. Pierpont was a connoisseur of art, rare manuscripts, gemstones, and antiquities, and he spent much of his later life collecting priceless works that became centerpieces of the collections of major museums.

J. P. Morgan seemed omnipresent. By the turn of the twentieth century, he directly controlled at least one-fifth of the nation's railroad trackage, had created the trusts known as United States Steel, General Electric, International Harvester, Amalgamated Copper, and International Mercantile Marine and owned or controlled many of the largest banks, trust companies, and life insurance companies in the country. His power was conjoined with philanthropy. He helped fund New York City's Public Library, Metropolitan Museum, Museum of Natural History, and Cathedral of St. John the Divine, not to mention Harvard Medical School's original campus and various Episcopal seminaries, churches, rectories, and annexes. He was a nonpareil yachtsman and clubman and responsible for the construction of the classic headquarters of the New York Yacht Club and New York's Metropolitan Club. He commissioned construction of several of the largest private yachts afloat; the Navy later commandeered two of them for use as warships. He was a personal friend of Britain's King Edward VII and Germany's Kaiser Wilhelm II, and on good terms with Pope Pius X. Morgan was an early financial backer of Thomas Edison; his home and offices were illuminated by electric lights; and he was one of the first people in the world to have a home telephone.

Pierpont entered the banking business in New York in the 1860s. In 1871, Junius arranged a partnership between Pierpont and Philadelphia banker Anthony Drexel, creating Drexel, Morgan & Company. By the time of Drexel's death, Pierpont was clearly in charge of the bank, which became J. P. Morgan & Company in 1895.

THE ALBANY & SUSQUEHANNA

The biggest industry in the United States in the last half of the nineteenth century was railroads. The growth of the nation's railroads, however, had been chaotic, leading to years of "railroad wars" where competing operators, using bare-knuckle tactics and all manner of political and financial subterfuge, fought for control of strategic lines. For decades, much of the work of Morgan's lawyers revolved around financing, reorganizing, and consolidating railroads.

In 1869, the speculator Jay Gould decided to take over the Albany & Susquehanna Railroad. The A&S was the brainchild of New York politician Joseph Ramsey, who coaxed the legislature into funding it, cajoled municipalities to buy stock in the yet-to-be-built road to ensure themselves of a place along its route, and made himself the line's president. Gould began his assault by furtively buying the stock Ramsey had sold to the cities and towns along the railroad's route.[1] Upon learning of Gould's plans, Ramsey caused A&S to sell unissued treasury stock to sympathetic investors, preventing Gould from winning control. In response, Gould then induced one of Tammany Hall's stable of corrupt judges, George G. Barnard, to enjoin Ramsey from interfering with Gould or even from continuing to act as the A&S' president. Soon, the railroad's books were stolen from its offices, then recaptured and buried in a local cemetery. Each camp hired men to occupy railyards and tunnels, and armed clashes began. Finally, the governor called out the New York militia.

J. P. Morgan then entered the fray. Just before Gould mounted his raid on the A&S, Morgan had arranged a $500,000 mortgage loan to the railroad, and he also had interests in railroads that were themselves investors in the A&S. Ramsey saw Morgan as a logical ally, sold him a block of A&S stock, and asked for his advice. Morgan needed legal help and turned to his father-in-law. As it happened, Charles Tracy knew something about the subject because he already was in the midst of a battle of his own against Gould and Judge Barnard over the Union Pacific Railroad. Since the main legal proceedings were upstate, Charles Tracy engaged the prominent Albany lawyer Samuel Hand as his co-counsel and took over defense of the A&S.[2] Tracy and Hand prevailed, and Morgan then leased the A&S to the Delaware & Hudson Canal Company for 99 years, thus removing it forever from Gould's hands.[3]

PANIC OF 1873

In September 1873, the nation's economy fell into serious recession following failure of the Philadelphia bank of Jay Cooke & Company. Cooke had made millions selling U.S. government bonds to finance the Civil War and was now the promoter of the Northern Pacific Railroad, which was planned to connect the Great Lakes with the Pacific Northwest. Cooke's bank underwrote the Northern Pacific's bond issues, only to find itself unable to syndicate the bonds. Financial panic spread, and soon dozens of overextended railroads were bankrupt, drawing J. P. Morgan and other bankers involuntarily into the business of reorganizing them.

The legal arc of Charles Tracy's career followed that of Morgan. His law firm, now known as Tracy, Olmstead & Tracy, included his longtime partner, Dwight Olmstead (1826–1891), and his son Charlie, a recent Columbia Law School graduate. Tracy and his firm were responsible for several of Morgan's most complex reorganizations in those early years. One was the insolvency of the Cairo & Vincennes Railroad, which failed almost immediately after Junius Morgan sold £700,000 of the road's bonds to English investors. Tracy became one of the C&V's receivers and its main lawyer. It took him years to untangle the C&V's affairs; finally, he foreclosed upon its assets, which Morgan then leased to Jay Gould's Wabash, St. Louis and Pacific Railway.[4]

Tracy also handled the messy reorganization of the St. Louis Bridge Company and its related Tunnel Railroad Company. The Bridge Company had built the iconic Eads Bridge spanning the Mississippi but failed almost as soon as the bridge was completed. Morgan forced it into receivership in 1875, assembled a reorganization committee, and hired Tracy to represent it. After years of legal infighting, Tracy purchased the bridge at auction in 1878 and conveyed it to a newly formed company Morgan controlled, which then leased the bridge and its tunnel railroad to Gould.[5]

THE SOUTH PENNSYLVANIA RAILROAD FIGHT

After a series of epic battles with Gould, Cornelius Vanderbilt emerged triumphant from the railroad wars of the 1860s and 1870s. His New York Central dominated carriage of freight and passengers between New York and Chicago. Vanderbilt probably was the wealthiest man on earth when he died in 1877.

But even mightier than the New York Central was the Pennsylvania Railroad. By 1865, it already was the world's largest corporation with 30,000 employees and capitalization of $61 million.[6] There had, for years, been an uneasy peace between the New York Central and the Pennsylvania, with the former confining itself to its New York-Chicago route and the latter handling traffic between Philadelphia and Pittsburgh. In the early 1880s the Pennsylvania broke the truce by taking control of the New York, West Shore & Buffalo Railroad, whose tracks ran up the Hudson Valley across the river from the New York Central's lines (and, as it happened, down the bluff from Morgan's summer home). But the Pennsylvania had powerful enemies, including Andrew Carnegie and the Rockefeller brothers, who chafed at the Pennsylvania's high rates to their mines, mills, and oil fields. With Carnegie and Rockefeller's support, the New York Central retaliated by buying the charter of a defunct railroad called the South Pennsylvania and starting construction of a new railroad in the heart of the Pennsylvania's territory.

The prospect of a destructive rate war between the two railroad systems horrified Morgan because of the harm it inevitably would wreak upon the bond market, the mainstay of the Morgans' banking business. Morgan's solution to such problems invariably was to reach gentlemen's agreements to divide markets, and he did so here. Thus, on a steaming July day in 1885, Morgan invited New York Central president Chauncy Depew and the Pennsylvania's president, George Roberts, to a meeting on his yacht, the *Corsair*, in the Hudson River. There, after a day of intense discussion, the two sides agreed to a compromise: the New York Central would sell the South Pennsylvania Railroad to the Pennsylvania, and the Pennsylvania would sell its stock in the New York, West Shore & Buffalo to the New York Central. As simple as it appeared, the details of the compromise were complicated because it involved the sale of other lines in addition to the West Shore and the South Pennsylvania and numerous side deals and financial adjustments. Moreover, the transaction was quickly attacked by the Pennsylvania Attorney General as an unlawful monopoly.[7]

Ordinarily, Morgan would have been represented in the negotiations by his father-in-law, but Charles Tracy had died four months earlier. This left Charles' son, Charlie Tracy, to step into his father's shoes. The Vanderbilts were also represented by a new lawyer. This new face was Frank Stetson, a rising star in the New York bar, best known then as a trial lawyer. During the difficult negotiations and subsequent litigation, Morgan was impressed by Stetson's ability. Although he kept Charlie Tracy on retainer for another year, he increasingly relied upon Stetson for advice. Perhaps at Morgan's suggestion, Tracy and Stetson merged their law practices in 1887.

With this, Stetson and Morgan began a collaboration that lasted over twenty-five years. Stetson represented Morgan in court, superintended his bank's reorganization of dozens of railroads and industrial corporations, negotiated financings, handled mergers and acquisitions, and shepherded the Morgan empire through the political vicissitudes of the time. So complete was Stetson's representation of the Morgan interests that he came to be known as "Morgan's Attorney General." Yet Stetson and Morgan were not personal friends. Stetson was not part of Morgan's social circle—he did not join Morgan's entourage to Europe each year, he was not invited to Morgan's parties on the *Corsair*, he did not participate in Morgan's habitual afternoon gatherings with his friends uptown, and neither Stetson nor his wife appeared on the guest lists for the balls and assemblies of New York's social elite. Stetson resembled, if anything, one of the Morgan bank's trusted partners—indispensable, richly paid, and always at hand.

FRANK STETSON

Francis Lynde Stetson was born in 1846 in upstate New York. His father, Lemuel, was a lawyer and staunch Democrat who served as district attorney, county judge, state assemblyman, a member of the New York state constitutional convention of 1846 and, briefly, a U.S. congressman.

Frank Stetson graduated from Williams College in 1867 and Columbia Law School in 1869. The next year, he began a general practice in New York with his uncle, William Hascall. Stetson quickly showed aptitude as a courtroom lawyer. Years later, the great Joseph Hodges Choate wrote that the slow decline of the quality New York's trial bar was due in part to Stetson's later decision to abandon trial work to concentrate on corporate reorganizations and financings.

Stetson inherited his father's interest in Democratic politics. In New York City, the party was divided into two bitterly opposed wings—the Tammany Hall political machine and the party's conservative, pro-business faction. The political divide reflected an ethnic one. The Tammany Hall Democrats were largely Irish Catholic, with support from New York City's German and Jewish communities. The establishment Democrats, in turn, were largely Protestants of one denomination or another. Their leader was New York City lawyer Samuel J. Tilden.

Among the downtown lawyers, the issue coalesced around the corruption of Tammany judges, and in 1870 they organized the Bar Association of the City of New York partly as a vehicle for their attack on Tammany. Its first president was the eminent William Maxwell Evarts and its vice president was Tilden himself. In 1872, the Association submitted a report to the New York legislature on judicial corruption that ultimately led to the removal of four Tammany judges. One was the notorious George Barnard and another was Albert Cardozo, father of the future Supreme Court Justice Benjamin Cardozo.

Lemuel Stetson had once run on a statewide ticket with Samuel Tilden, so it is likely that young Frank had a ready introduction to the rising leader. Stetson soon joined the Bar Association's anti-Tammany efforts and became a Tilden confidant.[8] When Tilden became governor in 1874, he asked Stetson to serve as his private secretary, an offer Stetson declined.[9] Two years later, Tilden was the Democratic nominee for president, and Stetson worked on the campaign. Indeed, by one account, it was Stetson who brought Tilden the news on the evening of November 7, 1876, that Tilden had been elected president.[10] However, the election was contested because of allegations of massive voter fraud in the Southern states, resulting in the appointment by Congress of an electoral commission to sort out the returns. Florida sent two competing delegations of electors to Washington, and Stetson was put in charge of preparing the case for the Tilden slate. Although he was ultimately unsuccessful, Stetson's thoroughness in preparing the case marked him as an up-and-coming star among downtown lawyers.

After the smoke cleared on the 1876 election, Stetson's wealthy friend William C. Whitney offered him the job of assistant corporation counsel for New York City.[11] Stetson remained in Whitney's office until 1880, where he learned the intricacies of city, state and national politics and knew rising politicians of both parties. Stetson then entered into partnership with a leading litigator of the day, Francis N. Bangs (1828–1885). Bangs was born in New York in 1828, graduated from college in 1845, and received his law degree from Yale in 1847. Bangs had made his name as a bankruptcy lawyer. He came to prominence when he was chosen as counsel for the receiver of the merchant bank Ketchum, Son & Co., which collapsed in scandal in 1865 after the younger Ketchum embezzled money from his father and then forged $1.5 million of gold certificates. Bangs' practice grew with the passage of the Federal Bankruptcy Act in 1867, which extended the bankruptcy laws to corporations. Bangs was involved in the creation of the City Bar Association and took his turn as its president in 1882-83.

A half-generation older than Stetson, Bangs suffered from poor health, and his law practice was interrupted for long periods because of illness. His contemporaries considered him dour, if not simply disagreeable. According to one contemporary, "[I]n invective, Mr. Bangs had no superior."[12] During one trial, Bangs so violently assailed opposing counsel that his co-counsel vainly tugged at Bangs' coattails in an effort to restrain him.[13] Although Bangs & Stetson was never a large law office—besides

Bangs and Stetson, it only included Bangs' sons Francis S. and Charles W. Bangs—it was well regarded. [14] But the partnership lasted only five years because Bangs, almost literally, worked himself to death in 1885.[15]

The partnership articles of Bangs & Stetson contained a provision that captures ideals of personal and professional collegiality underpinning a law firm partnership. It read:

> The parties to this agreement mutually pledge to each other their best efforts, respectively, to aid each other's professional success and advancement during the continuance of the partnership hereby formed; so that in the manner within the limits and to the ends above set forth, each party shall receive from the others a fair opportunity to use his best faculties for the common benefit, and shall have an approximate if not complete or perfect compensation for his industry and abilities, out of the partnership funds, as far as such funds will go.[16]

This language remained in the partnership agreements of all of the successor firms of Bangs & Stetson, and apparently still is found in the Davis Polk's partnership agreement today. However, Frank Stetson seems to have largely ignored it during the thirty years he ran the firm.

BANGS, STETSON, TRACY & MacVEAGH

It is not surprising that J. P. Morgan decided to replace Charlie Tracy with Frank Stetson. Stetson was exceptionally capable, and Morgan consistently put talent before family in business affairs. While Morgan had little respect for politicians, he depended upon good relations with the federal and state governments, and Stetson was a leader of the New York Democratic Party. And, at a time when religion figured prominently in personal and public life, both Morgan and Stetson were active Episcopalians. Each made it a point to attend their church's triennial General Convention, and the two had undoubtedly met over the years.

Yet Charlie Tracy also was an excellent lawyer, and family politics may well have played a role. By the late 1880s, Pierpont's marriage to Fanny was all but finished. Within his circle of friends and companions, Morgan was obsessively gregarious, while Fanny was a homebody. Soon, Morgan began his cultivation of a series of mistresses and imposed an unwritten rule that, whenever feasible, he and Fanny should be on separate continents. Clearly, Charlie's loyalty to his sister was a problem. Compounding this was Morgan's unsatisfactory relationship with his son, Jack, whom he viewed as an inadequate successor to the empire he and Junius had created. Jack, understandably, identified with his mother, and Charlie was Jack's favorite uncle. (Charlie, in fact, made Jack the executor of his will.) With the death of the older Tracy, Morgan may have thought that the time had come for a transition.

The merger of Stetson and Tracy's practices also was timely for other reasons. The year after the senior Charles Tracy died, the firm's other partner, Dwight Olmstead, retired, relegating Charlie Tracy to a solo practice. This was also when Francis Bangs died, leaving Stetson in partnership with Bangs' two sons, neither of whom enjoyed his father's stature. In any event, the firm of Bangs, Stetson, Tracy & MacVeagh, 45 William Street, was formed on February 1, 1887, with the two Bangs brothers, Stetson, and Charlie Tracy as partners.

Frank Stetson was famously congenial, and there is no evidence that his relations with Charlie Tracy were anything other than friendly. And Charlie was an appealing, if old-fashioned, man: he enjoyed reading the Greek and Roman classics in their original and to the end of his days insisted on writing with a quill pen.[17] He and Frank Stetson remained in partnership for the better part of ten years, and Charlie continued to represent Morgan in railroad reorganizations until his health failed him in the early 1890s. He was a receiver of Jay Gould's Wabash, St. Louis & Pacific Railway when it collapsed in 1884, was a receiver of the Cairo, Vincennes & Chicago Railroad when it went bankrupt yet again in 1887, and represented the Morgan bank's committee of bondholders when it foreclosed on the Ohio, Indiana & Western Railroad in 1890.

The other name in the firm was Philadelphia lawyer Wayne MacVeagh. MacVeagh had represented the Pennsylvania Railroad in the South Pennsylvania matter, had ties to the Drexel side of the Morgan bank, and was a fixture in Pennsylvania Republican politics. He had briefly served as attorney general under Presidents Garfield and Arthur in 1881 and survived a famous, bitter intra-party fight with Pennsylvania political boss Simon Cameron, who happened also to be his father-in-law. Law firms being family affairs in those days, MacVeagh brought along his son Charles MacVeagh, who later became a partner as well.[18]

GROVER CLEVELAND AND THE ELECTION OF 1888

In 1882, Stetson met the rising politician and lawyer Grover Cleveland at a reception at the Manhattan Club (the Democratic Party's answer to the solidly Republican Union Club).[19] They became friends, and Stetson worked on Cleveland's successful presidential campaign in 1884. Stetson could certainly have claimed a plum job in the new administration but, according to Cleveland, never asked for one.

Cleveland came up for re-election in 1888, and Stetson was again active in the campaign. Cleveland won a majority of the popular vote, but lost in the Electoral College tabulation to Benjamin Harrison. Out of office, Cleveland returned to New York to plot his return to the White House. Seeing that Cleveland would need a place to land, Stetson offered him a position as counsel to his firm. It was little more than a rent-sharing arrangement, but having the leader of the national Democratic Party down the hall did no harm.

Stetson had now been practicing law for twenty years. He was only 43 but already was a wealthy man. The most powerful banker in America had made Stetson his "regular attorney in everything" and Stetson had the ex-president as a colleague.[20]

Stetson was a power in the Democratic Party in New York and beyond, and the Tammany wing was in retreat. Stetson had a wide circle of personal and business friends, several of whom were tied to the great fortunes of the day.

The few portraits we have of Stetson show a trim man of average height, prematurely gray, and sporting the mustache common to nineteenth-century gentlemen. His passport application said he had blue eyes, brown hair, a prominent nose, and a florid complexion. He was outgoing and said to be a wonderful conversationalist. Stetson was married, but he and his wife, the former Elizabeth Ruff, had no children. They had a large estate in New Jersey, where Frank bred prize Shropshire sheep.[21] The estate had roads through the woods for Elizabeth, a paraplegic, to drive her carriage and a private nine-hole golf course for Frank's relaxation. Just before the turn of the century, the Stetsons acquired an impressive townhouse at 4 East 74th Street that in later years became the home of Marc Chagall and Michael Jackson. Stetson belonged to a half-dozen clubs but was not active in formal society, possibly because of his wife's disability.

Despite his busy law practice, Stetson found time for other interests. He was a committed churchman, serving as a trustee of the General Theological Seminary and routinely attending the triennial Episcopal General Convention. In fact, it was Stetson who framed the Episcopal Church's longstanding canon on divorce and marriage. Stetson was interested in his genealogy and, with his distant cousin John B. Stetson (the Philadelphia maker of the famous cowboy hats), established the Stetson Kindred of America and purchased the Stetson family's ancestral home. Stetson's greatest passion was his alma mater, Williams College. He was a trustee for years and closely involved with the college's management and planning. Stetson left the bulk of his estate to Williams, and he and his wife are buried there.

Like other successful men, Stetson was intelligent, well organized, and indefatigable. What made him stand out as a lawyer, though, was his ability to listen to opposing counsel, appreciate the subtleties of their arguments, and either allay their concerns or devise a response. He was unfailingly courteous and fair, even to his most inveterate adversaries. He also had a gift for phrasing complex matters succinctly, and his legal drafting was considered a model of clarity. Perhaps this came from his days as a trial lawyer. As one of his partners later eulogized, "[t]he ultimate test of every agreement he drew, of every course of action he advised, was how would such agreement or such action affect the mind and even the heart of judge or jury."[22]

15 BROAD STREET

Perhaps to reinforce his close relationship with Morgan's bankers, Stetson moved his firm's offices to the seventh floor of the recently constructed Mills Building at 15 Broad Street around 1890. The Mills Building was a project of the California banker Darius Ogden Mills, a native New Yorker who had made a fortune supplying miners in the gold and silver rushes. The building was a marvel of its time: it cost $3 million, was eleven stories tall, boasted seven elevators, held 800 tenants, and had entrances on Broad Street, Wall Street, and Exchange Place. It dwarfed the Drexel, Morgan bank headquarters next door, and it was where J. P. Morgan chose to keep his personal office. Stetson ensconced Cleveland in the best part of the suite, a corner office that overlooked the Stock Exchange.

The rhythm of a law practice remained Dickensian. The business day officially began at 9:30 and ended at 5:30. If there was a receptionist, it was a middle-aged man in a suit at a small desk by the elevator. There were few telephones, and they were put in special booths. There was no such thing as making a quick phone call to learn a missing detail—routine communication was by letter, a handwritten note, or a personal visit. In the case of J. P. Morgan, a law clerk would hand-deliver letters and papers, then stand by Morgan's desk until the banker conveyed his answers and instructions.[23]

Typewriters were still a novelty and most firms employed only a few typists—"stenographers" as they were called—who were confined to a closed-off room to hide the clatter of their machines. Office machinery as we know it today did not exist. There were no copiers, so storing, locating, retrieving, and maintaining thick paper files was a constant burden. Devices as basic as staplers were not yet in common use, and an occupational hazard was getting stabbed by the straight pins that clerks used to fasten papers together. The mail came and went through a special door in the back of the offices so the bustle of the firm's logistics would remain invisible. Rarely were women employed in any capacity.

Routine legal work was handled by a cadre of law clerks. Except for the handful who themselves later became partners in law firms, they are largely unknown: the legal directories of the day did not list them. The clerks worked wherever room allowed. They were assigned desks in the library, a hallway, the bookkeeper's office, or an alcove. As an ex-clerk recalled the office of Bangs, Stetson, Tracy & MacVeagh in 1887:

> As you opened the entrance door you found yourself in a small space [with] a small desk for the office boy and a hard wood bench . . . where clients and messengers sat side by side. A low railing with a swinging gate separated this from the general office. In the general office were desks for Mr. Van Sinderen, the managing clerk, . . . Robert Hall, office assistant, Pat Nolan, court messenger, and a long high one for Bainton, the bookkeeper. James and Harry Garfield [sons of the late President] had to use the same desk. One attended law school in the morning and the other in the afternoon.[24]

If there were an available office, it was apt to be dim and cramped, and customarily a few law clerks would be crammed into whatever space was free. Occasionally, a clerk might be senior enough to have the privilege of sitting near a window that opened onto an air shaft.

Much of the work was tedious. The most profitable work was representing banks in large financings, and it fell to law clerks to comb through trust instruments, contracts, and mortgages for typographical errors. Since important documents and legal briefs generally were set in lead type and printed, it also was the job of law clerks to spend nights at the legal printers proofreading galleys and making eleventh-hour edits.

Pay was low. Young clerks typically worked for no salary for one year, and then earned $25 per month.[25] Austin Wakeman Scott, who later became the preeminent authority on the law of trusts and the longest-serving member of the Harvard Law School faculty, remembered clerking for James C. Carter's law firm in the early 1900s. In a speech he delivered in the mid-1970s, Scott told how, on Fridays, the law clerks lined up for their pay, which was dispensed from the bookkeeper's petty cash drawer. Not surprisingly, many law clerks continued to live with their parents for years after starting work.

STETSON JENNINGS & RUSSELL

Cleveland was renominated for the presidency in 1892. Stetson threw himself into the election, which turned out to be a muddy affair that Cleveland won by a small margin. Stetson turned down Cleveland's offer of the post of Treasury Secretary, preferring to be a behind-the-scenes counselor to Cleveland and, it is said, a dispenser of presidential patronage.[26]

A few months after Cleveland took office, yet another financial panic afflicted the country. Again, many financially overstretched railroads fell victim. On February 20, 1893, the Philadelphia & Reading Railroad went into receivership, followed by 191 other railroads in the next sixteen months, requiring workouts of their debts. Their finances had become, if anything, even more byzantine than before. Stetson's law firm handled many of the largest railroad reorganizations, including those of the Philadelphia & Reading, the Northern Pacific, the Erie, and the Southern Railway system. Several took years to complete, and the legal issues they raised remained unresolved for decades.

The growth of his practice led Stetson to reorganize his firm in 1894. The Bangs brothers stepped aside. Francis left to become president of a trust company, and his brother Charles remained at the firm, but not as a named partner.[27] Stetson then merged his firm with that of Frederic Jennings and Charles Russell, creating the partnership of Stetson, Tracy, Jennings & Russell. When Charlie Tracy died prematurely in January 1896—he was only 50—the firm became Stetson Jennings & Russell, and so remained for almost thirty years.

Charles Howland Russell was a graduate of Harvard College and Columbia Law School. After passing the bar, he became a law clerk at Evarts, Southmayd & Choate, which was generally regarded as the leading New York law firm of its time.[28] When newly elected President Rutherford B. Hayes appointed William Evarts Secretary of State in 1877, Russell followed Evarts to Washington as his private secretary. Russell returned to New York in 1880 to form his partnership with Frederic Jennings, another former Evarts, Southmayd & Choate clerk. Jennings was a graduate of Williams College and Harvard and New York University law schools. He was regarded as "the foremost legal expert in matters relating to the subways."[29]

Jennings and Russell were well connected. In 1880, Jennings had wed the heiress Laura Hall Park, daughter of a railroad magnate and granddaughter of a Vermont governor.[30] Russell's father had been president of the Morgan-affiliated National Bank of Commerce.[31] In 1890, Russell married Jane Potter, the daughter of the renowned and much-admired clergyman Henry Codman Potter, the Episcopal Bishop of New York and a close friend of J. P. Morgan.[32]

The fact that Stetson reorganized his law firm in 1894 did not mean he had decided to modernize it. Each of the partners had, in essence, his own set of clients and law practice. Each kept for himself the retainers paid by clients—Stetson, for example, was paid a personal retainer by Morgan of $50,000 each year—and the economic basis of the partnership was the sharing of expenses in proportion to the cost of each partner's practice.[33] In 1887 or so, Stetson had rewritten the partnership's articles, setting $15 per hour as the cost of each senior partner's practice, $7.50 for Francis S. Bangs, $5.00 for Charles MacVeagh, and $1.00 "for every line of register entries" concerning the work of the firm's lawyers.[34] Under this formula, by 1894 Stetson was responsible for almost half of the partnership expenses, implying that he had half of its practice.[35]

This Balkanized system made it difficult to share work, or even to share a client, since there was no simple way to determine the relative contribution made by each member of a legal team. (Lawyers did not routinely keep records of the hours they worked and the matters they worked on until a system of keeping time sheets was developed around 1915 by a Harvard Business School professor named William Morse Cole.)[36] Instead, clients were personal property, to be handed down if possible to family members or friends.

As a result, there was little incentive to expand the firm. Although the burdens of growth—such as increased rent or salaries—would be shared by all, there was no assurance that additional profits would be shared equitably. Thus, from the time it was organized until World War I, Stetson, Jennings & Russell barely grew. Notwithstanding the exponential growth of its clients, the number of active partners at the law firm did not exceed seven until 1914.

THE GOLD CRISIS OF 1895

In 1895 the United States faced a currency crisis that nearly destroyed the nation's credit. The main reason disaster was avoided was the legal creativity of the lawyers at Stetson's firm.

The United States was then on the gold standard: in theory every dollar in circulation was backed by a dollar's worth of gold and anyone could have greenbacks redeemed in gold coin.[37] During the Panic of 1893, foreign investors sold American investments and then presented the sale proceeds in dollars to the Treasury for conversion into gold. Gold reserves fell steadily during 1894. As investors doubted the adequacy of the nation's gold supply, redemptions increased to alarming levels. In January 1895, the Treasury's gold supply stood at only $68 million and fell to $45 million a week later. By early February, the Treasury was paying out over $2 million in gold each day, and default on the national debt was imminent.[38]

There was a cure for the problem: Congress could authorize the Treasury to issue bonds to buy gold overseas. "Silverites" in Congress, however, chafed at the gold standard and refused to pass legislation to sustain it. The Treasury then sought to arrange a loan from the Morgan and Rothschild banks, only to have the effort collapse at the last moment. Time had run out. Even if Congress were to pass legislation authorizing issuance of gold bonds, it would be too late to complete their public sale.

President Cleveland implored Morgan to find a solution. At a White House meeting on the morning of February 5, Morgan, Stetson and Morgan bank partner Robert Bacon met in secret with Cleveland, Attorney General Richard Olney, and others in the White House library. There, Morgan offered a solution that almost certainly originated with Stetson or one of his partners.[39] The lawyers had found a long-forgotten Civil War statute that authorized the Treasury to purchase gold coins with any bonds or notes it wished and at whatever rates and terms the Secretary found advantageous.[40] Using this loophole, Morgan agreed to sell the government $65 million in gold in exchange for 30-year bonds, repayable in gold or in silver, bearing 4 percent interest. Stetson quickly drew up a contract reflecting this arrangement.[41] The contract also provided that the Morgan-Rothschild syndicate would use its clout to prevent further exports of gold from the United States Treasury until things stabilized. "Since they controlled the exchange market, Cleveland knew they could make good this promise."[42]

The plan worked. As soon as news of the loan spread, the run on gold stopped. When the bonds were later offered to the public, they sold out in twenty minutes.[43] Morgan made little profit on the deal but reaped the incalculable benefit of preserving public confidence in the bond markets. Stetson, Jennings & Russell, it was said, declined to charge a fee for its work, viewing it as a public service.[44]

4

Railroads and Railroad Reorganizations

Until quite recently, establishment New York law firms disdained the lower realms of legal practice. Foremost among these was bankruptcy work. This field seemed beneath the dignity of Wall Street practitioners, who dealt with higher matters of corporate finance, bank loans, stock and bond underwriting, mergers and acquisitions, and high stakes lawsuits. Bankruptcy was instead a field relegated to small law firms, usually run by Jewish lawyers, that were willing and able to handle matters that large law firms shunned.

It is one of the great ironies of legal history that Wall Street law firms first became ascendant largely because of their bankruptcy work. Until they were, essentially, foreclosed by legislation championed by former Cravath associate (and later Supreme Court Justice) William O. Douglas during the New Deal, downtown law firms built much of their practices around corporate reorganizations, mainly of railroads. In fact, Frank Stetson, William Nelson Cromwell, and Robert T. Swaine each cut his teeth on railroad reorganizations, and their firms for many years maintained departments devoted almost exclusively to railroad work.

Yet this should hardly be surprising. In the years after the Civil War, railroads were the centerpiece of the U.S. economy. By the 1880s, 80 percent of the New York Stock Exchange listings were of railroad securities.[1] Aside from agriculture, railroads were the nation's largest single industry, its largest employer, and the subject of more invested capital than any other part of the economy. Railroads were the lifeblood of commerce and communication and the indispensable economic link to distant communities that became viable only when connected by rail. Railroads also were enormous consumers of the coal, iron, and timber that came from the nation's mines, furnaces, and forests, and a driver of technological progress in steel production, telecommunications, and machinery. Thomas Edison, Andrew Carnegie, and countless others got their start working for the railroads.

Few enterprises were more capital intensive than the railroad business. Between 1870 and 1890, American railroads laid over 110,000 miles of track, at an average cost of $2 million per mile in today's dollars.[2] Generally, railroads were financed by bonds sold on the exchanges of London, Paris and Frankfurt. These instruments—known as American Railroad Bonds—were among the most traded securities of their time. They yielded as much as 8 percent and were widely held even among the European middle classes. The Rothschilds, Baring Brothers, J.S. Morgan, M.M. Warburg, and other European banking houses formed syndicates to float issues of railroad bonds and such New York financiers as J. P. Morgan, August Belmont, and Jacob Schiff made fortunes on the American side from financing the construction and growth of railroads.

Enthusiasm for its securities belied serious fault lines in the railroad business and the United States economy. Excessive government subsidies had resulted in chronic overexpansion. Rail lines had been financed with high-priced debt, which required a reliable stream of income from freight and passenger service. However, overbuilding meant that some roads serviced the largely empty West, while those in the East faced intense competition from parallel lines. The result was decades of economic instability as railroad after railroad failed.

It was no easy feat to reorganize a railroad, whose capital structure was often fiendishly difficult. Securing the railroads' bonds were mortgages on discrete portions of track. (The Wabash railroad, for example, had almost forty mortgages covering different elements of its asset base.) If the railroad defaulted on its debt, bondholders had an absolute right to foreclose on and liquidate their collateral. But this was an illusory remedy, since foreclosing upon disconnected miles of track simply destroyed the railroad's enterprise value. Bondholders who successfully foreclosed upon their collateral might find themselves owning interrupted segments of a rail line or a series of freight depots that were nearly worthless standing alone. Moreover, most railroads were actually agglomerations of smaller railroads captive to the main road because of a financing device known as the railroad lease. To raise money for the rapid build-out of rail lines, railroads in the nineteenth century arranged with their bankers to create special purpose financing vehicles to sell bonds, build new connecting rail lines, and purchase locomotives and rolling stock, and then lease the entire enterprise back to the parent railroad for periods of up to 999 years, with the parent guaranteeing the debts of the leased line in the bargain. Since the insolvency of the parent line usually resulted in the collapse of the leased railroad as well, one railroad's bankruptcy quickly infected others.[3]

The task of untangling insolvencies of this complexity and magnitude would have required exceptional legal talent in the best of times. However, in the years between the Civil War and the New Deal, much lawyering occurred in a legal vacuum. There was no federal bankruptcy law at all in the twenty years between 1878 and 1898, and there was no statute covering railroad bankruptcies until 1933. Although bondholders were, at least in theory, secured creditors with a senior claim upon the assets of the railroad, their rights were difficult to enforce. Railroad balance sheets could not be trusted, both because of outright fraud and the undeveloped accounting rules of the day. (The roads, for example, did not generally recognize depreciation of their assets.) The railroads' tangible assets were therefore difficult to value. Rolling stock was easily removed beyond the reach of creditors and not readily saleable anyway because different railroads had incommensurate technical standards.

Although railroads had plenty of trackage, stations, depots, and maintenance facilities, these assets were spread across state lines, requiring creditors of a failing line to bring a succession of state court receivership proceedings. Lawyers were remitted to the devices of the time—common-law causes of action, petitions in courts of equity, appointment of receivers and issuance of a bewildering array of writs, injunctions, and stays and an equally confusing set of state and federal courts with jurisdiction that was, at once, overlapping, incomplete, and unclear, and procedural practices that varied from state to state, court to court, and judge to judge. It was not unusual for different constituencies of creditors to seek the appointment of competing receivers, for one court to vacate the appointments made by another, or for receivers in different states to fight with one another.

Bankers—whose profits depended upon stable bond markets—found this intolerable and demanded that their lawyers solve the problem. In response, Stetson, Cravath and Cromwell—among many others—perfected a device called the equity receivership, designed to bring railroad reorganizations under control. When a railroad fell into financial distress, a creditor, typically with the consent of its management, would ask a court to appoint an officer to take charge of—to "receive"—the railroad's mortgaged assets. Although this alone did not prevent different groups of creditors from attempting to foreclose upon the railroad's assets, the receiver was an officer of the court and could readily obtain an injunction to prevent creditors or other third parties from attaching the railroad's assets. These injunctions—which resemble the automatic stays imposed by the Bankruptcy Code today—mitigated the risk that the railroad would be summarily put out of business, or that one group of creditors would steal a march on another.

With peace thus temporarily imposed, bondholders would start a foreclosure proceeding, but not with any intention of forcing a premature sale of the railroad's property. Instead they would seek to renegotiate the railroad's obligations. A manager of the railroad, acting as the receiver, would postpone the foreclosure sale indefinitely. The banks that had syndicated the railroad's stock or bonds would then organize committees to represent each class of securities and require the holders to deposit their securities with the committees. Thus assured, the railroad and its banks, overseen by the banks' counsel, would negotiate the restructuring terms. When final agreement was reached, the bankers would then combine all the committees into a single reorganization committee, which would request the court to proceed with the foreclosure sale.

The sole bidder at the sale would be the reorganization committee itself. It would offer to buy the railroad's assets, using as currency the deposited stocks and bonds and enough additional cash for a modest payment to those investors who had declined to participate in the transaction. It was a foregone conclusion that the reorganization committee's bid would succeed because it would almost surely be the only one. "Counsel who have acted frequently for reorganization committees have spent a great many anxious hours preparing for the unexpected bidder," Paul Cravath once noted, "but in my own experience he has never appeared."[4]

The dynamics of the equity receivership made an independent bid unnecessary. Instead banks intervened when a railroad defaulted to protect scattered investors who owned its stock and bonds. Reaping large fees along the way, the banks propounded a myth, the Bank Paternalism narrative, that they were investors' champions. Rescuing a railroad from financial dismemberment, they argued, was nothing less than a public service. As a leading reorganization lawyer, Cravath had an insider's view of the process. "While you have been preparing the receivership papers," he wrote, "it may be assumed that your client, the banker, has been engaged in forming a bondholders' protective committee, in which event it becomes part of your task to draw the Bondholders' Protective Agreement appointing the committee, defining its powers and providing for the deposits of bonds thereunder." The primary objective of the agreement, he explained, "is to confer upon the committee the power to take any action it may deem necessary or proper for the protection of the bondholders and the enforcement of their rights." Because this agreement is the source of the bank's authority, he concluded, the "powers conferred . . . cannot well be too broad."[5]

This lofty view of the reorganization process provided a self-justifying rationale for the equity receivership and the dominant role of its bankers and lawyers, who drew on long experience in similar cases. "Do not attempt to evolve the agreement out of your own consciousness," Cravath said, "for it would take you days to work out clauses covering half of the contingencies for which provision should be made." The boilerplate elements of the reorganization agreement were in his view "the result of the experience and prophetic vision of a great many able lawyers." The railroad's bankers and lawyers were presumed to have a moral commitment to its investors.

Reorganizations could be windfalls for bankers. The legal work was demanding. To justify a sizable fee in one case, Cravath wrote that "the Western Pacific business proved to be unusually complicated. . . . We had to deal with four railroad corporations each organized under the laws of a different state. . . . [A] great deal of the negotiating which is usually done by the principals fell upon the lawyers, and many days were spent in consultations and negotiations." Cravath and his name partner Henderson were among the luminaries of the reorganization bar, but their protégé, Robert Swaine, who would one day step into Cravath's shoes, was even more influential.[6] Implementation of the reorganization plan ordinarily involved the issuance of new securities to replace the old ones and to raise money to finance the reorganization and provide working capital to the reorganized railroad. Usually, this meant dealing with J. P. Morgan, Kuhn, Loeb or a few other banks that had underwritten the bonds and served as bond trustees. The amount of the new securities typically was large, and the syndicate fees could be as high as 6 percent of par value of the new bonds and stocks. In addition, if—but only if—a reorganization was successful, the bankers were paid fees for their work as depositories of securities, advisers to committees, and executors of the plan. In the case of the Erie Railroad's reorganization in 1895, for example, the Morgan banks were paid $500,000 plus expenses.[7]

Contrary opinions were less benign. In *Other People's Money*, a muckraking book published in 1914, Louis Brandeis argued that certain banks controlled the nation's finances and the receivership process for their own benefit. A later critic, Max Lowenthal, authored a book, *The Investor Pays*, criticizing the fictitious drama staged by railroad reorganization bankers and their lawyers for judicial and public consumption. In reality, he wrote, insiders precipitated the receivership, decided on a plan and implemented it without regard to the rights of dissenters or the public. Reorganization lawyers were seen as subservient to their Wall Street bank clients and unconcerned about the fate of small investors who required protection. In fact, the investment banks that had underwritten railroad bonds looked for support to the same Wall Street firms that handled their securities issuances. Because Cravath represented Kuhn, Loeb in many of its railroad bond offerings, for example, it made sense for the firm to act as reorganization counsel if the railroad defaulted on the bonds. Control of receivership reinforced the bankers' grip on major sources of capital, and Wall Street professionals paid themselves handsomely. The fees in reorganization cases could be enormous; they amounted, New Dealer Thurman Arnold later wrote, to "high-class boondoggling."[8]

The large number of railroad failures created a need for well-trained corporate lawyers. The lawyer-intensive receivership practice of the Wall Street bar placed Stetson, Cravath and Cromwell's firms at the pinnacle of the profession. Since legal fees were awarded as part of the final decree approving the reorganization, lawyers were not paid unless the reorganization was successful. Thus, the reorganization bar was confined to lawyers who could work for years without being paid, and could risk never getting paid at all. The barriers to competition became nearly insurmountable. " . . . [A] limited number of law firms, mostly in New York City . . . became expert in reorganization practice," wrote Robert Swaine, "and were retained . . . in nearly every railroad receivership." No firm gained more than Cravath. During the first two decades of the twentieth century, it grew from five to thirteen partners, supported by forty-six associates. The firm's practice was based upon its relationship with Kuhn, Loeb, as Frank Stetson's was with J. P. Morgan.

RAILROAD CONSOLIDATION

Most of the nation's railroads were reorganized during the financial panics in the late nineteenth century. With each successive reorganization, a railroad became more and more beholden to its bankers. (Indeed, one wit called the entire process "Morganization.") But the collapse of so many rail lines gave financiers the opening they had been looking for to fix the railroads' structural problems.

Reorganization committees were able to eliminate inefficiencies, sell off unneeded assets, combine branch lines, and otherwise rationalize the country's rail industry. When the dust cleared at the end of the century, American railroads had been consolidated into six large groups—Morgan, Vanderbilt, Pennsylvania, Gould-Rockefeller, Harriman-Kuhn-Loeb, and Moore. Collectively, these groups controlled 165,000 of the 204,000 miles of railroad track in the United States.

Morgan and his lieutenants were the largest, directly in charge of one-fifth of the nation's trackage and indirectly influencing much more. Some groups, like Morgan and Harriman or Vanderbilt and Gould, were inveterate antagonists. Others, such as the Morgan, Vanderbilt, and Pennsylvania groups and the Harriman-Kuhn-Loeb and Moore groups had some measure of cross-ownership and common interest. The scope of the consolidation was astonishing. The Morgan group had five rail systems and 225 operating railroads under its control and the Pennsylvania four systems and 280 operating railroads.[9]

THE NORTHERN PACIFIC RAILROAD

Although each reorganization was a saga of its own, the insolvency of the Northern Pacific, was one of the most complicated. The Northern Pacific was an ambitious transcontinental line that had been organized in the mid-1860s to connect the northern Great Lakes to the Pacific Northwest. A project of Civil War financier Jay Cooke, the Northern Pacific was the nation's second transcontinental railroad. President Lincoln—a former railroad lawyer himself—signed its charter during the Civil War, contemplating a route that would link Lake Superior to the port waters of Puget Sound. Congress approved the charter, giving the company land grants of almost forty million acres, which it used to raise money from European investors. The company started construction in 1870, but soon was overextended, ruining Cooke and sparking the Panic of 1873. Finally, in 1883, under the leadership of Henry Villard, a German aristocrat and railroad promoter, the Northern Pacific completed its rail line, with borrowed millions, as Villard himself drove the symbolic final spike. A few months later, the company's stock crashed as investors realized it was hopelessly in debt and its West Coast terminus, Portland, Oregon, resembled an undeveloped wilderness.[10]

Villard had risked his personal fortune on the Northern Pacific venture. When disappointed creditors threatened to seize his mansion on Madison Avenue in New York City, he turned for help to William Nelson Cromwell, who arranged a loan from Drexel, Morgan & Co., evidenced by a note in Villard's wife's name and secured by his house as collateral, thus frustrating importunate creditors. Cromwell later negotiated a sale of the property to Whitelaw Reid, the newspaper publisher. Villard, suitably impressed, engaged Cromwell as counsel for the Northern Pacific Railroad, where his own tenure was to be short-lived. Accused in the press of hopeless speculation and a cycle of extravagance and folly, Villard resigned as president of the Northern Pacific to escape his growing debts and left for Germany to seek new investors and recover from a nervous breakdown. Cromwell spent the next three years threatening to give the railroad's creditors even less if they failed to settle. Meanwhile he and Drexel, Morgan took the opportunity to consolidate control over the Northern Pacific. Much more than a mere lawyer, Cromwell wore a principal's hat. Shrewdly, he also anticipated that Villard would resurrect his finances and return with well-funded allies. "I was imbued with an abiding faith in your future," he wrote to Villard. "Your desire for a continuance of my connection with your affairs . . . is appreciated."[11]

Cromwell's faith was well placed. In 1886, just two years after his ignominious departure, Villard returned to New York. Acting for Deutsche Bank, he purchased a major stake in the Northern Pacific and once again became a director of the railroad; two years later, he became president of its affiliate, the Oregon and Transcontinental Company. "For the second time," wrote the *Albany Journal*, "Mr. Henry Villard finds himself at the head, or almost at the head, of the great Northern Pacific railroad company. . . . There was no loss of confidence in him among his friends. The best proof of this is the fact that he returned after a few years as the representative of German capital sufficient to put him in control. . . ."[12] Now fortified with new investment, Cromwell executed the next phase of his plan, incorporating Oregon & Transcontinental Company in 1890 as a holding company in order to exercise control over the railroad and enable its reach into the Midwest. To the press Villard appeared in charge, but it was Cromwell, not Villard, who effectively controlled the railroad's business. Regarding Villard as a figurehead, Cromwell justified his role. "What we needed most was a leader," he wrote, "through whom alone negotiations could be conducted. . . . I had my own methods of working . . . in carrying out my own views and plans. . . . I must be allowed my own way of working it out." Cromwell's strategic intervention was indispensable as the Northern Pacific confronted its first major competitor, the Canadian James J. Hill's Great Northern Railway, in the race to extend its rail lines to Chicago.[13]

In the event, and despite Cromwell's vaunted managerial skill, Northern Pacific incurred huge costs in building parallel lines to compete with the Great Northern. Its timing was unfortunate. Laid low by the Panic of 1893, the Northern Pacific had to declare bankruptcy again. For a second time Villard contemplated resignation, regretting his connection with the Northern Pacific. Aided by Cromwell, he nonetheless was able to sell a large block of company stock before its bankruptcy. The well-timed sale raised suspicions he had early knowledge of the railroad's imminent demise. Although Cromwell was able to protect Villard from angry investors seeking damages for their losses, the intimation of fraud remained.[14]

When receivership appeared inevitable, the Northern Pacific engaged Cromwell and Alfred Jaretski of Sullivan & Cromwell as reorganization counsel. To stop creditors from attaching parts of the railroad, Cromwell had to appoint a receiver in each state where it operated. He sent lawyers across the country to prepare and file the necessary papers and then telegraphed his associates simultaneously to file. No less an observer than Robert T. Swaine of Cravath, Swaine & Moore wrote many years later: "They did an excellent job of procuring the simultaneous appointment of the same receivers in all the judicial districts through which the road ran. . . . He and Jaretski had arranged with several circuit judges in advance. . . . '[I]nside of two hours from the time of filing the papers in Milwaukee, the entire system had been legally put under the control of the receivers, and reports of the accomplishment of the work had been received in the office of the counsel here in New York.'"[15]

Despite the brilliant precision with which Cromwell and Jaretzki launched their attack, the reorganization floundered as the receivers fell into irreconcilable differences with the railroad's management, and competing sets of receivers were appointed to manage some of the Northern Pacific's branch lines.[16] Composition of the reorganization committee changed as the battle over the Northern Pacific raged, and at one point Morgan himself was a member.[17] Stetson, as expected, was the committee's counsel at the time the plan was floated, but in the course of the reorganization he began his lasting association with Victor Morawetz, who had recently left the Seward firm to become one of J. P. Morgan's chosen railroad executives.[18]

Although Morawetz never joined Stetson's law firm, the names of Stetson and Morawetz began to appear together on major deals, and Stetson involved Morawetz whenever he faced a novel challenge. In the Northern Pacific bankruptcy, Stetson and Morawetz devised a solution to one such intractable problem. Even during reorganization, railroads were reluctant to surrender their original charters, granted by the state legislature years before, and conferring broad powers that no legislature would now give. Problematically, the Northern Pacific's charter limited the railroad's ability to borrow money to refinance previous debt.[19] Stetson and Morawetz circumvented these constraints by finding an unbuilt railroad in Wisconsin—the Superior & St. Croix—that had a more forgiving charter, changing the Superior's name to the Northern Pacific *Railway* and having the new railway buy the assets of the old railroad.[20] A reorganization plan was approved in 1895, and the Northern Pacific emerged from receivership the next year, financed by new securities syndicated by Morgan and Deutsche Bank.[21]

Reverberations of the Northern Pacific reorganization lasted for years. One feature of the plan of reorganization that Stetson and Morawetz developed was that stockholders of the Northern Pacific Railroad would, upon paying an assessment, receive stock in the new Northern Pacific *Railway*. This caused them to become senior in the distribution of the railroad's property to the rights of unsecured creditors. One such creditor, Joseph Boyd, sued many years later alleging that his rights to the property of the railroad's estate should be senior to those of its stockholders. The case made its way to the Supreme Court where Stetson, now an elder statesman at the bar, personally argued it on behalf of the railway in November 1912. In April 1913, the Court sided with Boyd, establishing what came to be known as the absolute priority rule and greatly complicating future reorganizations.[22] Dealing with the implications of *Boyd* became a preoccupation of the Wall Street bar for the next twenty-five years.

TEMPLATE FOR COMBINATIONS

The systematic reorganization of the railroads was an object lesson for the bankers and lawyers of Wall Street. Their ability to combine disparate railroads into large integrated networks, to raise the money to restore the roads' finances, and to manage such enormous companies successfully was a blueprint for other sectors of the economy as well. Consolidation of the railroads presaged the creation of the great industrial trusts.

Assemblages of companies, however, were not feasible unless they could be financed, and the legal infrastructure of the late nineteenth century was inadequate for the enormous financings that were necessary to create giant corporations. There was still no national bankruptcy law, nor were there federal laws regulating stocks, bonds, or other securities. The patchwork of state laws and inadequacy of the courts meant that investors were justifiably anxious about parting with their capital. It was the immaturity of the law that impeded concentration of the economy.

Frank Stetson pioneered a creative and enduring solution to this dilemma. Corporate assets long had been posted as collateral to secure loans and bond issues using an instrument known as the corporate mortgage. Historically, this was a simple affair, resembling an ordinary real estate mortgage and seldom running more than a few pages. Stetson realized, though, that the corporate mortgage could become far more. As a contract between a creditor and a debtor, it could be expanded to cover other matters besides a description of the collateral and its conveyance to a trustee. There was no particular reason that the mortgage could not be expanded to include more than one creditor and thus dictate relationships among different classes of creditors. Nor, for that matter, was there any reason why the mortgage could not extend to corporate assets beyond real estate. Ultimately, Stetson realized that the corporate mortgage could do far more than convey a security interest. Instead, the document could become a legal system in and of itself, governing almost all aspects of debtor-creditor relations.

Under Stetson's hand, the corporate mortgage ballooned to what we know today as the corporate trust indenture. Stetson changed it from a four- or five-page document to one often running to 200 pages. He found he could add provisions to extend the creditor's security interest to such things as after-acquired property, proceeds of the sale of assets, franchise rights, the common stock and internal debt of subsidiaries, leasehold rights, and even intellectual property. Stetson decided he could almost create a private bankruptcy code by setting forth in detail the conditions upon which a receiver could be appointed and the rights the receiver could exercise. He prevented renegade creditors from besieging faltering debtors by denying creditors the right to take direct action against a debtor and instead obligating them to work through the mortgage trustee. Similarly, he concluded that he could define by contract what was and what was not an event of default, whether there should be a right to cure, and the conditions under which the indenture trustee might grant waivers. At the same time, he made standard the acceleration clause, meaning that the rights of all bondholders matured simultaneously, preventing a debtor from selectively manipulating different classes of creditors. Working around "contentions which previously had been made in reported cases," Stetson found that he could determine by contract such perplexing questions as the effect upon conversion rights of corporate consolidations or the issuance of preferred stock.[23] His indenture specified that the trustee could foreclose by lawsuit, sell all pledged assets as a single package, apply for a receiver, and recover a deficiency judgment. The indenture could require the borrower to waive its rights to seek stays or to claim the benefits of appraisal laws. Similarly, Stetson added covenants requiring the borrower to keep its premises in good condition, maintain a level of current assets, and refrain from conduct that undermined the priority or integrity of the lien. As if this were not enough, Stetson decided that the indenture also was a good place to specify the priority of recoveries among different classes of creditors, or even dictate that in some circumstances a stockholder or junior creditor could take precedence over a creditor with senior rights.

Few legal instruments have been more successful than Stetson's corporate trust indenture. It was a solution to a plethora of legal and practical problems that had plagued bankers and lawyers for years, and it is still a foundation of corporate finance today. Many of its features found their way into subsequent bankruptcy codes, and it became such a powerful instrument in the hands of bankers that Congress passed the Trust Indenture Act of 1939 to rein it in. It was trust indenture that enabled the enormous aggregations of capital without which the creation of the behemoth corporations of the Trust Era could not have happened.

Stetson's conception of the trust indenture did not lie only in his talents as a corporate lawyer. Instead, it harkened back to his days as a litigator and his frustrating experience brokering the negotiations among creditors in railroad reorganizations. Knowing the inherent limitations of litigation and the unpredictability of courts, Stetson believed that the uncertainties of the judicial system could be circumvented if bankers and their lawyers, *ab initio*, set down clear rules and defined legal rights long before any crisis arose. With the scope of uncertainty narrowed, many previously intractable issues simply never arose.

5

The Age of Trusts and The Progressive Era

Expansion of the nation's economy in the last decades of the nineteenth century exposed its greatest anomaly: the nation's industrial base was growing explosively, yet remained inefficient and dispersed. Business in the last decades of the nineteenth century required economies of scale and visionaries ready to build and organize large projects. The consolidation of hundreds of fragmented railroads into large regional rail systems in the mid-1890s became an obvious model for other industries, and bankers now had the means of raising the enormous amounts of capital required to finance giant enterprises. One of the main impediments to the creation of large enterprises was the state of corporate law.

BUSINESS TRUSTS AND HOLDING COMPANIES

Stubborn legal questions impeded the organization of large companies. Some states, for example, did not allow foreign corporations to own real estate within their boundaries, while others imposed artificial constraints upon how much capital a business could have. Most state laws prohibited one corporation from owning another.

In 1882, Pittsburgh lawyer Samuel C. T. Dodd devised a structure called the "business trust"—a short-lived solution that nonetheless gave its name to an economic era. Tasked by John D. Rockefeller to circumvent state laws preventing Standard Oil from absorbing its rivals, Dodd found a simple expedient. Since the offending state laws applied only to corporations, Dodd suggested that Rockefeller create a *trust* to hold the stock of the companies Standard Oil had gobbled up. Shareholders in companies would exchange their share certificates for an instrument called a dividend-payment certificate, which evidenced their ownership of an interest in the trust, conferred some voting rights, and provided for the payment of dividends. The trustees—Rockefeller and his colleagues—would then vote the shares to elect slates of directors to manage the constituent companies.

Dodd's innovation came at an opportune time. The nation's boom-and-bust business cycles all but forced companies to combine. Initially, they did so in loose cartels to limit production, divide markets, and maintain prices. Ultimately, they simply merged to form huge combinations in oil, tobacco, steel, and other commodities. "The day of combination," Rockefeller boasted, "is here to stay." It represented "survival of the fittest," he said, "the working out of a law of nature and a law of god." Trusts promoted ruthless business practices: degradation of human labor, unscrupulous manipulation of stocks and bonds, and freewheeling monopolies whose resources often dwarfed those of city and even state governments.[1] Standard Oil, American Tobacco, and other huge consolidations—tightly organized, horizontally and vertically integrated giants—swallowed up competitors and marginalized competing small producers, wholesalers and retailers. Inspired by Standard Oil's example other industries soon established trusts of their own.[2]

This consolidation was troubling to many in the Victorian age. Two years before he died in 1887, Algernon Sullivan stated his misgivings about the trusts. "I regard them with apprehension," he said. "I think it is good public policy to restrict and regulate them and I shall so speak." His partner thought otherwise; Cromwell was too ambitious a lawyer to let this opportunity pass by. Once Sullivan was gone, Cromwell felt free to realize his vision of the firm as a leader in corporate consolidation.[3] He developed a reputation as a clever lawyer, one who taught robber barons how to rob. Under Cromwell's management Sullivan & Cromwell became a change agent that stood apart from comparable law firms and gained a reputation as a devious corporate strategist.[4]

In 1892, the Ohio Supreme Court determined that Dodd's trust device was illegal as a matter of corporate law.[5] But, by then, the issue was largely moot. In 1888, New Jersey Governor Robert Stockton Green asked a flamboyant lawyer named James Brooks Dill how New Jersey might increase its revenues to pay off its remaining Civil War debts.[6] Dill suggested that New Jersey could become a safe haven for big business by offering an alternative to a trust, namely a corporate holding company.[7] In 1889, the legislature amended New Jersey's corporate code to enact Dill's proposal, thus permitting a New Jersey corporation to own the stock of other corporations with a view to controlling their affairs.[8] The results were remarkable. In five years, corporate filing fees and franchise taxes paid to New Jersey grew from $800,000 to over $2 million and accounted for more than half of the state's revenues. By the turn of the century almost all the nation's large corporations were domiciled in New Jersey, allowing it to pay off the state debt and abolish property taxes.

William Nelson Cromwell was the first to capitalize upon the change of law. A year after the death of Algernon Sullivan, Cromwell made William J. Curtis a partner in the firm. Cromwell intended to train Curtis as a business lawyer and was keenly aware of the shortcomings of the trust structure.[9] Cromwell tasked Curtis, who happened to be a New Jersey resident, to work with Dill in developing the holding company structure and convincing the New Jersey legislature to liberalize its corporation laws.

Allowing one corporation to own the shares of another begged the question whether the resulting firm might be an illegal monopoly. The Antitrust Act of 1890, popularly known as the Sherman Act, declared that every combination in restraint of trade was illegal and further made it a crime for any person to monopolize trade. But neither "combination" nor "monopolize" had a clear or accepted meaning, and it seemed easy to sidestep the law. Thus, after the Ohio Supreme Court ordered the Standard Oil Trust dissolved, Samuel Dodd simply arranged to vest control of its sixty-four companies in twenty new corporations, each controlled by the same members of the Rockefeller group. Similarly, it was not uncommon for a single director to sit on dozens of boards to ensure that different companies acted in harmony. Chauncey Depew, for example, sat on well over 100 corporate boards over the years, and continued to serve on over seventy even after he was elected to the United States Senate.[10] Moreover, as a general matter, monopolization was thought to require some level of collusion between legally distinct competitors. In early cases, courts found that elements of a single firm, no matter how large, could take concerted action without restraining trade.[11]

It was an irony of the age that most of the great monopolies were assembled only after the Sherman Act was passed. Although some arose when one corporation drove its rivals out of business or cornered them into merging, it became common to organize trusts as roll-ups of whole industries. By the turn of the twentieth century, promoters had created hundreds of trusts, ranging from the massive firms monopolizing the copper, sugar, and tobacco businesses to such oddities as the Fire-Brick Trust, the Baking Powder Trust, the Button Trust, the Paper Envelope Trust, and the Bobbin & Shuttle Trust.

The downtown law firms were at the center of the trust frenzy. Not surprisingly, the first two trusts to incorporate in New Jersey were Sullivan & Cromwell clients. Within three years fifty companies, including Morganized railroads, the sugar trust, and the tobacco trust, converted to the corporate holding company form under New Jersey law, many of them choosing at the same time to headquarter in New York. Never shy about self-promotion, in 1911 Cromwell published a retrospective chronicle of his most signal cases, not in a legal register, but instead, and characteristically, in *Who's Who in Finance*. Far from a dry catalogue of ancient triumphs, the listing reveals Cromwell (and by implication Sullivan & Cromwell) as an aggressive player in the nation's unfettered capital markets before World War I. His clientele included railroads, brokerage firms, insurance companies, banks, and shipbuilders in battles for control, reorganization in bankruptcy, and receiverships. Cromwell was also present at the creation of major corporations including American Cotton Oil Co., National Tube Co., and U.S. Steel Corporation. "Every one of these transactions was a battle," Cromwell recalled, " . . . a battle in which there was never a moment to be lost, and during the fighting of which I never permitted anything to interfere for a moment."[12]

Frank Stetson was equally active. In 1892, his firm helped financiers Charles R. Flint and August Belmont consolidate nine failed rubber companies into United States Rubber. In the following years, it also was general counsel to the Paper Trust—International Paper Company—and involved in the creation of the farm machinery trust (International Harvester) and the Nickel Trust (International Nickel) in 1902.[13] Stetson also was central to J. P. Morgan's efforts in 1901 and 1902 to create an "Ocean Shipping Trust" to monopolize passenger and freight traffic in the North Atlantic. The result, International Mercantile Marine, was one of the first truly multinational companies, and Morgan's threat to British dominance of North Atlantic shipping led to an escalating race to build larger and larger ocean liners, culminating in the construction of the White Star Line's *Titanic* and Cunard's equally ill-fated competitor, the *Lusitania*.

THE STEEL TRUST

The greatest trust of all, however, was the mammoth combination Morgan assembled to dominate the mining, transportation, making, and fabrication of iron and steel. The result was the United States Steel Corporation.

The iron and steel business had come to rival the railroads as the United States' largest industry. Andrew Carnegie had, for years, been building an empire in western Pennsylvania that included coal mines, coking ovens, smelting plants, steel mills, and fabrication plants. By the 1880s, though, mines had opened in Minnesota to exploit the rich iron ore deposits of the Mesabi, Vermillion, and Cuyuna ranges, and a competing steel industry had emerged around Chicago.

The largest of these new companies was Illinois Steel, run by an outspoken promoter known as "Bet-a-Million" Gates, but represented by a solemn and shrewd former county judge named Elbert H. Gary. In 1898, Gary approached Morgan with a proposal to merge Illinois Steel with other regional companies to create a single firm that would control ore deposits, railroads, ships, docks, mills and production plants in the Midwest. Morgan agreed, and he formed a syndicate to finance the consolidation of four steel companies, two railroads, and other assets into a new entity called Federal Steel. Stetson was counsel to the syndicate and organized Federal Steel as a New Jersey holding company in September 1898. With Gary as its president, Federal Steel aggressively expanded its operations. Gary merged fourteen manufacturers into a newly formed National Tube Company and twenty-five other firms into the American Bridge Company. Predictably, this inflamed Andrew Carnegie, who instructed his brash 38-year-old president, Charles M. Schwab, to retaliate with newer, larger, and more efficient facilities.

This, of course, was the very type of ruinous competition J. P. Morgan abhorred. As it happened, in December 1900, he attended a dinner in Schwab's honor and learned that Schwab believed that the steel business could use further consolidation.[14] Following surreptitious meetings with Morgan's bankers, Schwab gingerly approached Carnegie about selling out to Morgan. After sleeping on it, Carnegie agreed to sell for $480 million. Morgan immediately accepted the price and dispatched Stetson and bankers Charles Steele and Robert Bacon to take the elevated train to Carnegie's mansion to get the deal signed up.[15]

The size of the U.S. Steel deal was unprecedented; in addition to buying out Carnegie, Morgan also had to finance the merger with Federal Steel and roll up dozens of other businesses. U.S. Steel's total capitalization was $1.4 billion, and to fund it Morgan had to organize a syndicate to underwrite $200 million of U.S. Steel securities.[16] Although the securities were quickly sold, there were persistent rumors that the company was overcapitalized and that its assets were worth no more than $1 billion. Future events proved those predictions wrong, since Morgan, ahead of his time, calculated the enterprise's value as a function of its earning power, and not its asset base.

The deal was a windfall for lawyers. Most leading corporate lawyers and their firms got a piece of the action precisely because so many different individuals and companies were involved. Cromwell, for example, represented National Sheet & Tube, while his partner, William Curtis, was instrumental in forming U.S. Steel's holding company. Most of the work related to financing the deal, and whatever antitrust analysis anyone did, was done by Stetson and Victor Morawetz. Stetson drafted the foundational document, the mortgage by which U.S. Steel pledged its assets to secure the $300 million bond issue that would help pay off Carnegie, as well as any future debt U.S. Steel would sell.[17] For this, he was handsomely paid. It was said that it took Stetson, working with Morawetz, eleven days to draft the papers to assemble U.S. Steel, and that the two men took home $500,000 in fees for that task alone.[18] Stetson also seems to have taken some of his fees in kind. Papers filed in a lawsuit in 1902 show that he owned about 8,000 shares of U.S. Steel preferred and common stock, with a par value of $800,000. For his part, Cromwell received 2,500 shares valued at $2 million at his death in 1948.

Stetson kept a firm grasp on the client. Initially he made himself the general counsel of the company but soon had his hands full with lawsuits by stockholders, investigations by state and federal authorities and, ultimately, the Justice Department's antitrust case to break up the company altogether. When the press of other business became too much, he installed his partner Charles MacVeagh, who held the job for nearly twenty years.

THE NORTHERN SECURITIES RAILROAD TRUST

The legal issues surrounding the trust movement and the antitrust laws came to a head in an unlikely way. The trust that may have brought the Age of Trusts to an end was a railroad trust that Frank Stetson organized almost by accident.

As was usually the case when J. P. Morgan reorganized a railroad, he ended up controlling it, and he did so after the successful reorganization of the Northern Pacific in

1895. Yet, in Morgan's eyes, the Northern Pacific was afflicted with one of the worst failings a railroad might have, namely, James J. Hill's competing Great Northern. In 1895, Hill proposed to merge the Northern Pacific and the Great Northern, only to have Stetson veto the plan on grounds it would violate the Sherman Antitrust Act. When court decisions soon proved Stetson right, officers of the Northern Pacific and the Great Northern gathered in London to hammer out an agreement to divide the market. Morgan assigned Stetson the job of arbitrating differences between the two railroads when disagreements occurred.[19]

Morgan had just left for his annual European vacation in 1901 when he learned that the Northern Pacific was under attack by one of the few men Morgan genuinely despised, Edward H. Harriman. Harriman controlled the Union Pacific, which operated the eastern half of the original transcontinental railroad running from Kansas City to Utah. The Northern Pacific had just beaten Harriman in a fight over the Chicago, Burlington & Quincy Railroad, and Harriman decided to recapture the CB&Q by taking over the Northern Pacific itself. Harriman enlisted the help of a coalition of bankers who had long resented Morgan. One was Kuhn, Loeb's Jacob Schiff, who until then had stayed out of Morgan's way. Another was the assertive James Stillman, the head of the burgeoning National City Bank, where the Rockefellers put their money. As soon as Morgan left New York, Schiff began scooping up shares of the Northern Pacific.

By the time the Morgan bankers learned of the raid, Harriman's group held a majority of Northern Pacific's preferred shares and were within 30,000 shares of controlling the common as well. Yet careful study of the legal documents revealed that the Northern Pacific's preferred stock would become redeemable in a few months, before the next meeting of stockholders. Thus, if Morgan could maintain a majority of the common stock, he could force the Northern Pacific to redeem the preferred stock and maintain control. Using a bottomless war chest loaned to him by the New York Life Insurance Company (whose president, George Perkins, as it happened, was a recently made partner in the Morgan bank) Morgan bought as much Northern Pacific stock he could find. At the end of the day, Morgan had won by a hair, with 52.5 percent of the common stock.

Schiff promptly wrote Morgan a letter all but apologizing for his role in the matter, and Morgan made clear that there were no hard feelings. He instructed Stetson to create a new, mega-holding company that would own the Northern Pacific, the Great Northern, and the CB&Q. Besides being too large a target for a hostile takeover, the combination would ensure permanent railroad peace in the Northwest. The entity, formed in November 1901, was a New Jersey holding company named the Northern Securities Company. Its assets went far beyond railroads to embrace coal and iron mines, timber properties, steamships, and land.

The antitrust implications of the plan were obvious. Even Stetson's then-associate, the diminutive George Gardiner, blurted out to Morgan "What do you want to do? Do you want to go to jail?"[20] However, there was ambiguity in the law. The competing railroads were neither merged nor combined. Instead, the controlling shareholders of each exchanged their shares for shares of Northern Securities, which was nothing more than an investor in these railroads. Mere investment, the argument went, was not illegal, could not form an illegal combination, and might not even constitute interstate commerce.

President Theodore Roosevelt disagreed. Working with Attorney General Philander Knox, he announced in February 1902 that the government would prosecute Northern Securities under the Sherman Act as an unlawful restraint of trade. Morgan, and the markets as a whole, were shocked, since the structure of Northern Securities had been carefully designed to circumvent the Act and many other trusts used the same approach. Morgan famously asked Roosevelt—referring to Knox and Stetson—"if we have done anything wrong, send your man to my man and they can fix it up."[21] Roosevelt refused—he was offended that Morgan considered him just another businessman to be mollified—and the case was filed the next month.

As usual, Stetson assembled a large team of lawyers—none from his own law firm—to handle the case. At trial, they offered various arguments why the Sherman Act should not apply. The first was that Northern Securities was not an illegal combination because it was a corporation organized under New Jersey to perform a lawful act. A second was that the railroads within the group had taken no action whatsoever; any actions were those taken by stockholders, who were legally distinct from the railroads and whose rights and powers were entirely distinct from those of the corporation itself.[22] These arguments seem almost frivolous today, and they failed then as well. Northern Securities lost badly in the trial court, which enjoined Northern Securities from voting its stock in the railroads, from paying dividends, or from exercising control over the Northern Pacific or Great Northern.[23] Morgan was blindsided by the result, worrying how the complex deal possibly could be unwound. There were complex issues of tracking down the original owners of the stock, determining how to adjust the prices at which the exchange had been made, paying off loans that had been secured upon the stock, and handling other adjustments. After learning of the decision, Morgan turned to Stetson and said, "You will have a pretty job, unscrambling the eggs and putting them into their shells and getting them back to the original hens!"[24]

Stetson did better than simply unscrambling the eggs; he also made sure most of them ended up in J. P. Morgan's basket. In addition to being Morgan's lawyer, Stetson was the general counsel of Northern Securities itself. After the Supreme Court narrowly affirmed the circuit court in 1904,[25] Stetson called a shareholders meeting to vote upon a proposal to recapitalize the company. The resolution proposed a hundredfold reduction in the capital stock of the company, meaning that for each 100 shares a stockholder owned, he or she now would have only one. The other 99 shares were to be surrendered to the company in return for $39.27 of stock in the Northern Pacific and $30.17 in the Great Northern.

However fair this might seem on its face, this proposal was a direct attack on Harriman. Harriman and his allies, of course, once owned almost half of the Northern Pacific's stock, and if they could have it back they could again put the railroad into play. However, in the creation of Northern Securities, Morgan, Hill and Harriman each had contributed all of their stock in the Northern Pacific and Great Northern. When combined, Morgan and Hill together owned over two-thirds of Northern Securities; conversely, the Harriman faction that had owned almost half of the Northern Pacific's stock now owned less than a quarter of Northern Securities. (Apparently, Morgan had purchased Schiff's Northern Securities shares, either to make peace or further outflank Harriman.) Thus, under cover of complying with the court's decree, Stetson ensured that Harriman now would be a minority stockholder of each of the two railroads and never again a threat to either.[26]

The Supreme Court's decision in *Northern Securities* is viewed as one of the seminal cases in the history of antitrust law. Putting to one side Stetson's skillful response to his client's defeat, *Northern Securities* set off a wave of trust-busting. Although it remained an open issue for years whether sheer size violated the Sherman Act, *Northern Securities* made it clear that combinations of competitors—whether in trusts, holding companies or otherwise—were illegal.

THE "MONEY TRUST"

J. P. Morgan abhorred disorganization as much as he coveted power and wealth. Notwithstanding his setback in *Northern Securities*, Morgan continued in his resolve to bring order to the nation's chaotic economy.

The "Trio"

Although J. P. Morgan was generally viewed as a man of unbounded wealth, in truth his bank provided only a fraction of the capital needed for its financings, reorganizations, and consolidations. Putting their own personal wealth at risk, Morgan and his partners financed deals by borrowing much of the money they needed from commercial banks. Morgan's banker was George Fisher Baker, who had cofounded the First National Bank of New York in 1863. Habitually opposing Morgan and Baker was a group of rivals that consisted of Jacob Schiff of Kuhn, Loeb and the Rockefeller family, who relied upon James Stillman's National City Bank.[27]

By the 1890s trust companies had emerged as powerful financial institutions. Creatures of state law intended to handle such sedate matters as wills, trusts, and estates, trust companies were not subject to banking laws or regulations. In this vacuum, trust companies had begun to act like banks, accepting money from small depositors and making large commercial loans. On Wednesday, October 16, 1907, an effort to corner the copper market failed, sparking yet another financial panic.[28] As fear spread, depositors demanded their money and the overextended trust companies failed one after the other. Morgan—now a man of 70—famously stopped the panic by summoning New York's bankers to his house and demanding that they make large loans to supply the troubled trust companies with the liquidity they needed to avoid collapse. Afterward,

Morgan resolved to impose the same discipline upon the financial markets as he had imposed upon railroads, the steel industry, and other sectors of the economy.

Morgan formed a partnership with his ally Baker and chronic foe Stillman to create an informal cartel to stabilize—or, perhaps, dominate—financial markets. Morgan, Baker and Stillman called their arrangement the "Trio."[29] They agreed to divide the securities markets using a formula that gave the bank that originated any new issue of securities half the issue and the rest equally to the other two. Between 1908 and 1912, the Trio underwrote—by itself and in conjunction with other banks—87 new issues worth over $1.3 billion.[30] Meanwhile, Morgan systematically took control of many of the trust companies and life insurance companies that had come to rival the banks' own power.

The Trio's control over the United States' finances caused widespread alarm about the creation of a "Money Trust." Journalists, politicians associated with the Progressive movement and, perhaps most of all, financiers excluded from the Trio began lobbying for Congress to do something. In 1913, Louis Brandeis serialized his muckraking book *Other People's Money*, arguing that these few banks controlled the nation's finances for their own benefit. "We must break the Money Trust," he concluded, "or the Money Trust will break us."[31]

The "Insurgents"

Stetson had remained politically active through the years. In 1911, he was pulled into a seemingly unrelated controversy that would have serious consequences for his main client. Until ratification of the Seventeenth Amendment in 1913, U.S. senators were elected by state legislatures or referenda; New York chose its senators in a joint session of its Assembly and Senate. Its incumbent senator at the time was Republican Chauncey Depew, whose term would expire in March 1911. The legislature's composition assured that his successor would be a Democrat.

Politicking to name the new senator began in January 1911. Tammany's preferred replacement was William F. Sheehan, a Buffalo politician who had been a bitter antagonist of Grover Cleveland and Stetson alike. Feeling they were being railroaded by Tammany, a group of Assemblymen and state senators organized to defeat Sheehan's nomination. The group came to be known as the "Insurgents," and soon it had a leader in the 29-year-old freshman Senator Franklin D. Roosevelt.[32]

The stalemate reached a crisis point in March. An extraordinary session of Congress was to begin in April and, unless the legislature acted quickly, New York would have but one seated senator. In the middle of the fight, Stetson appeared in Albany, hoping to broker a compromise between the warring Democratic factions. The Insurgents offered a list of four candidates whom they would support, and it appeared that a consensus candidate would be the wealthy New York lawyer Samuel Untermyer, who openly longed for public office.

Untermyer was an experienced trial lawyer who, like Stetson, had gone on to specialize in corporate finance. He cultivated the image of an aristocratic gentleman although, as one author observed, "he was arrogant, humorless, dictatorial, patronizing, and, not surprisingly, almost universally disliked."[33] More problematically, Untermyer had long been a thorn in the Morgans' side.[34] Untermyer had, for years, criticized the monopolies Morgan had assembled, and in 1911 he gave a series of speeches calling upon the government to break them up. Beyond being an enemy of the Morgan bank, Untermyer was viewed as a cat's paw for Tammany Hall. As a young lawyer, Untermyer had worked for Tammany boss Richard Croker, and it was Untermyer who was Tammany's emissary in Croker's ham-handed effort to solicit a bribe from Adolph Ochs by promising the *New York Times* all of the city's advertising if Ochs would hire, for $10,000 annually, a journalist of Croker's choosing.[35]

Stetson rejected Untermyer out of hand, summarily ending his hopes of a Senate seat. Soon, rumors circulated that Stetson had other motives, namely, that the new Senator must oppose Progressive legislation and impede Congress' efforts to implement the new federal income tax so reviled by Wall Street bankers. Tammany attacked Stetson as nothing but a front for Morgan interests. Frustrated in his efforts to broker a deal, Stetson soon packed his bags and returned to New York City.[36] Despite Roosevelt's continued efforts, the Insurgents failed and, on March 31, 1911, the legislature approved the respected, if Tammany-affiliated, Judge James Aloysius O'Gorman on the 62nd ballot.

The Pujo Committee

Stetson's veto of Untermyer's candidacy came at a bad time. In July 1911, Minnesota congressman Charles Lindbergh Sr. (the aviator's father) called for an investigation into the Money Trust. Early the next year, Congress created a subcommittee, chaired by Louisiana Democrat Arsène Pujo, to hold hearings. Soon, the subcommittee hired a large staff, and its chief counsel turned out to be none other than Samuel Untermyer.

Untermyer was a dangerous adversary. He was a brilliant examiner and skilled at cultivating the press. And if Untermyer had simply been a Morgan opponent before, it was now a grudge match. Making no secret of his hostility, Untermyer maintained that there was now a money oligarchy—a "system, vicious and dangerous beyond conception"—through which a small cabal of millionaires effectively ruled the American economy.[37] Untermyer and his staff spent months poring over documents and preparing a compelling case against the financial oligarchy. They demonstrated the concentration of wealth, the web of interlocking directorships, and the uncontrolled financial abuses of Wall Street. The Pujo Committee held public hearings in May and June of 1912, then recessed for the elections. Morgan's turn to testify was set for December 18.

By now, though, J. P. Morgan was mainly a figurehead. He had turned over leadership of his bank to his son Jack and its management to a small core of exceptional men such as Henry Davison and Thomas W. Lamont. Morgan was in failing health and depressed by the loss of the *Titanic* (a ship owned by his White Star line) and the deaths of his friends on board. Morgan was bored by the preparation for his testimony, gloomy about being a witness, and resentful at his public vilification.[38]

It fell to Stetson to organize Morgan's defense. He recruited a battery of lawyers as notable for its political weight as for its legal expertise. Defense counsel included the venerable Joseph Hodges Choate; Morgan's close friend and personal lawyer, Lewis Cass Ledyard; Wisconsin's ex-senator and political boss John Coit Spooner; New York lawyer George B. Case; and—surprisingly—Tammany politician William F. Sheehan, whose Senate, chances Stetson had labored so hard to thwart the year before.[39] With Stetson at his side, Morgan testified for two days. Untermyer confined the first day of questioning to details about Morgan's bank and its relationships to other banks, using charts and diagrams to make his point about the endless connections among the Wall Street banks. Like the seasoned trial lawyer that he was, Untermyer pushed the substance of his examination to the next day, when Morgan would be tired and the background facts nailed down.

The December 19 examination lasted about five hours and somewhat bewildered everyone involved. Untermyer's thesis was that it was all but impossible for a businessman to obtain financing unless he already was a member of the financial oligopoly. Morgan stoutly denied this, insisting instead that the touchstone of credit was personal character. There was some truth in Morgan's position—he had, for decades, been punctilious about the men with whom he did business—but he also had formed syndicates for the likes of Jay Gould. In any event, Morgan's unshakable self-righteousness flustered Untermyer, who became angry and sarcastic. It became a stalemate: Untermyer accused Morgan of refusing to do business with those who were not already wealthy, while Morgan insisted that he only did business with men of high character, most of whom happened to be wealthy precisely because of their high character.[40]

Both men made their point, but Untermyer's side ultimately prevailed. Morgan received accolades for his performance in front of the Pujo Committee and his refusal to concede that the bankers of Wall Street were anything other than the keel of America's financial system. Yet Untermyer demonstrated convincingly the scope of the self-dealing and collusion on Wall Street and the lassitude of regulation. A few weeks later, J. P. Morgan left for his overseas annual trip. In March, Morgan suffered the first of a series of strokes while sailing on the Nile, and he died in Rome on March 31, 1913.

Congress soon passed reforms to address concentration of economic power. In December 1913, President Woodrow Wilson signed the Federal Reserve Act, which established a national central bank and limited the power of the Morgan and other New York banks. In October 1914, the Wilson administration enacted the Clayton Antitrust Act, which gave teeth to the Sherman Act by explicitly banning anticompetitive mergers and interlocking directorships and imposing treble damages for violations of the Sherman Act. This, and the advent of World War I, effectively ended the era.

6

William Nelson Cromwell and The Panama Canal

Cromwell's career paralleled, and was a factor in, the huge growth of U.S. industry after the Civil War.[1] He allied himself with and worked unstintingly for the most fearsome capitalists of his time and often took control of events, not as an agent but instead as a prime mover. He was not shy about using whatever tactics might win the day. Ethical constraint was not his long suit. One biographical account accuses him of "deceit, bribery, and trickery."[2] A fairer description would state that he had an overwhelming desire to prevail, usually did and often used devious but not necessarily illegal means to that end. These character traits gave Cromwell a unique advantage in the convoluted dealings that led to construction of the Panama Canal, which he described as planning and conducting "the campaign for the adoption, purchase and building by the United States of the Panama Canal. . . . " It is an irony that a man of such Napoleonic ego and instinct for unilateral action could have developed a premier institutional law firm. For many years Sullivan & Cromwell was the elongated shadow of a single man.

The railroad business led Cromwell to his fateful connection with the Panama Canal. The Panama Railroad traversed the Isthmus of Panama from Atlantic to Pacific, enabling gold-seeking prospectors on their way to California to shorten their journey. It also marked the route of the failed Panama Canal project undertaken by the French in the 1880s. The Panama Railroad controlled access to the intended route through a concession granted by Colombia (of which Panama was then a province). A majority interest in the Panama Railroad was sold for $25 million to Compagnie Universelle du Canal de Panama, the French company managed by Ferdinand de Lesseps that tried to reproduce in Panama his success in building the Suez Canal in 1869 but instead precipitated a disaster, causing the disease-related and accidental deaths of over 20,000 workers and a scandalous loss of close to $300 million. Cromwell served as general counsel and director of the Panama Railroad. The Compagnie

Universelle du Canal de Panama, bankrupt as a result of its epic failure, became the ward of French receivers, who formed the Nouvelle Compagnie du Canal in 1894 as its successor, capitalized by forced investments from large shareholders of the old company. The Nouvelle Compagnie acquired its assets and launched a quixotic campaign to restart construction of the canal.[3]

In 1896 the Nouvelle Compagnie sent its director general, Marcel Hutin, to Washington in a vain attempt to convince the United States to buy the remains of de Lesseps' disaster.[4] A contemporary newspaper account said there was not "one chance in a hundred that the United States government would ever purchase the company's interest in a half completed ditch . . . ,"[5] instead preferring Nicaragua as the site for the canal. Needing an exceptional advocate to undertake a seemingly impossible task, on behalf of the Nouvelle Compagnie Hutin engaged Cromwell. One newspaper later called him "the man whose masterful mind, whetted on the grindstone of corporate cunning, conceived and carried out the rape of the Isthmus."[6] Cromwell sensed an opportunity to make an enormous amount of money and began devising a plan to sell the new company and the large amount of land it controlled in Panama to the United States. He promised his client an audacious and aggressive campaign. In pursuing it, he would project his already formidable business influence (and that of Sullivan & Cromwell) into the innermost corners of high government policy-making.[7]

To overcome the reputational burden of the French disaster, Cromwell suggested formation of a U.S. company owned by prominent financiers (including himself) that would buy all the Nouvelle Compagnie's assets related to the Panama Canal including, not least, its shares of stock in the Panama Railroad and all lands ceded by the Colombian government and sell them to the United States. Hutin thought it nothing more than a scheme to buy the assets cheap and resell them at a much higher price. Undeterred, Cromwell approached the Compagnie Nouvelle's largest shareholders to endorse his plan, warning that the United States would never otherwise buy the French "junk heap" in Panama. On December 27, 1899 Cromwell and Frank Stetson, J. P. Morgan's counsel, organized the Panama Canal Company of America to acquire and complete a canal across the Isthmus of Panama. Subscribers included J. P. Morgan and other prominent financial grandees. In the event, the liquidator of the Nouvelle Compagnie obtained a court decree forbidding sale of its assets to an American company without the consent of its shareholders, which was not forthcoming. Although the Panama Canal Company of America never progressed beyond its corporate filing, Cromwell later formed a syndicate, including J. P. Morgan & Co. and President Roosevelt's brother-in-law, Douglas Robinson, among others, to buy Nouvelle Compagnie shares for an estimated $5 million, anticipating a hugely profitable resale of the underlying assets to the United States for as much as $40 million.[8]

"Few lobbyists," writes historian David McCullough, "had ever gone about their task with such intensity or imagination."[9] Cromwell (together with his partner, William Curtis, and Roger Farnham, a newspaperman) inundated editors and congressman with materials on Panama, pursued Cabinet secretaries including Elihu Root and Philander Knox, arranged a meeting with President McKinley, negotiated with Colombian officials, and was the moving force behind McKinley's appointment of the Isthmian Canal Commission, charged with weighing the merits of both the Panama and Nicaragua routes. Despite these efforts, Cromwell was unable to prevent the Commission from issuing a report favoring Nicaragua during the presidential election year of 1900. Meanwhile President McKinley urged the Senate to enact legislation supporting a Nicaraguan waterway. Confident nonetheless, Cromwell was able to persuade Marcus Alonzo Hanna, an enormously influential U.S. senator, chairman of the Republican National Committee, and close personal friend of President McKinley, to amend the party platform in an election year by substituting a plank in favor of an Isthmian canal for one in favor of Nicaragua. Cromwell paid handsomely for Hanna's intervention by delivering a $60,000 check to the Republican campaign fund, charged to the Compagnie Nouvelle as a necessary expense. Hanna, who had once declared his support for the Nicaraguan route, later became a principal advocate in the Senate for the Panama Canal.[10]

CROMWELL IS DISMISSED BUT RETURNS TO FIGHT AGAIN

The conversion of Mark Hanna, not immediately evident, failed to spare Cromwell from reprisal. Rumors of Cromwell's plan to form a syndicate to buy Nouvelle Compagnie shares reached Marcel Hutin, who dispatched Baron Eugene Oppenheim to investigate. When Oppenheim reported the $60,000 donation, on July 1, 1901, Hutin, furious, dismissed Cromwell as general counsel of Compagnie Nouvelle and as its representative in the United States. Cromwell's dismissal was ill-timed, closely preceding Theodore Roosevelt's elevation to the presidency upon President McKinley's assassination and the Commission's unanimous approval of a Nicaragua canal, largely based on rejection of the Nouvelle Compagnie's improvident demand of $110 million for its assets, almost three times what Cromwell had proposed. Financial overreach, not the intrinsic merits of the Nicaragua route, had predisposed the Commission to decide in favor of Nicaragua. Without Cromwell's guiding hand, the Panama cause seemed bleak.[11]

At this moment a new actor and co-adventurer appeared on the scene. A graduate of the elite École des Ponts et Chaussees, Phillippe Bunau-Varilla had briefly served de Lesseps as an engineer on construction of the Panama Canal but was stigmatized as a "Panamiste" when the undertaking failed ignominiously. French courts accused Bunau-Varilla of fraud and compelled him, his brother, and several associates, among other penalty stockholders in the prior company, to purchase Nouvelle Compagnie shares but denied them any voice in management. There was little chance that the Nouvelle Compagnie could complete work on the canal, but Bunau-Varilla (like Cromwell) harbored hope that the United States might be a purchaser of last resort and had already visited the United States to make the Panama case to influential power brokers there, including Mark Hanna, J. P. Morgan, and President McKinley. An enigmatic figure, born out of wedlock and raised in modest circumstances, Bunau-Varilla presented himself as an aristocrat. "He didn't just come into a room," recalled Alice Roosevelt Longworth, "he made an entrance." With thinning dark hair and a waxed Hercule Poirot mustache, he seemed an unlikely tribune but was (again like Cromwell) astute, audacious, brilliant, and convincing. He had emerged, mysteriously, from the wreckage of the canal project a well-to-do man with a mansion on the fashionable Avenue d'Iena in Paris, near the Arc de Triomphe. His driving ambition, he said, was to vindicate French honor as a "soldier of the 'Idea of the Canal.'" If the United States were to acquire the Nouvelle Compagnie's assets, he would also be a very rich man.[12]

Recent events in Washington made the prospect of such a payday unlikely. Representative William Hepburn had introduced a bill in Congress authorizing appropriation of $180 million for a Nicaraguan canal shortly after President Roosevelt, in his annual address to Congress, urged the strategic importance and early completion of an Isthmian canal (thought to be a veiled reference to Nicaragua). In Cromwell's absence the case for Panama depended on Bunau-Varilla, who realized the Nouvelle Compagnie's management had made a serious error in proposing an unacceptably high valuation. He returned to Paris from the United States in December 1901 in time to force Hutin's resignation as president, install as his replacement the president of Credit Lyonnais, and authorize the company's sale. In early January of the next year the Nouvelle Compagnie cabled the Commission an offer to sell its assets to the United States for $40 million. The Commission's chairman, Admiral John Walker, conveyed the offer to Secretary of State John Hay, who rushed it to President Roosevelt. In mid-January the president reconvened the Commission, which unanimously reversed its earlier decision. Senator Hanna then asked Bunau-Varilla to have the Nouvelle Compagnie's board reinstate Cromwell as general counsel and representative in the United States. "[L]eaving aside all our other business," Cromwell said, "we acceded to this request."[13]

CROMWELL FOMENTS A REVOLUTION

Aided by Bunau-Varilla, Cromwell then embarked on the critical leg of an extraordinary journey. His fingerprints were everywhere. No mere lawyer or lobbyist, he became a de facto foreign secretary of the U.S. government, driven by the lure of big money. Described by a contemporary journalist as "the most powerful figure in the meeting places of American politico-finance," Cromwell made the Panama Canal happen, in the process establishing Sullivan & Cromwell's reputation as the go-to international law firm. Senator Hanna urged President Roosevelt to rely heavily on Cromwell. "You want to be very careful, Theodore," he said. "This is very ticklish business. You had better be guided by Cromwell; he knows all about the subject and all about those people down there." The president replied, "The trouble with

Cromwell is he overestimates his relation to the cosmos." "Cosmos?" Hanna said. "I don't know him—I don't know any of those South Americans, but Cromwell knows them all. You stick close to Cromwell."[14]

Roosevelt's accidental presidency had not at first blush seemed an advantage to the Panama lobby. While he was vice president, neither Cromwell nor Bunau-Varilla approached him. But Roosevelt was impetuous, with an expansive view of the United States as a world power, and had publicly supported the annexation of Cuba, Puerto Rico, Hawaii, and the Philippines. He viewed an Isthmian canal as the key to the nation's dominance of the Western Hemisphere and also had personal reasons to prefer Panama in the first major decision of his administration. He was almost certainly aware that Cromwell's syndicate had been formed to purchase shares of the Nouvelle Compagnie. Cromwell had sent his partner, William Curtis, to France, ostensibly to solicit the consent of the Nouvelle Compagnie's shareholders for sale of its assets to the United States, but in fact to buy company shares from scattered small-holders. A press report alleged that Cromwell and Bunau-Varilla were agents for J. P. Morgan's "gigantic Wall Street syndicate to gain control of the French concession and sell it to the U.S."[15]

President Roosevelt had Senator John Coit Spooner, a friend, introduce a bill proposing a Panama Canal and directing the president to buy the properties of the Nouvelle Compagnie for $40 million. The bill contemplated that Colombia would cede "perpetual control" of a canal zone in Panama. Proponents of Nicaragua were angry and upset. Senator John Tyler Morgan of Alabama, a leading supporter of the Nicaraguan cause, promised a vicious attack and got the Committee on Interoceanic Canals, which he chaired, to recommend Nicaragua and adoption of the Hepburn bill. Morgan castigated Cromwell for his intrusion into decisions and policies of the U.S. government.[16] Despite presidential support, Panama's prospects again seemed in jeopardy. A single factor turned the tide. Mark Hanna, coached by Cromwell, made the best speech of his career in support of Panama. Cromwell had prepared research material and placed junior associates at Hanna's side, ready to locate books and pamphlets for quotations. Hanna was no orator, but he made a formidable case. "All engineering and practical questions involved in the construction of the Panama Canal," he said, "are satisfactorily settled and assured. . . . " After furious debate, including Senator Morgan's allegation of "unlawful and corrupt methods," the Congress narrowly voted in favor of the Spooner bill, which gave preference to Panama but only if an acceptable treaty could be negotiated with Colombia.[17]

Colombia proposed a six-mile-wide canal zone leased to the United States for 100 years but over which it would retain sovereignty. For this it would receive $20 million upon signing a treaty and $600,000 annually after the canal had repaid its costs. Colombia would remain responsible for the zone's defense. Under the Spooner Act the United States required not a lease but an absolute conveyance of the land underlying the zone. Contemptuous of "dago ambassadors from powerless, insignificant countries," Secretary Hay authorized Cromwell to negotiate the treaty on behalf of the United States. Cromwell's counterproposal empowered the Compagnie Nouvelle to sell its rights, privileges, properties, and concessions to the United States and offered an up-front payment of $10 million, an annual payment of $250,000, and a 100-year renewable lease. Under extreme pressure Tomas Herran, the Colombian ambassador, agreed. The parties signed the Hay-Herran Treaty in January 1903 at Hay's Lafayette Square house, with Cromwell as the only witness. Recognizing his key contribution, Hay presented Cromwell with the signing pen. Two months later, overcoming last-ditch opposition from Senator Morgan, the Senate ratified the Hay-Herran Treaty and waited for Colombia's congress to do likewise.[18]

It was then up to Colombia's president to convene a special session of the Colombian congress. In a blunt message drafted by Cromwell, Secretary Hay warned Colombia not to reject the treaty or unduly delay its ratification. In June Cromwell spent a day at the White House meeting with President Roosevelt and afterward dispatched his press agent, Roger Farnham, to the *New York World*'s Washington bureau. The next day the *World* published an extraordinary front-page declaration. "President Roosevelt," it wrote, "is determined to have the Panama Canal route. . . . The State of Panama will secede if the Colombian Congress fails to ratify the canal treaty. . . . The citizens of Panama propose, after seceding, to make a treaty with the United States, giving this government the equivalent of absolute sovereignty over the Canal Zone. . . . In return the President of the United States would promptly recognize the new Government." Seldom, if ever, had a private individual, particularly one positioned to benefit from the action he proposed, had such direct influence on the U.S. government.[19]

The Colombian congress, jealous of its sovereignty and having been denied at Cromwell's urging a requested $15 million indemnity from the Nouvelle Compagnie in exchange for its consent, voted to a man against the treaty. Simply by deferring negotiations for a year, Colombia could have reached the end of its Panama Canal concession, taken control of the canal assets, and sold them to the United States. Meanwhile it could hold out for payment from the United States and the Compagnie Nouvelle. President Roosevelt was incensed. " . . . I do not think that the Bogota lot of jackrabbits," he wrote to Secretary Hay, "should be allowed permanently to bar one of the future highways of civilization." Roosevelt chose to overlook Secretary Hay's advice to Colombia—a main cause of the treaty's defeat—that Cromwell's clients would not part with a cent of their $40 million. Roosevelt now confronted several unpalatable options, the best of which, in the words of Shelby Cullom, the chair of the Senate Foreign Relations Committee, would be to "make another treaty, not with Colombia, but with Panama." Cullom's words echoed Cromwell's plan.[20]

Cromwell had great influence in Panama, where leading citizens viewed the canal as its economic lifeline and had long entertained the mirage of independence from Bogota's control. When Colombia rejected the Hay-Herran Treaty, Cromwell provoked a secessionist movement, mobilized key employees of the Panama Railroad, interceded with the Secretary of State, arranged critical financing, continued through his syndicate to acquire shares of the Nouvelle Compagnie and dispatched Bunau-Varilla from Paris to secure a further meeting with President Roosevelt and Secretary

Hay. Bunau-Varilla warned of revolution in Panama. " . . . [W]e shall not be caught napping," Hay replied. "Orders have been given to naval forces on the Pacific to sail toward the Isthmus." The United States, it appeared, would indeed support the revolution. Bunau-Varilla's revolutionary plan called for the rebels to seize the cities of Panama and Colon and the Panama Railroad line. The United States would dispatch a warship to prevent Colombia from taking any retaliatory measures and would quickly recognize the new state. Bunau-Varilla supplied a proclamation of independence, draft constitution, national flag, and a promise of $100,000 (funded by Cromwell's transfer from Credit Lyonnais) to underwrite the revolutionary government upon its formation. In return he extracted a promise that the Panamanian government would appoint him minister plenipotentiary of Panama with power to represent it in Washington and to draft and ratify a treaty with the United States.[21]

The USS *Nashville* arrived in Colon on November 2 with orders to keep the railroad open, occupy it if service was threatened, and prevent the landing of any forces "with hostile intent." The *Nashville*'s timely arrival was a tangible emblem of U.S. support, later seen as gunboat diplomacy. On November 3, exactly as Cromwell had planned, the revolutionary junta carried out a successful uprising against the Colombian government. Barely three days later President Roosevelt recognized the junta as Panama's de facto government, and formal recognition followed within a week. As Panama's minister plenipotentiary (a role he had purchased through financial assistance to the rebels), Bunau-Varilla met in New York with J. P. Morgan to confirm his prospective appointment (per Cromwell's plan) as Panama's financial agent with the exclusive right to cash and disburse the $10 million payment Panama would receive when it signed the canal treaty. Bunau-Varilla then hastily negotiated the Isthmian Canal Convention with Secretary of State Hay in Washington to preclude any objections an arriving Panamanian delegation might raise. Panama reluctantly ratified the treaty on December 2; the U.S. Senate ratification followed on February 23, 1904. The Hay-Bunau-Varilla Treaty included a grant "in perpetuity of the use, occupation, and control" of a ten-mile wide strip of territory within which the United States acquired sovereign "rights, power, and authority." The treaty was much more favorable to the United States than the aborted Hay-Herran Treaty and made Panama a virtual protectorate. Most important to Cromwell, the United States also purchased the rights and properties of the Nouvelle Compagnie for $40 million, then the largest real estate transaction in history.[22]

A FULMINATING SCANDAL

The purchase realized Cromwell's intricate plan of enrichment but became a fulminating scandal beginning with the Senate debate that led to ratification of the Hay-Bunau-Varilla Treaty. John Tyler Morgan, Cromwell's dedicated senatorial foe, contended Cromwell had organized a secret syndicate to profit from the Panama Canal. Two years later Morgan conducted hearings at which Cromwell was the chief witness but refused to testify. In 1908 the *New York World* charged that a syndicate of American investors, including J. P. Morgan, Cromwell, and the president's brother-in-law, Douglas Robinson, had made a handsome profit from the $40 million paid by the United States for the assets of the Nouvelle Compagnie, but all evidence of the syndicate membership mysteriously vanished. The *World* reporters later unearthed a copy of a massive brief filed by Cromwell to the French arbitration court in an effort to justify his $800,000 legal fee to the Nouvelle Compagnie (settled for $200,000). The brief explained Cromwell's efforts in instigating the revolution in Panama and creating the American syndicate that purchased at great discount the shares of the Nouvelle Compagnie and sold its assets to the United States. Perhaps to discredit Bunau-Varilla's parallel role, the brief concluded: "Messrs. Sullivan & Cromwell . . . planned everything, directed everything, and obtained everything; . . nothing was done without them, nor by anybody but themselves."[23]

The syndicate memorandum of agreement dated May 25, 1900, and collateral documents, later discovered by the *World* reporters, proved the existence of the syndicate and Cromwell's key role as organizer and stakeholder. Cromwell's scheme also addressed the mechanics of disbursement of the $40 million purchase price. As fiscal agent overseen by Cromwell, J. P. Morgan & Co. paid 30 percent to the penalized shareholders of the Nouvelle Compagnie and the balance to the syndicate members, including, among others, Cromwell himself (under the name "Nelson P. Cromwell"). Since the syndicate had acquired the remaining shares of the Nouvelle Compagnie, its members received around $25 million, a huge return on their investment. Cromwell became Panama's general counsel, fiscal agent, and United States representative and governed the nation's fiscal affairs for more than a decade, confirming his reputation as the man who "conceived and carried out the rape of the Isthmus." Two congressional investigations and a libel suit before the United States Supreme Court failed to prove conclusively that he had received an illicit profit. But the aura of rascality lingered. "How we romanticize men like Cromwell," wrote Louis Auchincloss many years later. "'Empire builders,' 'men of vision,' or even lovingly 'pirates.' And if one examines a single transaction carefully, what is Cromwell but a crook?"[24]

More important than Cromwell's singular quest for personal enrichment was his successful pursuit of influence in great affairs of state, shared by Sullivan & Cromwell, which through Cromwell was able to penetrate the inner sanctum of national politics. Cromwell had advised the president and the secretary of state, lobbied the Senate to choose Panama over Nicaragua, negotiated a treaty on behalf of the government and singlehandedly fomented a revolution. Panama was a consuming passion that occupied Cromwell full-time for almost four years. He was a champion puller of strings, damned as a "paid schemer," but became an indispensable actor in the nation's acquisition of the canal zone. Sullivan & Cromwell was now free to work with whomever it wanted. Starting as a local firm in New York City, it had become national counsel to major corporate clients during industrial consolidation at the turn of the century, and finally achieved global scale with the Panama Canal affair. Its rise to prominence was largely an individual, not an institutional, triumph. Cromwell would remain a central figure in the firm for many years to come, although his hands-on participation diminished after Panama as he sought new leadership for his twenty-lawyer firm in the first decade of the twentieth century.

7

Sullivan & Cromwell, an International Law Firm

Under Cromwell's aegis his firm now worked at the intersection of national politics and global business. Sullivan & Cromwell hosted a "web of relationships that constituted power, carefully crafted to accrue and endure over sovereign borders."[1] After the all-consuming Panama exercise, however, Cromwell needed to rebuild his firm, still largely populated by first-generation partners—William Curtis, Alfred Jaretski, George Sullivan (son of the founder), and Cromwell himself. In the decade between 1898 and 1908 the firm had made only one partner. Unlike Cravath, Sullivan & Cromwell did not systematically recruit high-stand law school graduates and lacked a pipeline of able acolytes. Instead associates came and went randomly, some remaining for many years as associates and others (including Harlan Fiske Stone, who became Chief Justice of the Supreme Court) departing after short stints. Cromwell's focus was primarily transactional, not organizational. The task of nurturing an institutional law firm was left to others.[2]

JOHN FOSTER DULLES

In 1911 Sullivan & Cromwell received an application for employment from John Foster Dulles, the grandson of John Watson Foster, Benjamin Harrison's Secretary of State, and a recent honors graduate of Princeton and a student at George Washington University Law School (from which he did not receive a law degree until many years later). Dulles was soon to be married to Janet Avery, from a distinguished upstate New York family and a first cousin of John D. Rockefeller Jr. Despite his credentials and family connections young Dulles found it difficult to attract an offer from New York firms that favored graduates of Harvard, Yale, and Columbia Law Schools. His craggy brow, aquiline nose, and strong jaw conveyed gravity and puritanical reserve but not sociability. He had already failed to interest Cotton & Franklin (the predecessor of Cahill, Gordon & Reindel). ". . . [S]omething about this clumsy youngster's presentation—big, tense, righteous, a world-class word-swallower . . . —put off the interviewing partner at Sullivan and Cromwell," who also turned thumbs down. Dulles then asked his grandfather, who had known Algernon Sullivan, to intercede with Cromwell. Mindful of the value of well-placed contacts, Cromwell overruled his partner in deference to a former associate of beloved Algernon Sullivan. Dulles went onto the firm's rolls at fifty dollars a month. "I had a desk in what was known as the 'Bullpen,'" he recalled long after in the firm's tribute to Cromwell. "Six recruits of that and the preceding year had desks which encircled the telephone switchboard and operator, located in the center of the room." He was to remain at the firm for forty years, a dour, moralistic, and dynamic presence who rose to be managing partner and eventually Secretary of State by exploiting Sullivan & Cromwell's international reputation and his own exceptional political connections.[3]

Sullivan & Cromwell was a platform for the ambitions of certain anointed partners, first Cromwell himself and then John Foster Dulles and his brother, Allen Dulles, but it was also a conventional Wall Street law firm dependent on securities issuances, corporate consolidations, and major litigation. To Royall Victor, who became managing partner in 1915 at the age of 38, fell the task of recruiting recent law school graduates, outplacing rejected associates with client companies, and making new partners. Not surprisingly, for the time, there were family connections among them: Henry Hill Pierce, son-in-law of William Curtis; Edward H. Green, cousin of Alfred Jaretski Sr.; and Jaretski's son, Alfred Jaretski Jr., his cousin, Edward H. Green, and his son-in-law, Eustace Seligman—thought to be an unusually large Jewish contingent for a Wall Street firm of that era when its main competitors were entirely WASP. Victor and the new partners turned their attention to utilities, which were then replacing railroads as the business vehicle of choice, including North American Company, a paradigmatic multi-tiered utility holding company that issued preferred stock and bonds without voting rights, not common stock, to concentrate managerial control. The new partners served on the boards of multiple utilities and perfected the open-end mortgage as a financing device. Important though it was, such activity was not the practice imagined by John Foster Dulles and, later, by his brother. They envisioned Sullivan & Cromwell as a means to shape world affairs for the benefit of the select, their roster of international clients.[4]

Dulles quickly demonstrated his use to the firm as counsel to the New York Produce Exchange, the Fiscal Agent of Panama (from which post a New York banker tried unsuccessfully to remove Cromwell), other Panamanian clients, French banks that were reorganizing Brazilian railways, and clients with large financial interests in Cuba. On a business trip to British Guiana, to oppose a tariff on imports of U.S. flour, he contracted malaria and nearly died. A massive dose of quinine saved his life but damaged his optic nerve, leaving him with excess tearing and a tic in his left eye—Foster's crocodile tears as critics would later describe them. The impairment ruled out active military duty, but the outbreak of war in 1914 accelerated Dulles' career thanks to another close family connection, his uncle Robert Lansing, who became President Wilson's Secretary of State in 1915. Like Wilson, whom he knew and admired as a student at Princeton, Dulles was infused with missionary zeal.[5]

Dulles was a third-year associate at Sullivan & Cromwell on the eve of the First World War in August 1914. Just a few months later, despite hostilities, he arranged a business trip to Europe to seek war risk insurance for firm clients and prospect for business. His uncle Robert Lansing, then Counselor at the Department of State but soon to become Secretary, equipped Dulles with letters of introduction to U.S. ambassadors in London and Paris vouching for the truth of any representations he might make. After he returned, Dulles continued work for clients with European interests, foreshadowing the international bent of his legal career, aided immeasurably by the influence of his grandfather (John Watson Foster) and uncle, both secretaries of state, and dynamic expansion of the United States economy. Washington exerted gravitational pull. At Lansing's behest Dulles became involved in a contested election in Cuba as a quasi-official intermediary (whose primary task was to protect the substantial interests of Sullivan & Cromwell clients in that country). At a breakfast meeting with his uncle, taking a page from Cromwell's playbook, Dulles urged that the Navy dispatch two fast destroyers to Cuba where a faction of the Liberal Party was in revolt against a recent election result. Within hours, Lansing directed the Secretary of the Navy to send the ships. Decrying the Liberal revolt as lawless and unconstitutional, President Wilson ordered Marines into the Cuban countryside, where, ostensibly to protect the sugar industry, they remained for five years.[6]

In March 1917, shortly before the United States entered the war, Lansing impressed his nephew into further service as a special emissary to Costa Rica, Nicaragua, and Panama to counteract German influence in the region. Lansing wanted these countries to declare war on Germany as soon as Congress acted. Dulles was well suited for the assignment. His firm had been instrumental in creating and was legal counsel to the Republic of Panama. He could easily justify his presence. As Lansing's envoy Dulles extracted from Nicaragua a proclamation suspending diplomatic relations with Germany and from Panama a declaration of war against Germany. In Costa Rica, ruled by General Federico Tinoco, a brutal dictator who had seized power in a coup orchestrated by United Fruit Company, a Sullivan & Cromwell client, Dulles promised U.S. recognition of his government in return for Tinoco's display of sincere friendliness. The Costa Rican Minister in Washington warned the State Department of Tinoco's assistance to the United Fruit Company, and President Wilson withheld recognition. Notwithstanding this rejection, Dulles remained in the president's good graces. With influential connections, he saw major opportunities as the United States went to war.[7]

DULLES AT VERSAILLES

Dulles has been described as a "frighteningly ambitious man . . . carefully calculating every step of his career, developing simultaneously the skills of a ruthless legal tactician and deeply held but simplistic moral convictions." Wartime led him into the epicenter of world politics. Ineligible for military service because of poor eyesight, he became (thanks again to his uncle) a legal adviser to Vance McCormick, chair of the War Trade Board, which was responsible for policing trading with the enemy acts and negotiation with neutrals to enforce the Allied blockade, including interdiction of trade with Leninists in Russia. Dulles used his position with the War Trade Board to renew his friendship with Bernard Baruch, the legendary Wall Street speculator, appointed by President Wilson in January 1919 as principal U.S. delegate to the Reparations Commission to determine the penalty Germany would pay after the war. Drawing on an old acquaintance, Dulles convinced Baruch to appoint him as his assistant and over the next eight months, in Paris at the peace conference, became the primary spokesman and draftsman for the U.S. delegation. Almost immediately he joined the cadre of economic advisers surrounding President Wilson. His European counterparts were John Maynard Keynes and Jean Monnet, each to have a decisive impact on global economic and political affairs. Dulles was no longer simply a junior lawyer with influential relatives. "His months in Paris," wrote one observer years later, "legitimized Foster to the emerging postwar power structure, kept him in daily working contact with leaders who appreciated that milling-machine intellect, his gift for breaking down and reconciling positions, his chilly, assured touch." Among those leaders, at one signal dinner party he organized, were Secretary of State Lansing, William Nelson Cromwell, Foreign Minister Lou Tsen-Tsiang of China, and William Graves Sharp, the American ambassador to France. So social had the Peace Conference become that Dulles had his wife Janet join him.[8]

German reparations became a bone of contention at the peace conference. Britain and France demanded that Germany reimburse them for the entire cost of the war—a huge sum including all expenses for arms, munitions, and supplies plus replacement of lost or damaged property. The Americans proposed reparations at one-tenth of that amount, believing anything larger would crater the German economy and lead to radical political backlash. Dulles became the point man for the American countervailing view, citing the Pre-Armistice Agreement signed by Germany and the Allies in November 1918, which required German reparations only for loss of civilian property. Dulles also took the lead in drafting the treaty clauses concerning German reparations, cleverly dividing the subject in two. One clause stated that Germany would make reparation for the entire cost of the war; the other stated that Germany's ability to do so would be limited "to such extent as will render the making of such complete reparation impractical." Dulles' legal sophistry was simply a band-aid. Bernard Baruch, his boss, saw the problem clearly. "[I]n the reparation clauses," Baruch said, "the conference was not writing a mere contract of dollars and cents; it was dealing with blood-raw passions still pulsing through the people's veins."

Later revisions transformed Dulles' formulation into Article 231 of the final treaty, denounced by Hitler as the war guilt clause, which made Germany responsible for all the loss and damage the Allies suffered as a result of German aggression. In May 1921, the Allied Reparations Committee issued an ultimatum that imposed on Germany a reparations bill of 132 billion marks, payable in gold, more than three times the maximum Germany could possibly pay according to Keynes. Within three years the Weimar Republic experienced hyperinflation, suspended reparations payments, and watched French and Belgian forces occupy the Ruhr Valley.[9]

On June 28, 1919, the Weimar delegate, under extreme pressure including the threat of Allied invasion, signed the treaty. Allen Dulles, present with his brother at the fateful ceremony in the Hall of Mirrors at Versailles, recalled that the German signatory was so affected with emotion he could hardly stand. Count Brockdorff-Rantzau, the Foreign Secretary, saw the treaty as a death sentence for millions of German men, women, and children. He declined to sign. Dulles himself, unhappy with the turn of events, was eager to return home to his law practice at Sullivan & Cromwell; but just the day before he had received a letter from President Wilson asking him to remain in Paris to continue his work. Dulles sent a copy of the president's letter to Cromwell and remained in Europe through the summer and fall as U.S. representative on the Reparations Committee, work that gave him face time with the French finance minister and the chief justice of England, to whom he argued the need for stability of government and a new basis of credit. On Bastille Day the French government made Dulles a member of the Legion of Honor. During his final weeks in Paris, Thomas Lamont, a Morgan partner and senior advisor to President Wilson, arranged for Dulles to be offered a partnership in a leading New York law firm at three times his pre-war salary. Dulles was careful to pass word of the offer to Sullivan & Cromwell, which made him a partner as soon as he returned to New York. He was 31 years old. Like his mentor Cromwell, Dulles "had learned to thrive in those lucrative thickets where business, politics, and diplomacy overlap."[10]

8

The Cravath System and Cravath the Man

THE CRAVATH SYSTEM

It is not an exaggeration to say that most institutional law firms, even today, embrace the system of law firm organization devised by Paul Cravath at the turn of the twentieth century. The Cravath system rationalized and perfected his firm's recruitment, promotion, specialization, outplacement, and branding, policies that came to characterize much of contemporary big law practice. Given the enormous success of Cravath's invention, it is tempting in hindsight to take it for granted. It was, however, a revolutionary step forward in its day—a radical renunciation of the idiosyncratic and casual patterns of practice the legal profession had followed for centuries. Paul Cravath saw the indispensable need for efficiency and organization if law firms were to serve an ever more complex corporate clientele. He was, without doubt, the herald of the modern age.

Robert T. Swaine, Cravath's successor and the author of a three-volume firm history, devotes the first twelve pages of the second volume of that history to the Cravath system. Cravath wanted only the best and brightest. A Phi Beta Kappa man from a good college who had become a law review editor at Harvard, Columbia, or Yale was the first choice. Colorless, narrow-minded bookworms need not apply (nor, for many years women, Jews, Blacks, and others not of WASP origins). He valued warmth, force of personality, and physical stamina. An ideal candidate, he once said at the Harvard Law School, must have "character, industry and intellectual thoroughness, qualities that do not make for charm but go far to make up that indefinable something that we call efficiency. Brilliant intellectual powers are not essential." Young lawyers did not specialize at first but were trained by working on smaller elements of large, complex corporate deals. "Cravath believed," Swaine wrote, "that the man who learns to analyze the component parts of a large problem involving complicated facts, and to do each detailed part well, becomes a better lawyer faster. . . ."[1] Responsibility would grow in accordance with competence; and each associate would in principle have an unimpeded opportunity for advancement based on talent.[2] After several years, those who learned to delegate, i.e., to expand their own activities by using younger assistants whom they have trained, may leap ahead. ". . . [T]he greater the amount of effective work a man can turn out," Cravath opined, ". . . the greater his value to the firm."[3] To ensure quality, Cravath put each lawyer on salary. "Because the demands in time, energy and competence are heavy," Swaine wrote, "the Cravath office tries to keep annual advancements and ultimate compensation at least as high as those of any other office in the city."[4]

Once hired, associates embarked on a quest for partnership, a goal achieved by only a few after an apprenticeship of six to ten years, called by latter-day commentators the "promotion to partner tournament."[5] Under the Cravath system associates remained for only as long as they were growing in responsibility. "A man who is not growing professionally," Swaine observed, "creates a barrier to the progress of younger men within the organization. . . ."[6] Those who leave do so for many reasons and are often welcomed by the firm's corporate clients or, as one of the authors did, form law firms of their own. But the reason some are chosen and many others are not often seems arbitrary or at least shrouded in mystery. According to Swaine, "[t]he choice is difficult; factors which control ultimate decisions are intangible; admittedly they are affected by the idiosyncrasies of the existing partners. Mental ability there must be, but in addition, personality, judgment, character. No pretense is made that the ultimate decisions are infallible."[7]

The Cravath system requires each lawyer in the firm to devote himself (only latterly, herself) to the practice of law as a member of the Cravath team. "There are no half-time partners nor associates," Swaine warned. "Nor is there any such thing as the business of individual partners or associates: all the business in the office must be firm business. . . . Hence, business-getting ability is not a factor in the advancement of a man within the office at any level, except . . . out of competence in doing law work, as contrasted with family or social connections."[8]

Cravath weighed lineage, personality, and ability when hiring new lawyers, but merit counted more than blood ties. This meritocratic policy set Cravath's firm apart from many competitors and became a touchstone in its search for talent. It was also the basis for lockstep compensation of partners, largely based on seniority, enabled by the firm's great profitability and its relentless drive for efficiency. The firm did not believe in star power. "There was a time when the lawyer was a gentleman, and the shopkeeper was a shopkeeper," Swaine recalled. "The lawyer is still sometimes a gentleman. But the shopkeeper's business has attained a size, value, and an influence which overshadows any individual attorney, whatever his skill."[9] Swaine's comment addressed rapidly changing professional terms of engagement. The elite practice of law soon grew to encompass more than common-law matters. It extended instead into the board rooms and executive suites of large corporations and required expertise in arcane areas of transactional law. Lawyers at Cravath and peer firms became planners, negotiators, and executors of complex deals, having long since outgrown the model of a small general partnership. Cravath, individually, was the progenitor of the institutional law firm, rationalizing for the twentieth century a relic of the nineteenth.

Only a large, specialized firm like Cravath could service the mergers and acquisitions, securities issuances, and bankruptcy reorganizations that increasingly characterized corporate law practice in the Gilded Age. By doing so, Cravath and a few other peer firms controlled the market for high-end legal services as part of an informal law firm cartel and helped determine the course of structural change in the U.S. economy. Ultimately, however, the Cravath firm and its WASP Wall Street cohorts found they could not remain competitive by applying the social standards of a gentlemen's club to a tough, relentless profession critically dependent on talent. The embargo on Jewish lawyers (Cravath did not make its first Jewish partner until 1958) and certain lines of business meant that up-start firms in New York, fortified by bright Ivy League law school graduates spurned by the establishment, became formidable competition with a focus on bankruptcy, strike suits and proxy contests. Change was imperative but slow to come.[10]

CRAVATH, THE MAN

For all his intense devotion to business Cravath was not a social cipher. Described in his obituary as a "globetrotter, diner-out [and] music lover,"[11] he married Agnes Huntington, an operetta star, became chairman of the Metropolitan Opera, was a founder of Long Island's Piping Rock Club (to which firm lawyers repair for a summer outing each year), perfectionist designer of several Locust Valley estates, and passionate gardener at the same venues. The *New York Times* said he knew the joys of art and the collection of precious things. "It was part of Mr. Cravath's nature," wrote another account of his life, "to hurl himself with unquenchable energy into any cause that he took up." His leisure pursuits and professional life reflected a singular intensity. "Cravath builds a house," said one observer, "as he does everything else—fiercely and with unholy efficiency. Everything must be perfect. There are always bitter clashes, feuds, with architects and landscape gardeners; repeatedly he discharges workmen who do not satisfy him. But he gets what he wants—and what he wants is gold-plated perfection."[12]

Cravath often combined his sidebar activities with his business interests. A social animal, he seldom spent an evening at home. In the first decade of his firm, Swaine recounts, he worked with associates late at night at his home after returning from a dinner party, the theater, the opera, or a concert. His house on East Thirty-Eighth Street had a gym, a well-stocked legal library and a comfortable lounge. Young lawyers from the firm, awaiting his return, spent an hour or two reviewing documents or discussing a point of law. They were then dispatched to the office, there to prepare a new draft or a legal conclusion for presentation early the following morning. In the summers before World War I, Cravath and other moguls commuted on a yacht, *The Flying Fox*, from the foot of Wall Street to the north shore of Long Island. Young associates often discussed business with the master on the deck of the yacht, "followed by a good dinner at Cravath's country home, a ride back to the City on a smoky Long Island train, and hours at the office to have papers ready for the next morning."[13] But any implication of bonhomie, prompted by nautical surroundings, would be misleading. "In those years," Swaine notes, "Cravath was imperious and given to outbursts of temper. . . . Deadly serious in his work, he showed little human warmth and still less humor. . . ."[14] But distant events portended change. The First World War—and Cravath's role in it—thrust him into the broader avenues of public life and marked a decisive change in his career, interests, and life experience. His law firm, long the center of his universe, now ran smoothly enough without hands-on guidance. He became free to entertain other quests.

As the war in Europe unfolded in a bloody stalemate between entrenched German and French armies, the trajectory of Cravath's career and even his personality underwent a change. Robert T. Swaine, who had almost left the firm to escape his boss' obsessive oversight, recalled that "[t]he Cravath who returned from World War I was a much more human person than the prewar Cravath. His role during the war was that of an adviser, constantly seeking to reconcile the differing points of view of strong men of vigorous personalities. He acquired tolerance. He learned that few men are unfailing in their judgments and he became less sure of his own and less insistent that everything be done his way. He mellowed and was less irascible; there were fewer outbursts of temper. His whole outlook on life broadened. His public contacts expanded."[15]

At the outbreak of hostilities an elite circle of New York politicians, bankers, and lawyers promoted the Allied cause. In doing so, Cravath joined, among others, Theodore Roosevelt and his younger cousin Franklin; Benjamin Strong, governor of the Federal Reserve Bank of New York; various Morgan partners; and leading lawyers such as Henry Stimson, Elihu Root, and George W. Wickersham. This influential group of insiders ardently sought a German defeat enabled by an alliance with Britain and France. Viewing the war in Manichean or even biblical terms, they castigated the Kaiser's Germany as a bloodthirsty warmonger and found President Wilson's neutrality diplomacy sterile and weak-kneed. Instead they urged American intervention and mounted a campaign in favor of defense spending and universal military training. They lobbied the government to relax controls on domestic firms providing war matériel to the Allies while J. P. Morgan arranged loans to finance war purchases. The pervasive belief in an Anglo-American alliance, already widespread among conservatives on either side of the Atlantic before the war, only grew more compelling as it ground on. Cravath was among the most committed supporters of the alliance, in part for reasons of WASP solidarity and also because several firm clients, including Bethlehem Steel and Westinghouse, had received procurement contracts from the British and French. Interviewed by the *New York Times* in 1916 after his return from a European trip, he said U.S. neutrality "[imperiled] our friendship with France and England, to say nothing of [its] deadening effect upon the spiritual life of the Nation. . . ." In a book published shortly thereafter, he said the Allies had a righteous cause "because they are fighting for the salvation of Christendom." When the United States finally intervened in April 1917, Cravath "found it a great relief that we are finally in the war with France and England. . . ."[16]

In October 1917, at the urging of Russell Leffingwell, a former Cravath partner then serving as Assistant Secretary of the Treasury, Cravath embarked secretly on a cruiser for Europe as a presidential appointee and advisory counsel to the sole U.S. representative on the Inter-Allied Council on War Purchases and Finance. Exposed to the grim reality of the trenches, which he visited several times in December 1917, Cravath said no "experience in my life . . . has left in my memory a more depressing impression than this visit to the battlefronts in winter." Otherwise, however, he welcomed his new obligations. For more than a year, enjoying "himself more than he ever did in his life," Cravath helped coordinate the war efforts of the United States and the Allies, shuttling between London and Paris, where the Council's finance section was based. In this work he was often a useful intermediary who favored British economic interests. In January 1918 John Maynard Keynes told a fellow Treasury official: "Our great standby [on the Inter-Allied Council on War Purchases and Finance] . . . is Cravath, who is perfectly admirable in every way and the savior of all difficult situations. The cause of the allies owes a great deal to his wise, upright and straightforward character." By contrast a U.S Treasury official said that Cravath "was indiscreet, told almost everything, and [is] disposed to be too pro-British."[17]

In the course of his work Cravath met with an array of notables, among them Bonar Law, then Chancellor of the Exchequer, Arthur Balfour, Secretary for Foreign Affairs, General John Pershing, commander of U.S. forces, and Lloyd George, British Prime Minister. Never shy, Cravath told Lloyd George that "the military victory for which we hope may prove to be a barren victory unless it be followed by a sound and lasting Anglo-American friendship; and that no effort should be spared to avoid misunderstandings which might imperil that friendship."[18] Cravath applauded the appointment of John W. Davis as U.S. Ambassador to Great Britain in 1918 (a position he once hoped to get for himself). He thought Davis could smooth out Anglo-American postwar disagreements and urged Secretary of Treasury McAdoo to extend the Inter-Allied machinery after the war to avoid "an unparalleled orgy of profiteering and economic confusion."[19] In 1918 Cravath helped found the English-Speaking Union and cultivated well-connected British politicians including Lord Beaverbrook, John Maynard Keynes, F. E. Smith, the Earl of Birkenhead, and Lord Buckmaster (the British Solicitor-General and Lord Chancellor). Margot Asquith, wife of the former Liberal prime minister, called Cravath her "tall and beloved American friend."[20] In the course of little more than a year he had become a prominent public figure. He was awarded the Distinguished Service Medal, became an Honorary Bencher of Gray's Inn, and received the Order of Chevalier of the Legion of Honor of France.[21]

After the war Cravath's interests were decidedly international. In the next two decades he traveled widely in Europe and Asia, including Soviet Russia, and authored prolix letters, later privately printed, supporting Western dominance, ignoring rising nationalist movements and advocating diplomatic relations with Soviet Russia. Cravath embraced British imperialism, anathema to Woodrow Wilson and other American liberals but deemed a force for international stability by advocates of the Anglo-American alliance. To advance his worldview, he joined John W. Davis in founding the Council on Foreign Relations, which stood for the nation's involvement in world affairs alongside Great Britain and opposed the rising tide of domestic isolationism. For twenty years Cravath he was active in the Council, suggesting speakers, and raising money for its journal, *Foreign Affairs.* He became a severe critic of the Treaty of Versailles as "unfitted to cure the economic ills of Europe, but cunningly devised to create new ones." The only reasonable chance of the Allies collecting an indemnity from Germany, he thought, was to keep it within such modest limits that the burden of paying it would be less appalling to the Germans than the consequences of default. Cravath described the Treaty of Versailles as a "Carthaginian peace," whose economic terms should be renegotiated.[22]

Together with Senator Henry Cabot Lodge of Massachusetts, former Secretary of State Elihu Root, and Morgan partners Dwight Morrow and Thomas Lamont, Cravath supported an Anglo-American guarantee of France's security against future German aggression. At Paris President Wilson had negotiated such a treaty, but the Senate refused to ratify it. Cravath at first supported Wilson's League of Nations but accepted reservations required by Senate Republicans and urged the Allies to go along. "The future of the world seems to me," he said, "to be full of danger unless the League of Nations can be set up with American participation." To Cravath, however, the League was little more than a means of Anglo-American cooperation, unbound by the technical provisions of the Treaty and focused instead on the pragmatic accommodations of its two most important stakeholders. In the election of 1920 Cravath was one of several Republicans (including lawyers Stimson, Coudert, and Wickersham) who signed a public statement declaring President Wilson's League of Nations to be so gravely flawed they preferred to begin again under President Harding. On a personal level Cravath forged friendships with Jean Monnet of France and Morgan partner Dwight Morrow, both internationalists. Together they envisioned creation, in Dean Acheson's words, of "a new world order" based on reason and knowledge.[23] While Cravath the man became more humane in the wake of world war, Cravath the law firm lost none of its institutional rigor and remained a formidable bastion of muscular law practice.[24]

9

Early Cravath Alumni

A law firm may be judged not only by the talent and capacity of the lawyers laboring within it but also by the careers some achieved after leaving the firm. Among the most significant leavers during and between two world wars were Russell C. Leffingwell, S. Parker Gilbert, and John J. McCloy, each of whom played an important role in government and business after Cravath and set a precedent for later generations of firm lawyers. Gilbert and McCloy became pivotal actors in German affairs before and after the Second World War. All three held high office, McCloy several times. Leffingwell and McCloy ascended to the very top of the financial world. All got early footing at Cravath, Wall Street's forcing house, and used it as a launching pad at time of war and thereafter to the inner councils of the business world. Each was driven by a ferocious work ethic and will to succeed. Collectively, they and their counterparts in elite law firms and investment banks defined an American establishment.

Leffingwell, described by Swaine as "the ninth generation of Leffingwells in this country," graduated from Yale and Columbia Law School, where he was editor-in-chief of the *Law Review* and became a partner in Cravath, Henderson & de Gersdorff in 1907 after Guthrie had left the firm. Leffingwell seems to have led a charmed life as the youngest partner. It was left to him to screen his assistants and choose those who worked directly for Cravath or Henderson. He was regarded as an exact draftsman and keen analyst of the economic implications of corporate transactions. " . . . [H]e acted as a restraining influence on his seniors and clients," Swaine recalled, "and taught his juniors the importance of recognizing that not all of the lawyer's problems in matters of corporate finance lie within the statute and cases." Having suffered under the hypercritical regime of Cravath, Guthrie and Henderson, he was restrained in commenting on juniors' work and gave "encouragement and self-confidence to timid but able men, who would have broken under Cravath or Henderson."[1]

In the winter of 1914-1915 after the onset of war, Leffingwell, burned out from hard work, planned to quit the firm in order to teach or write. Cravath urged him to take a six-month leave before coming to a decision. After spending the winter at Lake George, he returned to the office, but his resumed practice was cut short by America's entry into the war in 1917. Although 38, he applied for a commission as a reserve officer at the Plattsburg training camp in upstate New York. Appalled that someone of such promise would devote himself to "teaching American young men how to stick their bayonets through the bodies of imaginary huns," Cravath urged friends in Washington to find him a suitable government job. William Gibbs McAdoo, Secretary of the Treasury and a neighbor of Leffingwell, summoned him to Washington on the eve of his departure to Plattsburg. Starting as a dollar-a-year man in the Treasury Department, he became Assistant Secretary of the Treasury in charge of a portfolio that included massive issuance of Liberty Bonds and $11 billion in credits to Allied governments. With snow-white hair and a pointed nose, he had the gravitas of an elder statesman and looked older than his years. He was also a wide-ranging intellectual, a hard practical man who loved the cut and thrust of debate. The Treasury was to be a key post in a nation transformed by war.[2]

The government now controlled the U.S. economy. To support the Allied Expeditionary Forces, federal spending increased enormously, and new agencies proliferated. Financing the requirements of total mobilization was a duty thrust on the Treasury, which had to find new sources of money. Although income taxes accounted for half of federal revenue, public debt and rampant inflation also became essential elements of wartime finance. McAdoo, himself a lawyer, turned to fellow lawyers to fill key Treasury positions. Leffingwell was by far his most important recruit and became the de facto undersecretary of the Treasury during most of the war. As counsel for Kuhn Loeb and other New York banks, he was intimately conversant with the inner workings of corporate reorganizations and major underwritings. Cravath called him "one of the best lawyers at our Bar, with no superior as a contract lawyer."[3]

His initial job at Treasury was the First Liberty Loan for $2 billion. Sceptics doubted raising such a huge amount was possible but were proven wrong when Liberty Loan Committees easily sold the bonds. During the war government debt increased from $1 billion to over $26 billion. Reliance on bonds rather than tax revenues confronted Leffingwell, a Wall Street Republican, with a difficult problem. Surprisingly, he argued for taxation. "The sound rule to stick to," he reminded McAdoo, "is that taxes should be as heavy as they can safely be levied." Unpersuaded, McAdoo set off on a nationwide speaking tour to publicize the sale of government bonds. Leffingwell reminded him that taxes could raise revenue, curtail consumption, and distribute the costs of the war. Inducing the public to take bonds would require taxpayers to pay back war loans and finance the postwar recovery. Saturating the market with government loans, he thought, would inevitably lead to financial ruin. Thirty years later, Leffingwell had a similar view. "Economically speaking," he said in a speech to the Academy of Political Science, "war is the business of destruction. To engage in the business of destruction prudently and conservatively, avoiding any greater government expenditure than the taxpayers of the country can meet out of current taxes, means that we shall send our sons and grandsons to war with bare fists, and lose the war, prudently, with a balanced budget and a dear-money policy; and leave it to our conquerors to inflate us."[4]

After the war most Treasury lawyers returned to the private sector. Leffingwell remained at Treasury, working under McAdoo and his immediate successor Carter Glass. When Glass resigned from Treasury in 1920, he and McAdoo urged President Wilson to name Leffingwell as secretary. Leffingwell did not hide his disappointment when Wilson selected the secretary of agriculture as Glass' successor but was not surprised to learn that Wilson had done so. In 1920, after a summer vacation, Leffingwell returned to the firm, now clumsily renamed Cravath, Henderson, Leffingwell & de Gersdorff. He quickly resumed his former pace and often worked late, much to the dismay of his associates, who could not leave before he did. But life as a lawyer had palled. Leffingwell found drafting corporate mortgages far less compelling than managing Liberty Loans and financing the Allies at the Treasury.[5]

In 1923, like Charles Steele before him, he accepted a partnership at J. P. Morgan & Co., where he served for more than thirty years, eventually becoming board chairman. Along the way, he chaired the Carnegie Corporation, helped found the Council on Foreign Relations, and advised everyone from the president in Washington to junior officers at Broad and Wall.

J. P. Morgan was not merely a leading investment bank. It also discharged obligations later borne by federal agencies and international organizations. As he gained seniority in this pivotal institution, Leffingwell became a key partner, together with Thomas Lamont and Dwight Morrow, and earned a reputation as a business intellectual, writing and speaking widely. He was also one of the few partners with access to the Democratic Party, having formed a friendship with Franklin Roosevelt through the "assistant secretaries' club." Unlike many of his peers, he approved the reflationary policies of the First New Deal and Roosevelt's decision to take the dollar off the gold standard, a policy shift that lifted the stock market by 15 percent and broke the psychology of deflation. "Your action in going off gold," he wrote the president, "saved the country from complete collapse." During the long Depression years that followed, Leffingwell helped Roosevelt maintain open lines of communication to the banking establishment but remained, at bottom, an ardent proponent of corporate capitalism opposed to the New Deal and its liberal advocates. Leffingwell particularly mistrusted Supreme Court Justice Louis Brandeis. He viewed Brandeis as a behind-the-scenes author of the Glass-Steagall Act, which mandated separation of investment from commercial banking and required J. P. Morgan & Co. to split itself in two. "The Jews do not forget," he wrote his partner, Thomas Lamont. "They are relentless. . . . [W]e are confronted with the profound political-economic philosophy, matured in the wood for twenty years, of the finest brain and the most powerful personality in the Democratic Party, who happens to be a Justice of the Supreme Court."[6]

S. Parker Gilbert Jr., a Leffingwell protégé, entered the Cravath office in 1915, having graduated from Rutgers and Harvard Law School. "Tall, slim and pale," in

Swaine's recollection, "Gilbert was shy, serious-minded and distinguished by unusual industry." His intellect and capacity for hard work were soon to be legendary. When the United States declared war, Gilbert tried to enlist but failed to qualify for military service. With Leffingwell's help, the young lawyer instead became counsel to the War Loan staff at the Treasury. Upon Leffingwell's return to private practice in 1920, Gilbert, all of 27, succeeded him as Assistant Secretary of the Treasury for fiscal affairs. Work consumed him. He rarely left his office before midnight, often remaining until early morning. He soon became indispensable. A year later Andrew W. Mellon, shortly to take office as Secretary of the Treasury, persuaded him to remain with the incoming Republican administration as Under Secretary to work on refunding war debts. His meteoric rise inspired ecstatic press coverage. He was called "a youthful prodigy," a "thinking machine," and a "phenomenon."[7]

In 1923 he returned to Cravath as a partner but found it difficult to transition from high-level policy-making to the nuts and bolts of corporate practice. As it happened, economic developments then brewing in Europe eclipsed his humdrum legal concerns and catapulted him into a position of unique power. In 1924 a committee of experts sitting in Paris, chaired by Charles G. Dawes, proposed a plan to resolve the German reparations crisis traceable to the Treaty of Versailles. When Germany failed to pay reparations required by the treaty, French and Belgian military forces occupied the Ruhr, causing hyperinflation and disabling the German economy. The Dawes plan called for an end to the Allied occupation, a major loan to Germany, and a staggered payment plan for its discharge of war reparations. The plan's most novel feature was a mechanism designed to prevent reparations from again destabilizing the mark. The German government was to raise required funds in marks and pay them into a special escrow account in the Reichsbank under the control of an agent-general for reparations. The agent-general would then decide how to apply these funds—whether to pay them abroad, use them to buy German goods, or loan them to local businesses. Under the plan the agent-general would occupy a position of enormous leverage over the German economy, a proconsul or viceroy deciding that nation's fate and, as recommended by the Dawes committee, an American.[8]

Designation of the agent-general, an economic czar, became the subject of international log-rolling among major international financial players. Wall Street wanted one of its own, Dwight Morrow, a Morgan partner, for the post. Morrow enjoyed support from Jack Morgan, Dawes, and Hughes and Hoover in the Coolidge cabinet and seemed an obvious choice. The White House assumed his appointment would ensure success of the critical Dawes loan, to be underwritten by a Morgan bank syndicate. The U.S. ambassador to Germany, Alanson Houghton, was not so sure. He argued that choosing a Morgan partner would inflame German right-wing politics. The Morgan bank was also unloved by German-American communities in the Midwest, a warning surfaced by Coolidge's staff, but it was Houghton's cautionary view that sank Morrow's candidacy. This set off an international scramble among potential aspirants for the agent-general's position and their backers, including the Bank of England. The Morgan partners said the ideal candidate would have experience in the financial field, be well-known in the United States in order to reassure American investors in German bonds, and have sufficient character and reputation not to be wholly dependent upon others in arriving at financial or economic decisions. They wanted someone who could command confidence in the domestic marketplace and stand up to the French. When other candidates failed to attract decisive support, the Morgan partners proposed Parker Gilbert, who had served for five years at Treasury under Democrats and Republicans and achieved the rank of undersecretary.[9]

An economic expert whose primary interests were financial, not political, he was quickly approved. As agent-general, his brief was to manage Germany's reparation payments and decide how much it could afford to transfer into dollars each year. At 32, he was responsible for the world's third largest economy. During the next five years in Berlin he continued his zealous work habits and monastic lifestyle as he transferred $2 billion in German reparations (most of which supported the Allies' repayment of U.S. war loans). Reserved and taciturn, he did not socialize or learn German and worked without interruption. In the words of the German finance minister, "No theater, no concert, no other cultural events intruded into his life. . . ." He was a stern taskmaster and accused the Germans of fiscal extravagance. His minatory reports on Germany's economic policy gained him a tremendous following in Anglo-American financial circles and among Germany's creditors. But he was bitterly resented by many Germans, who burned him in effigy as a new kaiser "with a top hat for a crown and a coupon clipper for a scepter." Gilbert thought foreign bankers were too eager to lend and Germany too willing to accumulate foreign debt. The Dawes plan, he believed, had served its purpose, and he urged a more definite plan for the settlement of reparations. By 1928 he had persuaded the Allies to convene a further conference to determine, finally, what Germany would owe. The result was the Young plan, which reduced and stretched out reparations payments and converted German monetary obligations into tradable bonds. Germany would not pay the Allies directly but instead through a Bank for International Settlements, a change that eliminated the agent-general's office and allowed Gilbert to accept an offer of partnership from J. P. Morgan & Co., which he joined in 1931. By then the Depression had devastated world economies, Hitler had become a potent political force in Germany, and the revised reparations plan was close to collapse. Parker Gilbert died young, at 45, in 1938, a victim of his prodigious labors. His widow married Harold Stanley, of Morgan Stanley, of which her son, S. Parker Gilbert Jr., became chairman in the 1980s.[10]

John J. McCloy took a circuitous route to Cravath. After graduating from Harvard Law School in 1921, he was granted an audience by George Wharton Pepper, the leading lawyer in Philadelphia, McCloy's hometown, and an ornament of its bar. McCloy asked Pepper to which firms he should apply. Pepper's answer, candidly offered, was that, despite his credentials, as a striver from the wrong side of the tracks McCloy would never become a partner in a blue-chip Philadelphia firm. Pepper told McCloy instead to try New York, the national center of talent and finance, where law firms, even very good ones, were likely to be somewhat less concerned with social pedigree and more appreciative of hard work. That night McCloy took the train to New York and later joined Cadwalader, Wickersham & Taft, an old-line Wall Street law firm whose snobbish style evoked the Philadelphia McCloy had left behind. In December 1924 through Donald Swatland, a law school classmate, McCloy was able to transfer to Cravath, whose offices were just around the corner at 52 William Street. The firm weighed WASP lineage when hiring new lawyers, but merit counted more than blood ties. With relaxed common sense and an appetite for intense work, McCloy fit the Cravath mold. "I knew I could accomplish any task," he recalled, "that I could be the type of person others depended on, rather than the type that had to depend on others."[11]

McCloy was also lucky. His early years at Cravath coincided with a period of rapid growth for the firm, whose headcount expanded by almost half, driven by international business. McCloy's clients were investment banks, major corporations, and railroads. In 1925 Cravath managed a $30 million bond offering placed by Brown Brothers Harriman. This threw McCloy into contact with Robert Lovett, a tall handsome Yale graduate, then working for Brown Brothers as a runner, whose father was chairman of the Union Pacific Railroad and a neighbor of Paul Cravath on Long Island. Through Lovett McCloy also met Averell Harriman, who had inherited a fortune from his father, E. H. Harriman, and F. Trubee Davison, son of a Morgan partner and Assistant Secretary of War in the Coolidge administration, who invited McCloy to play tennis on the grass courts at his Peacock Point mansion. McCloy had been captain of the Amherst tennis team and used his prowess at the game to great advantage. His social horizons expanded as he gained entree to a wealthy elite circle he had once admired from afar.[12]

He soon became a regular at Long Island house parties where Lovett and Harriman were also guests. Memberships in the Grolier, University, Anglers, and Broad Street clubs followed, as did white tie evenings at the Metropolitan Opera. Work also continued apace. McCloy was kept busy by a rising tide of European business. His securities clients took him to Italy, Greece, France, and Germany. "Practically every merchant bank and Wall Street firm, from J. P. Morgan and Brown Brothers on down, was over there picking up loans," he recalled. "We were all very European in our outlook, and our goal was to see it rebuilt." In 1929, less than five years after joining the firm, McCloy became a Cravath partner. At about that time he met his future wife, Ellen Zinsser, whom he married the following year. Almost immediately McCloy and his bride departed for France, where he replaced Tex Moore in the firm's small Paris office on 3 Rue Taitbout as counsel for investment banking clients, notably J. P. Morgan and Kuhn, Loeb. Francis Plimpton and Allen Dulles, then also working in Paris, became close social friends.[13]

Shortly after his arrival in Paris, the firm's New York office dispatched McCloy to The Hague, where Bethlehem Steel had a case before the Mixed Claims Commission that was to alter the course of his career. An unexplained explosion in July 1916 had ripped through a munitions depot on Black Tom Island in New York Harbor. The press called it the "Black Tom" disaster. Bethlehem Steel, which had manufactured the munitions, and other claimants suspected German sabotage and were trying to collect damages from German funds held in the United States. The case had a long and winding history dating from the early 1920s. Intercepted German cable and radio messages from the First World War showed that the German government had authorized sabotage before the outbreak of hostilities, but the evidence did not conclusively prove German agents had set the fires leading to the explosion. After attending the hearings, McCloy predicted the claims would be denied but asked for assignment to the case and set about getting a rehearing. In 1932, after returning from Paris, he prepared the case for rehearing before the Commission in Washington but again lost. "Jack suffered from only one thing in the office," a summer intern recalled. " . . . [H]e had the Black Tom thing for so long it just looked hopeless to so many. Swaine was getting discouraged. . . ."[14]

Characteristically stubborn, McCloy refused to give up. He got Congress to pass legislation giving the government power to examine hostile witnesses under subpoena and compel production of documents. Later he defended constitutionality of the law, discovered further evidence of German collusion and fraud, and successfully reopened the case before the Commission in 1933. On the day the Commission's reopening decision was announced, McCloy boarded a ship for Ireland to interview Irish nationalist James K. Larkin, a legendary radical who had worked closely with German officials during the neutrality period and implicated Franz von Papen and other senior officials in Black Tom sabotage. McCloy spent months reviewing the voluminous case record and preparing the next brief before the Commission, a 380-page document. After eleven days of argument in 1936, the Commission set aside its 1932 decision and reinstated the case. Reinstatement altered the view of the German government. Hermann Goering signaled a willingness to entertain an out-of-court settlement. McCloy traveled to Germany with his wife to obtain final agreement, even attending the 1936 Olympics in a box next to Goering's as a guest of the German Foreign Office.[15]

In the event, the settlement unraveled, attacked by the Chase National Bank and other claimants whose unpaid balances would have been diminished by the sabotage awards. Litigation before the Commission resumed. Fortuitously, among papers filed with the Commission, a lawyer for the U.S. claimants discovered what came to be called the "Ahrendt postscript," an inadvertent handwritten admission by an official of a German shipping company that linked German agents to the explosion. In 1938 McCloy produced the final Black Tom brief, a catalogue of unmistakable proof of German guilt in what seemed an interminable case. The U.S. Attorney General argued on behalf of the U.S. claimants, who received awards of nearly $23.5 million, upheld by the U.S. Supreme Court on appeal.[16]

After a decade of dead ends and false starts, McCloy had prevailed. The Black Tom case launched his public career, aided by recent membership in the Council for Foreign Relations, a fount of internationalist foreign policy opinion. In pursuing an apparently unwinnable cause, he had acquired a reputation for expertise in German spy-craft at a time just before the Second World War when the United States had no intelligence service.

After the outbreak of World War II in Europe, President Roosevelt called Wall Street lawyer Henry Stimson back to Washington. Stimson was the classic example of the well-connected establishment lawyer who passed back and forth between Wall Street and Washington. He had served as Secretary of War under President Taft and Secretary of State in the Hoover administration. Now Roosevelt asked Stimson to again serve as the War Secretary. Stimson attracted a cadre of younger men with credentials similar to McCloy's, including Harvey Bundy, Robert Lovett, and Robert Patterson. A Cravath man (Al McCormack) directed Army intelligence, another Cravath man (Benjamin Shute) was responsible for distribution of Magic and Ultra intercepts, and a third Cravath man (Donald Swatland) procured airplanes for the Army Air Forces. Establishment lawyers were found throughout the entire upper echelon of the War Department. "Whenever we needed a man," said McCloy, "we thumbed through the roll of Council [on Foreign Relations] members and put through a call to New York."

In 1940, Stimson summoned McCloy to Washington as a special consultant on German espionage. Within a few months McCloy became assistant secretary for political and military affairs. His career and credentials conveyed a dynamic presence, even though he was short and compact. "His energy was enormous," Stimson later wrote, "and his optimism almost unquenchable."[17] McCloy became Stimson's alter ego, instrumental in passage of the Lend-Lease Act, selection of field commanders, and construction of the Pentagon itself. He also found himself at the center of contentious domestic issues, notably internment of Japanese Americans, where he facilitated questionable government action "to please the generals and make things easy for Stimson." He declined to authorize Allied bombing of Nazi concentration camps, opposed Secretary Morgenthau's proposal to limit German industry after the war, and took part in the decision to drop the atomic bomb on Japan (suggesting specific advance warning, retention of the emperor, and modification of unconditional surrender—all rejected by Truman's "assistant president" Secretary of State James F. Byrnes). By the end of the war he was widely regarded within the War Department as the ultimate point man to fix bureaucratic problems.[18]

In 1946, at war's end, McCloy returned to the practice of law on Wall Street. "No Cravath partner," wrote Swaine, "has had greater popularity in the firm than McCloy." Still, he craved more recognition, money, and freedom of action than was possible under Swaine's austere regime. In the end he had a falling out with Swaine, turned down several other attractive offers, and joined Milbank, Tweed & Hope, the Rockefeller family's law firm, which changed its name to Milbank, Tweed, Hope, Hadley & McCloy. His renewed stay in the private sector was contingent. In 1947 President Truman appointed McCloy to head the World Bank, the first of many public interest undertakings, followed in 1949 by appointment as High Commissioner for Germany and later chairmanship of Chase Manhattan Bank, the Ford Foundation, the Council on Foreign Relations, and Amherst's board of trustees. His principal biographer said of McCloy that he had "earned a position for himself as lawyer-servant for some of the most powerful private interests in America . . . in part because he was just a very good lawyer, but also because . . . he was the kind of man who could tell rich men what he really thought. He could be disarmingly frank, even critical, and yet . . . his loyalties were to their class."[19]

CRAVATH ALUMNI REDUX

Thirty years after his tour as a Cravath associate, in 1995, one of the authors received an invitation to attend a reception in Manhattan for its numerous alumni.[20] The invitation prompted apprehension since the firm, never known for its indulgence of associates, had pioneered an up-or-out hiring policy that compelled most associates eventually to seek work elsewhere—a diaspora that populated law firms, corporations, investment banks, government offices, and the judiciary. Why was the firm suddenly solicitous, one wondered, of those it had chosen not to keep? Having lost contact with his former colleagues over the intervening decades, the author was curious to see what changes the shifting tides of fortune had wrought. He approached the New York Public Library's vast chambers, the reception venue, at the appointed time in early December, amid a throng of legal humanity.

Several things became clear at once. An army of lawyers had come and gone since his own four-year stint, ending in the 1960s. One could only guess at their successes, failures, and careers. So many lawyers, so little time. The author moved on to his own cohort. The grayer heads did not all bristle with late-life accomplishments. Some were retired, several were engaged in down-market nonlegal pursuits, and—alas—at least three contemporaries had died unexpectedly within the last year. *Sic transit gloria mundi.* The pervasive atmosphere among the returnees was cautious, tentative, and watchful. Workaholics all, the alumni became associates again, if just for the night. Few had abandoned the law for a life of leisure. A retired general counsel for a Fortune 100 company was teaching at a law school to keep busy; a soon-to-retire corporate practitioner, after many years in harness, seemed almost panicked by the prospect of a life without deals, process, deadlines. No returning associate of the author's vintage bore any visible scars inflicted by Cravath's institutionalized system of rejection. Would they have done better at another, less ferociously competitive firm? If so, they were not speculating and seemed happy enough to have been connected to a deep well of legal prestige, whatever their present circumstances.

The most illustrious returning associate was Lloyd Cutler, founder of Wilmer, Cutler & Pickering in Washington, D.C., a leader of the bar and counsel to several presidents. Cutler had been a Cravath associate from 1940 until the early days of World War II and had worked for Robert Swaine on complex railroad reorganizations. Shortly after Pearl Harbor, Cutler told Swaine he was leaving for a job in Washington with the Lend-Lease Administration. Swaine was not amused. After all, he said, the railroads were also essential to the war effort. Unconvinced, Cutler left.

At war's end he approached the firm about returning but was refused. Only those who had left for military service, he was told, were welcome back in the fold.

The official Cravath history casts an oblique light on this incident: "After V-J Day, the former associates began to return. Apart from its legal obligation to take them back, they were products of the 'Cravath system' and the firm wanted them. Of the seventy-nine associates in military or other Government service after leaving the office, thirty-seven returned. They created a difficult problem with relation to the wartime substitutes, for although nearly all the latter had been employed for the duration only, the firm was grateful for their help, without which the work could not have been carried on, and, besides, human decencies did not permit summary termination of their employment."[21]

Much progress having been made in human relations in the intervening decades, the alumni returning to Cravath's reception were now welcome—however summary their terminations may have been—since, without their help, the work indeed could not have been carried on. Many years later, in 2019, at the firm's two hundredth anniversary in New York's Museum of Natural History, the returning alumni, their number now much enlarged, had become an overwhelming, buzzing throng. The edifice created and dominated by Paul Cravath belonged in part to them, not just the current incumbents.

10

Robert Swaine and Cravath's Reorganization Practice

Robert T. Swaine was to become the most powerful Cravath partner after Cravath himself and succeeded to the firm leadership role after Cravath's death in 1940. Swaine was a formidable lawyer, an exacting taskmaster, and a fearsome presence with a commanding knowledge of the intricacies of railroad reorganization—a subject to which he returned many times in law reviews and legal publications. As Cravath's protégé and successor, Swaine drove the firm's lucrative railroad reorganization practice.

Swaine joined the firm in 1910, just out of Harvard Law School, where he had been president of the *Law Review* and had won the Fay Diploma, awarded to the member of the graduating class giving most promise of professional success. In 1915, impelled by the stress of working for Cravath himself, he prepared to leave the firm and open his own practice. Russell Leffingwell, a rising younger partner, noticed boxes of books removed from Swaine's office and insisted that he see Cravath himself. "In less than an hour," Swaine recalled, "succumbing to the dominating personality [I] had sought to escape and to the promise of a partnership, [I] had agreed to remain."[1] Years later, second only to Cravath on the firm letterhead, Swaine became the face of the railroad reorganization bar, doing battle with William O. Douglas (once an associate at the firm) and New Deal reformers who mounted a formidable campaign to destroy the lucrative Wall Street railroad practice.

Swaine reframed the rules of the equity receivership, which depended on active cooperation of the railroad's old shareholders as a potential source of funding. " . . . [T]he purpose of a reorganization plan," he wrote in the *Columbia Law Review*, "is not so much to settle present litigation as it is to build a sound business structure which can effectively operate in the future . . . " Swaine saw negotiation and compromise among counsel and bankers as an essential feature of corporate reorganization. It was not necessary, in his view, to extinguish a shareholder's interest when a firm's liabilities exceeded its assets. Shareholders would have no incentive to participate in the reorganization if it completely eliminated their interests. Equity receiverships therefore usually allowed the railroad's old shareholders to keep an equity interest in the railroad if they agreed to invest badly needed new funds. The reorganization committee could then make a winning bid for less than the going concern value of the railroad's assets while leaving the shareholders in place and paying unsecured creditors only a fraction of their claims or nothing at all. The ensuing judicial sale created a new railroad owner that took the old line's assets free of all preexisting claims.[2]

Swaine called this "relative priority" a regime in which Wall Street lawyers and investment bankers protected the interests of their clients and ensured that the railroads continued to run. In modern financial terminology, relative priority meant protecting the option value of the equity and not treating the reorganization as a recognition event. Although Swaine did not use these terms, his theory of relative priority was later criticized as incoherent and could not be rigorously defended. Opponents of relative priority looked instead to the Supreme Court's decision in *Northern Pacific Ry. v. Boyd*, the 1913 case unsuccessfully argued by Frank Stetson holding that a railroad reorganization could not simply wipe out an unsecured creditor's claim. *Boyd* forced reorganizers to deal with unsecured creditors and increased the number of interests to be satisfied from two (mortgage bondholders and shareholders) to three. Unsecured creditors had to be satisfied. Contrary to Swaine's conceptualization, *Boyd* stood for a theory of absolute priority. Cravath called *Boyd* "a veritable demon incarnate standing across the path of the reorganizer today."[3]

In early 1916, a month before his thirtieth birthday, Swaine traveled to Jefferson City, Missouri, charged with the task of persuading the district court there and the public service commissions of Missouri and Kansas to approve reorganization of the St. Louis and San Francisco Railroad (the Frisco). Bankers, large security holders, and counsel occupied private railroad cars, parked in the railroad yards, as their living quarters. The Frisco had outstanding thirty different issues of mortgage bonds, totaling $200 million, secured by liens on single constituent lines. The plan of reorganization contained no specific provision for unsecured creditors although it reserved new securities for settlement with them. The judge presiding over the foreclosure proceedings, keenly aware of the *Boyd* case, at first insisted on paying unsecured creditors in cash. Appearing for the reorganization managers, Swaine undertook "three days of friendly debate in the [judge's] chambers . . . [and] persuaded [him to approve] what became the standard practice for dealing with the Boyd Case problem in equity reorganizations." Rather than cash, the reorganizers offered unsecured creditors a continuing interest as long as they paid a cash assessment. The resulting judicial decree took a potential cash drain and converted it into a cash infusion. "On a blistering day in August, 1916," according to Swaine's recounting, "at a St. Louis roundhouse filled with steaming engines, the property was sold by the special master to nominees of the reorganization managers; and on August 29 Judge Sanborn entered an order of confirmation, holding that the contentions of the many objecting creditors were untenable and the rule of the Boyd Case had been satisfied." The equity receivership bar was quick to adopt the technique in many future cases, not least the reorganization a decade later of the Chicago, Milwaukee and St. Paul Railroad, the largest in history.[4]

Once one of the nation's premier railroads, the Milwaukee had paid dividends continuously over many years but, in a fit of managerial megalomania, had built a $250 million line from Chicago to Seattle for which there was no traffic. It compounded this mistake by financing the line with bonded indebtedness. This led to years of decline under lethargic management that allowed the line to drift into receivership in 1925. In that year the Milwaukee had over 10,000 miles of track, $750 million in assets, and 40,000 widely dispersed security holders. It also had a $2 million annual operating deficit and $50 million in refunding bonds soon to mature. Management turned to Kuhn Loeb to handle the inevitable receivership. In such a major case Cravath himself and Robert Swaine made all major legal decisions, relying on a team of associates including Donald Swatland, John McCloy, and William O. Douglas.[5]

The Rockefeller and Armour families controlled the board but had quietly unloaded their holdings, and few of the railroad's remaining directors owned any shares. Their only allegiance was to the railroad's bankers, Kuhn Loeb and the National City Company. "Bill Douglas and I worked on the details of the St. Paul reorganization under Swatland's supervision," McCloy recalled. "Supervising the logistics of the massive reorganization was late night drudgery." Under Swaine's guiding eye, McCloy started work on the receivership papers months before there was any public hint the railroad was in distress. Cravath's strategy was promptness. Everything depended on being first in line.[6]

The firm had a friendly judge acquiesce in the receivership and appoint the president of the railroad as receiver. A new company was formed in Delaware to hold the railroad's assets. The bankers nominated committees to represent different groups of holders and induce deposit of their securities by threatening discrimination against nondepositors. Kuhn Loeb needed assurance that none of the railroad's many small shareholders would seek to exercise collective control over the reorganization. The committees soon held a majority of the outstanding shares. Cravath had used every legal device to obstruct dissatisfied security-holders and avoid government inquiry. "It seems practically certain," wrote the *New York Times*, "that the Reorganization Committee backed by Kuhn, Loeb & Co. and the National City Bank will buy in the property."

The auction took place in Butte, Montana, in November 1926 and consumed less than half an hour. As planned and anticipated, there was no bidder other than Kuhn Loeb at the proceedings. The bankers' fee for this work was just over $1 million. Cravath submitted bills for more than $450,000. Total fees came to more than $6 million, including large payments for nominal services to other financial institutions and law firms in New York. Swaine defended the fees as an "ordinary business arrangement"; but angry stockholders challenged them before the Supreme

Court, where they were barely upheld in a 5-3 decision. Justices Stone, Holmes and Brandeis dissented, charging Cravath with "failure to conform to . . . elementary standards of fairness and good conscience. . . ." The Milwaukee reorganization proved to be a landmark event with major repercussions for the Wall Street bar. Critics decried the artificiality of the consent receivership and the fictitious nature of the railroad foreclosure sale. "The controversies over the St. Paul reorganization," wrote Swaine, "had brought both private investors and public authorities to demand a substitute for the unsatisfactory equity procedure to meet the many impending railroad reorganization problems."[7]

The last act of Congress signed by President Hoover in 1933 addressed railroad reorganization by amending the Bankruptcy Act (Section 77) and giving the Interstate Commerce Commission broad authority to propose trustees, set limits on compensation, and pass judgment on any proposed reorganization plan. The purpose of the amendment, supported by New Dealers then coming into power, was in Swaine's view, "to eliminate those who had dominated railroad reorganizations in the past and to take the reorganization process under complete Governmental control."

The next year, the Act was further amended to add a new Chapter 77B that provided a jurisdictional basis to reorganize firms other than railroads. The 1934 amendments also bound dissenting creditors and ended the need for ancillary receiverships. However, unlike the railroad provisions, the 1934 amendments did not call for additional government oversight. It was not lost on Cravath or the reorganization bar that these reforms did little to address endemic protective committee abuses. Meanwhile, academic critics such as Thurmond Arnold, Jerome Frank, and William O. Douglas were mobilizing to attack the perceived evils of large-scale reorganizations run by investment banks and Wall Street counsel. "The stakes of participation in reorganization," wrote Thurman Arnold, "have become so high that they often are a greater objective than the reorganization itself."[8]

Douglas was at the time on the faculty of Yale Law School, revolutionizing the teaching of law. There, he had run an empirical study of bankruptcy filings as part of a campaign to become one of the first commissioners of the newly formed Securities and Exchange Commission. He was tapped instead to conduct the study of protective committees in bankruptcy that had been mandated by Congress when it passed the Securities Exchange Act of 1934. For the next several years Douglas commuted between New Haven and Washington directing a study team, one member of whom, Abe Fortas, would later sit with Douglas on the Supreme Court. When the study's first of eight volumes appeared, it gave traction to bankruptcy reform in Congress. Now Douglas' political star was rising. He had a seat on the SEC and would soon become its chairman. He regarded his study as an advocacy document for Congress, which then had three separate bankruptcy bills under consideration.[9]

Douglas supported the study by circulating an extensive questionnaire, sent to lawyers and banks nationwide for every large reorganization case, and interviewing leading practitioners. After cross-examination by Douglas, Swaine said that he felt shaken "until all his fillings fell out." The Chandler Act of 1938 carried into law

Douglas' animus against reorganization practice. No longer would existing managers run the business while their bankers ran the reorganization. The Chandler Act devolved these duties on a trustee with power to take over the business of the bankrupt firm and to formulate a reorganization plan. The SEC as a party in interest would scrutinize every reorganization plan involving a publicly held corporation. No Wall Street investment banker or its counsel could serve as trustee. Later, as a Justice of the Supreme Court, to complete his assault on Wall Street reorganization practice, Douglas ruled that a reorganization plan must be "fair and equitable." By that he meant the plan had to provide for absolute priority—the very result Swaine and Cravath had most feared. Still, the Chandler Act did not by its terms apply to railroad reorganizations, which were covered instead by earlier New Deal reforms. Nevertheless, the number of railroad cases began to decline, and Cravath and its peers in the reorganization bar turned to other targets of opportunity.[10]

Cravath's reorganization practice extended far beyond railroads. Hoyt A. Moore, who became a partner of the firm in 1913 and a name partner in 1943, devoted most of his time to Bethlehem Steel Corporation. "No lawyer," wrote Swaine, "ever unreservedly gave more of himself to a client than Hoyt Moore has given to Bethlehem." A Harvard Law School product with a constitution of iron and a pedant's eye for meticulous corporate documents, Moore was known for hard, driving work far into the night, through Sundays and holidays, outstaying a succession of the young associates under his command. When his partners suggested that the firm was under such pressure as to require further staff additions, Moore replied, "That's silly. No one is under pressure. There wasn't a light on when I left at two o'clock this morning." Moore's flinty personality was legendary. William O. Douglas, once a Cravath associate, recalled being with him when Moore received a telephone call from his wife that his house was on fire. "Why in hell bother me?" Moore replied. "Call the fire department."[11]

In 1932, on behalf of Bethlehem Steel, Moore commenced the receivership of Williamsport Wire Rope Company, which could not service outstanding bank loans and bonds during the dark days of the Depression. Bethlehem was a main supplier of steel to Williamsport, the principal purchaser of its wire rope output, a 25 percent owner of its common stock, a $700,000 creditor, and eventually a majority owner of its bonds. The presiding judge of the federal court for the Middle District of Pennsylvania, Albert W. Johnson, was corrupt. Complaints about his handling of bankruptcies and receiverships started soon after he took the oath of office. Of particular concern was his appointment of his son-in-law, Carl Schug, and his sons, Donald and Albert Jr., as trustees. Judge Johnson figured prominently in the Williamsport receivership, initially obstructing but ultimately approving its sale to Bethlehem Steel (represented by Moore) for $3.3 million, little, if any, of which was available for payment to other stockholders.

Under the foreclosure decree, drafted by Moore and signed by Judge Johnson, the buyer had to pay the costs of administration, thus discouraging bidders other than Bethlehem Steel who could not be certain what those costs might be. More to the point, this allowed the judge to approve his own bribe, since the costs of administration were a payoff to his henchmen by Bethlehem Steel. "Dexterity in drafting could not go much farther," wrote one commentator, "nor could effrontery." Federal investigation disclosed splits of receivers' and legal fees with two of Johnson's sons and an agreement for the unusual $250,000 "administration expense" of which $223,000 was to be paid by Bethlehem Steel out of court, evidence of counsel's criminal intent. Damning evidence of Moore's involvement was his meticulous recordation of the various ostensible fees, costs, and expenses of administration. Each line item in Moore's account was an odd and curious number, often expressed down to cents. Although Moore's accounting did not bother to add these items up, it just so happened that they totaled $250,000.00 to the penny. Reviewing the entire record, the Judiciary Committee of the House of Representatives concluded that Williamsport stockholders lost their equity as a result of "the corrupt connivance of John Memolo, attorney for the receivers; Hoyt A. Moore, attorney for Bethlehem Steel Co.; Judge Johnson; and his son, Donald Johnson. . . ."

When the receivership started, Moore feared that Bethlehem Steel faced judicial extortion but knew that a deal with Judge Johnson could let his client steal the wire rope company. Following suit by the Williamsport stockholders, the sale to Bethlehem was invalidated for fraud, and Bethlehem Steel paid the stockholders $6 million. Under threat of impeachment, Judge Johnson resigned, surrendering all salary and pension rights. In the subsequent criminal prosecution of Judge Johnson and his sons in *United States v. Johnson*, the court described a criminal conspiracy in which Judge Johnson, sitting as a judge of the District Court, received payment from Bethlehem Steel, facilitated by Moore, in the guise of fees and administrative expenses in return for action favorable to it in the Williamsport receivership. The court noted the "culpable participation of the defendant Moore" but concluded that prosecution was barred by the statute of limitations. A special master later determined that "Bethlehem improperly and illegally entered into a conspiracy with Judge Johnson and others . . . in the Williamsport receivership. . . ." Moore had attempted, with others, to bribe a federal judge—behavior that should have led to his disbarment, if not imprisonment—but narrowly escaped perdition because of a technicality and could thank his counsel, Theodore Kiendl and Ralph Carson of Davis Polk, for the reprieve. Moore had indeed gone the extra mile for his client. His later elevation to name partnership (not unlike John Foster Dulles' protection of his firm's Nazi clients) reflects the double moral standard that applied to such powerful partners.

11

The Creation of Davis Polk & Wardwell

The passing of J. P. Morgan should have had no immediate effect on Stetson, Jennings & Russell. Morgan's son, Jack, had been the senior figure at the bank for years, while a cadre of brilliant partners Pierpont had recruited now managed it. The institutional ties between the bank and the law firm were strong. Yet Morgan's death in 1913 and the outbreak of European war the next year coincided with a profound decline in Stetson, Jennings' fortunes.

Stetson now was an *eminence gris* of the bar. He had been president of the New York State Bar in 1909 and of the New York City Bar Association the next year. With his friend Victor Morawetz, he had written and testified extensively about reforms to corporate law and the Sherman Act. As a result of their efforts, New York became the first state to authorize the issuance of no-par stock in 1912.[1] That year, Stetson also served as Morgan's emissary to persuade President-elect Woodrow Wilson to adopt Wall Street's proposal for a "banking system fully controlled by bankers."[2] In November 1912, Stetson appeared before the Supreme Court to argue the seminal case of *Northern Pacific Railway v. Boyd* in an unsuccessful effort to defend the reorganization he and Morawetz had developed for the Northern Pacific a dozen years earlier. After World War I broke out in 1914, the Morgan bank hired his firm to handle negotiation of a $500 million loan to Britain and France, the largest bank loan ever made to that time, a matter that Stetson handled personally with the assistance of his 45-year-old associate, George Gardiner.[3]

But Stetson's successes masked how dysfunctional his law firm had become. For all his eminence as a lawyer, Stetson had made little effort to institutionalize his practice. When Stetson could not personally handle a matter, he often would refer it to another law firm without asking whether one of his partners might be interested in taking it on.[4] In 1909, for example, Stetson represented Morgan in the complex merger of Guaranty Trust Company, Morton Trust Company, and Fifth Avenue

Trust Company, but declined Morgan's request that he serve as counsel to the giant, combined institution. Stetson relented only after his partners Charles MacVeagh and Howland Russell begged him to let them represent the new client.[5] Early in World War I, Stetson passed on the chance to represent Morgan as the U.S. purchasing agent for Britain and France, which then sent the work to the up-and-coming firm of White & Case.

Not surprisingly, Stetson, Jennings & Russell had failed to grow. Between 1897 and 1907, it shrank from seven partners to six, and only four of those practiced law full time. Lansing P. Reed—who later became a named partner and managing partner of the firm—was told in 1908 to avoid the place. He later recalled that "there was no real partnership."[6] Although Allen Wardwell, Hall Park McCullough, and Edward R. Greene became partners in 1909, their promotion depended largely on personal connections, not an expanding firm practice. Wardwell was married to Stetson's niece, McCullough was Jennings' nephew, and Greene had been Russell's law clerk for 24 years. It was not until 1914 that the firm made another partner, and that was when the wealthy Ogden L. Mills became a partner upon the retirement of Henry L. Sprague.[7] The next year, the firm made two more partners, Lansing P. Reed and William C. Cannon, but to little effect, since Stetson now was approaching seventy and three other partners were in their sixties.[8] Financial results reflected this stagnation: in the years preceding World War I, the firm's average earnings were less than $300,000.[9]

ALLEN WARDWELL AND GEORGE GARDINER

If the evidence of decline was unmistakable, the seeds of the firm's ultimate renewal lay in two men of vastly different backgrounds who had been hired as law clerks at the turn of the century.

The more typical was Allen Wardwell. Wardwell was born in New York in 1873 to a well-to-do family. His father had a successful oil business in Buffalo and became the treasurer of a Standard Oil subsidiary.[10] Allen graduated from Yale in 1895 and received his law degree from Harvard Law School in 1898. He looked the part of an establishment lawyer—of average height with a square jaw, high forehead, and brown eyes and hair. He loved music, played the piano skillfully, and "heard with avidity serious music of every sort."[11] Wardwell was also a reticent and self-effacing man with an exceptional commitment to public service. When called upon to act, he did so with patience and quiet determination.

It is not entirely clear how Wardwell came to the attention of Frank Stetson. Perhaps it was a family connection since Frank Stetson's wife, Elizabeth, and Allen Wardwell's mother both were originally from Louisiana. In any event, living with the Stetsons was Elizabeth's widowed brother and his daughter Helen. Allen was introduced to Helen and became a frequent caller. The two were married in October 1903. Since the Stetsons had no children of their own, Allen and Helen were considered members of the family. There is little public record of Wardwell's early work at Stetson, Jennings & Russell. In all likelihood, given the way law firms operated in those days, Wardwell was attached to Frank Stetson's practice. He became a partner in 1909.

The second law clerk could not have been more different. George H. Gardiner had been born in Brooklyn in 1869, the third of seven children. All four of Gardiner's grandparents were immigrants from Ireland. Gardiner probably attended high school, but he never went to college. Until middle age, he lived with his widowed mother and younger siblings in Brooklyn. Unlike the handsome Wardwell, Gardiner did not fit the stereotype of a Wall Street lawyer. He suffered from curvature of the spine and stood barely five feet tall. In the parlance of the day, he would have been called a hunchback.

Gardiner came to the law in a roundabout way. Around 1890 he was hired as an assistant to the Ormsby brothers, resident court reporters at Bangs, Stetson, Tracy & MacVeagh.[12] He later became Frank Stetson's personal secretary and attended classes after work at nearby New York Law School.[13] He graduated in 1899, receiving the $100 prize awarded to the outstanding graduate of what was called the "evening school." In 1900, having been hired as a law clerk, he became Stetson's understudy, working at Stetson's side as he drafted the reorganization plans, indentures, and mortgages that were the foundation of his practice. As a result, Gardiner knew the documents from the ground up, possibly as well as Stetson himself. Gardiner became a partner in 1916 at the advanced age of 47.

THE RED CROSS MISSION TO RUSSIA

Wardwell was the closest thing Stetson had to a successor. He had been part of Stetson's practice since he joined the firm and was an expert in banking law, a centerpiece of the firm's practice. He was also a natural leader of the younger partners. It seemed clear that, if anyone were to step forward to steer the firm at this critical time, it would be Wardwell.

The First World War upset any such plans. Even before the United States declared war, Wardwell felt a call to duty and enlisted in the New York National Guard. Too old at 43 to do much more than sit at a desk, he yearned for a more active assignment, not unlike John Foster Dulles at Sullivan & Cromwell or Russell Leffingwell at Cravath. An opportunity presented itself when the United States entered the war in 1917. Refocusing its mission from simple humanitarian relief to military support, the American Red Cross reorganized itself along paramilitary lines under the leadership of Morgan senior partner, Henry P. Davison. Soon the Red Cross announced that it was recruiting men for a relief mission to Russia. With ties to both the Red Cross and the Morgan bank, Wardwell was able to hire on.

It is something of a mystery why Allen Wardwell chose to leave his wife, two young children, and faltering law firm to labor in wartime Russia, a nation he had never before visited and whose language he did not speak. In today's skeptical times, we might suspect an ulterior motive. But Wardwell was a man of classic sensibilities. He was idealistic, principled, and deeply religious. Before his life ended at age 80, Wardwell had devoted himself to countless public causes, ranging from the New York Legal Aid Society to the Metropolitan Opera. He had been president of the City Bar and a member of all manner of commissions, boards, and blue-ribbon panels.[14] Yet Wardwell closely guarded his personal privacy. In fact, it is almost impossible to locate an obituary of him, and no one seemed to know his middle name.

Given the rank (and uniform) of a major in the Red Cross, Wardwell joined a contingent of Red Cross officers who traveled to Petrograd (the wartime name of St. Petersburg) from Vladivostok on the Trans-Siberian railroad. There, he found chaos. Russia's transportation system had collapsed and, after the Bolshevik coup in November 1917, the Russian army disintegrated. Meanwhile the leader of the Red Cross mission quit, the new head began to dabble in Russian politics, and Russia soon dropped out of the war altogether.

We know intimate details of Wardwell's work because he kept a diary of his experiences in Russia, a document that became a valuable primary source for historians.[15] Shortly after arriving in Petrograd, he was sent south to reorganize the Red Cross' efforts in Romania. Wardwell then spent January and February 1918 north of the Arctic Circle in Murmansk, organizing shipments of supplies. This was Russia's lifeline to the west, and Wardwell found it overrun with refugees and adventurers of all descriptions, most desperately trying to escape. By the time spring arrived, the Red Cross' supplies were exhausted and most members of the mission were gone, leaving Wardwell in charge.

A civil war erupted as anti-Bolshevik forces rose against the new Communist regime, supported by Allied troops that had landed at Archangel. Soon the Bolsheviks were arresting British and French citizens. Wardwell delivered food and medicine to the prisoners and met with Lenin, Trotsky, and other senior Bolsheviks to urge the prisoners' release. For this, Wardwell was greatly appreciated and widely praised. "Wardwell, the American, had been heroic," wrote British diplomat R. H. Bruce Lockhart. "He had wrung concessions from the Bolsheviks. Daily he had fed all the prisoners. . . .'"[16] An imprisoned journalist wrote that Wardwell "literally slaved on behalf of the prisoners."[17]

Although he sought to avoid entanglement with Russian politics, Wardwell felt compelled to lodge a protest when Bolsheviks massacred hundreds of "counterrevolutionaries" after an assassination attempt on Lenin in August 1918. Wardwell's protest drew the wrath of Soviet foreign minister Georgi Chicherin, who excoriated the Red Cross' interference with Russian affairs. The Red Cross mission by now was obviously futile, and Wardwell left Russia in October, finally crossing no-man's-land into Finland on foot. He had no illusions that the mission had been a success. "It has all been so different from what we expected," he wrote. "Instead of definite relief work, with plenty of activity all the time, there has been this succession of upsets in Russia, changes in policy, long periods of waiting and then sudden surprises."[18]

Wardwell was obviously relieved when he finally made his way to France across war-torn Europe. There, he joined Henry Davison for the return to New York, and they left together from Bordeaux on November 16 on the steamship *Espagne*.

It was a fateful voyage. Also aboard the ship was the lawyer of exactly Wardwell's age who was returning from his work in Geneva as a commissioner to a conference on repatriation of prisoners. This man was from a small city in West Virginia and had lived there almost his entire life. Yet he had a distinguished record of public service—he had been a congressman and the United States Solicitor General, and he was about to become America's ambassador to Great Britain. He gave a brief shipboard talk about his work in Geneva, after which Wardwell introduced himself, commencing what became a long friendship with John W. Davis.[19]

JOHN W. DAVIS

At 45, John W. Davis already was one of the nation's most accomplished lawyers. Beyond his legal skills he had a natural grace and dignified bearing that inspired admiration and respect. He was cultivated, well spoken, handsome, and witty; he dressed well and his manners were impeccable. King George V called Davis "the most perfect gentleman I have ever met."[20]

John William Davis was born on April 13, 1873, in Clarksburg, West Virginia. His father, John James, was a leading lawyer in town and had served in both the Virginia and West Virginia legislatures and the U.S. House of Representatives. Davis' mother, Anna Kennedy, was college educated and a voracious reader; in fact, she was immersed in Gibbon's *Decline and Fall of the Roman Empire* when she went into labor the day her son was born.

Anna taught her son to read years before he was old enough to attend school, and encouraged him to study the volumes of poetry, history, and classics that lined her library. Davis had a prodigious memory—perhaps a photographic one—and for the rest of his life could recite long passages from the works of Carlyle, Dickens, Macaulay, and many others. He went to Washington & Lee University for college and law school, and briefly taught law there. He then joined his father in the firm of Davis & Davis.

Davis was famous for his powers of concentration and uncanny command of the case record. His colleagues observed that he could memorize hundreds of pages of material and recall where on each page a particular statement or fact could be found. In addressing a court, he seldom relied on more than a page or two of handwritten notes, and he rarely even looked at those. He had a powerful, sonorous voice that carried the courtroom and he could quote effortlessly from plays, novels, histories, classical philosophy, and contemporary literature. Davis' vocabulary was commanding, and he delivered arguments without hesitation, repetition, or indecision. He was especially skilled at marshaling the facts of his case; he often spent much of his allotted argument time guiding the court through layer upon layer of his case's factual underpinnings. However, Davis eschewed abstraction. He viewed lawyers, essentially, as mechanics; he did not see the law as a profession rooted in theory; and he seemed oblivious to the larger social implications of legal positions he advocated.

After the untimely death of his first wife in 1899, Davis lived with his parents and buried himself in his work. Davis' law practice had humble beginnings. One of his early cases was about the theft of a turkey and some chickens. Another was for the death of a cow that had been hit by a locomotive. He tried, and lost, a case where his client had bought a lame horse. Another time, he sued to recover a stolen pig. Clarksburg was becoming a small industrial city, though, and Davis soon began to represent the railroads and corporations that controlled West Virginia's timberlands, coal deposits, and gas formations. He began to attract attention for his skills as a lawyer, depth of preparation, and eloquence in the courtroom.

In those years, Davis became interested in Ellen (Nell) Bassell, a striking Clarksburg divorcee three years his senior and the daughter of his father's main rival at the bar. Nell was poorly educated, uninterested in ideas, and thought cold and calculating. Yet she had social skills and ambitions, including greater ambitions for Davis' future than Davis himself. Over his parents' opposition, they married in 1912.

Davis had already outgrown Clarksburg. In 1910 he won a seat in the U.S. House of Representatives. His reputation as a lawyer had preceded him, and he was assigned to the Judiciary Committee. Davis found the work tedious and exasperating. Much to his frustration, the Committee's chairman, Henry De Lamar Clayton Jr., delegated to Davis much of the work in framing the new antitrust act that would bear Clayton's name.

After Woodrow Wilson defeated William Howard Taft in the 1912 presidential election, the position of Solicitor General fell open. By then, Davis had earned a reputation as the ablest lawyer in Congress, and newly appointed Attorney General James C. McReynolds (a Kentuckian who had been practicing law with Guthrie, Cravath & Henderson for the past six years) offered him the post. Davis took the job at a time when a series of recently enacted Progressive measures were being challenged. His first argument took place in October 1913, in what were known as *The Pipe Line Cases*, where he defended the authority of the Interstate Commerce Commission to regulate oil pipelines as common carriers. The next day, he argued two civil rights cases involving state efforts to limit Black suffrage. Davis won all three.

In the next five years, Davis argued sixty-four more cases before the court, prevailing in forty-eight. His arguments included cases defending federal laws limiting child labor, fending off challenges to the eight-hour workday, enforcing the Sherman Act, and defining presidential power. Despite his defense of Progressive legislation, however, Davis never embraced Progressive ideals. He opposed women's suffrage; had few qualms about racial segregation; resented paying taxes; and opposed anything beyond minimal government spending on schools, roads, and other improvements. Although his circle of friends included such luminaries as Felix Frankfurter, Oliver Wendell Holmes, Charles C. Burlingham, Louis Brandeis, and Elihu Root, it did not cross his mind, then or later, that he might be out of step with the enlightened thinking of his age.

Davis and Nell enjoyed Washington. Davis played golf with Supreme Court justices, Nell became good friends with the wives of cabinet secretaries, and both enjoyed embassy functions and White House dinners. Nell helped Davis cultivate his social skills, and his innate shyness was seen as a form of self-assurance. The most significant connection they made was Nell's close friendship with Eleanor Foster Lansing, the wife of Secretary of State Robert Lansing, the daughter of former Secretary of State John W. Foster, and the aunt of future Secretary of State John Foster Dulles and future CIA Director Allen Welsh Dulles.

DIPLOMATIC DUTIES

Davis was constantly nervous about money. By 1917, he considered returning to private practice and interviewed with several law firms, including Cravath's. Davis had little compunction about working for the country's entrenched interests. He wrote his mother that Cravath's firm was "distinctly counsel for the predatory rich, railroads, Trust Co.'s, combines and such."[21] Davis changed his plans when the United States entered World War I, hoping somehow to join the war effort. In mid-1918 Secretary of State Lansing asked Davis to serve as one of the country's four commissioners to a conference in Berne, Switzerland to negotiate with Germany on the status of prisoners of war. In August 1918, Davis resigned as Solicitor General, imagining that he would be back in private practice soon enough. Davis had no sooner embarked for Berne than he received word that he was Lansing's choice to serve as the United States' ambassador to Great Britain. Taken aback and again worried about money, Davis initially rejected Lansing's proposal. He accepted the job only after Nell demanded he do so.

Davis was an unexpected success as ambassador, defusing tensions between the United States and Great Britain arising from the United States' burgeoning international aspirations, support for Irish independence, and various diplomatic gaffes by President Wilson and other politicians. The Davises came to know the leading figures of the British political establishment. Davis met Prime Minister Lloyd George, enjoyed the confidence of King George V, and spent weekends at the great country houses of the British elite. He could count the leading bankers and businessmen in London as personal friends, and he welcomed as houseguests rising stars in American business and politics. He developed a particularly close relationship with Lansing's nephew John Foster Dulles, who stayed with the Davises when in London.[22]

STETSON, JENNINGS & RUSSELL

Wardwell debarked from *The Espagne* upon its arrival in New York City on November 27, 1918, only to find that his law firm's affairs had gone from bad to worse. Jennings and Russell were semiretired; they came to the office infrequently, and did little when they were there.[23]

Stetson had suffered a stroke and was largely confined to his home. He also had shown signs of senility. In September 1917, he formally adopted as his daughter his late wife's 22-year-old secretary, Margery Hayhurst Lee. This was much to the astonishment of Miss Lee's biological parents, both of whom were still living and neither of whom had been consulted. When asked about the adoption by a newspaper reporter, Stetson replied only that his wife had been very fond of Miss Lee.[24]

The main reason the firm had survived in these lean years was not because of the polished partners with Ivy League credentials. Instead, the weight was borne by the humble and hardworking George Gardiner. After Gardiner's successful work on the massive Anglo-French loan, the firm had made him a partner in 1916, a quarter-century after he had first come to work as a stenographer. He had in that time become a master of his craft. When in 1916 Stetson joined leading New York lawyers—including Paul Cravath, George Wickersham, and William Guthrie—to deliver a series of lectures to the City Bar Association on corporation finance, it was almost certainly Gardiner who wrote Stetson's technical paper on the fine points of corporate bonds, mortgages, collateral trusts, and indentures. That same year, the Morgan bank asked Gardiner to prepare the deposit agreement for the reorganization of Mexico's external debt.[25] In 1918, Guaranty Trust Company dispatched Gardiner to Cuba to represent the syndicate the bank had organized at the U.S. government's request to finance that year's sugar crop. Gardiner was now indispensable to the firm's most important client. Lansing Reed later recalled that the "only reason we remained counsel to J. P. Morgan and Co. after Mr. Stetson's decline in health was that their admiration for the character and ability of Mr. Gardiner was such that they could not go to anyone else."[26]

With the three senior partners incapacitated or absent, Wardwell took steps in 1919 to turn Stetson, Jennings & Russell into a true partnership, instead of the cost-sharing and client-husbanding arrangement it had been for decades.[27] Although we can only guess at the changes Wardwell made, they probably reflected elements of the Cravath system. Among other things, Wardwell's reforms included according each partner an equal vote on matters of firm governance and elevation of new partners and, more fundamentally, setting each partner's ownership share of the firm—and, thus, his draw—based upon his seniority in the firm instead of the size of his book of business. This meant that rising lawyers without clients could take the risk of joining the firm.

The three named partners passed away in quick succession. Frederic Jennings and Frank Stetson died at home from strokes in May and December 1920, respectively. Howland Russell died in February 1921 from complications of a fall.[28]

RESUSCITATION

The 1918 bar directory lists dozens of law firms that have long since passed out of memory. In their day, firms such as Joline, Larkin & Rathbone or Hughes, Rounds,

Shurman & Dwight were respected and prosperous; their partners went to elite colleges and law schools; their client lists were impressive. But law firms are fragile institutions. The loss of a prominent leader or key client can result in an abrupt reversal of fortune, and there is a death spiral as one setback leads to another.

There is no particular reason that Stetson, Jennings & Russell should have survived. It had been moribund for years, its three leading partners were dead, its practice was dangerously dependent upon a single client, and it was not especially profitable. There were now new law firms on Wall Street and formidable lawyers—Cravath and Cromwell were only two—taking matters away. Clearly, something had to be done.

It fell to Allen Wardwell to revive the firm. Wardwell does not come across as a particularly calculating man, although perhaps his dealings with the Bolsheviks were a learning experience. He knew that resuscitation of his law firm would require bringing someone outstanding aboard, and he had his eye on John W. Davis. Stetson, Jennings & Russell was not a compelling enough opportunity to land Davis, however; Wardwell knew that, to recruit Davis, he must first build his case.

Wardwell began by recruiting a lawyer both he and Davis knew. Frank Polk had been one year ahead of Wardwell at Yale, where they had belonged to the same secret society. Although Polk had been an indifferent student, he was considered the most popular man in the class of '94. Polk began practicing law in 1897, but soon left to enlist in the cavalry in the Spanish-American War. At the war's end, he formed his own law firm and threw himself into various political and civic causes. In 1914, Polk was appointed the New York City's Corporation Counsel. A few months later, an unemployed (and nearsighted) blacksmith tried to assassinate Mayor John Purroy Mitchel, but instead shot Polk, shattering his jawbone. Polk recovered, but bore a scar for the rest of his life.

Polk was confirmed the following year as Counselor of the State Department. In 1919, he headed the American commission for the negotiation of the Treaty of Versailles, and in July of that year he was promoted to Undersecretary of State. In that position, he worked closely with John W. Davis, first when Davis was a commissioner to the Berne conference and then when Davis became Ambassador to Britain.

Wardwell approached Polk to join Stetson, Jennings & Russell in 1920. Polk's ties to Davis were the obvious reason for Wardwell's interest. Despite Polk's distinguished record of public service, it was not entirely clear what he would bring to the firm. He was nearing 50 and may have suffered a debilitating nervous disorder in 1918. Having Polk join the firm was an obvious next step in courting Davis, though, and given the state of things, Wardwell probably concluded that, if his law firm were to survive at all, it would have to be from some combination of Davis, Polk, and himself. Wardwell made, and Polk accepted, an offer of partnership in early 1920.

It was now common knowledge that Davis was planning to resign his ambassadorship. Davis was frustrated with President Wilson (who had, in pique, fired Davis' friend Lansing) and become increasingly irritated by the devious and supercilious British Foreign Secretary, Lord Curzon. Davis also wanted to make money. He was now in the prime of life—47—and thought the time had come to restore his finances.

Wardwell wrote Davis in March 1920 that the partners of Stetson, Jennings & Russell hoped Davis would join the firm. Polk concurred, writing to Davis that Stetson, Jennings & Russell had "a splendid name and a great reputation for conservatism" as well as "a wonderful business, and not only has your friends the Morgan people but . . . many other big concerns." "If they made you the head . . . that would be the most attractive position in New York."[29]

Other firms coveted Davis as well. Paul Cravath came to London and increased the offer he had made Davis a few years before. More offers came when Davis visited New York in August 1920. John Foster Dulles offered him a 10 percent interest in Sullivan & Cromwell. Davis' friend William Wallace Jr. proposed a one-third interest in Chadbourne, Babbitt & Wallace. Wardwell offered Davis leadership of Stetson, Jennings & Russell, a guarantee of $50,000 annually and 15 percent of the firm's net earnings. Given its revenues, Davis could expect upward of $150,000 a year.[30]

Paul Cravath then matched Wardwell's offer with a minimum guarantee of $50,000 a year and 15 percent of his firm's net profits, which certainly exceeded those of Stetson, Jennings & Russell. Unlike Wardwell, however, Cravath did not intend to give Davis a leadership role. He would remain the firm's managing partner and keep one-quarter of its profits.[31]

Wardwell countered by upping Davis' guarantee to $60,000 and his share of profits to eighteen per cent. More shrewdly, Wardwell coordinated a sustained lobbying effort among his firm's clients. The general manager of the Associated Press—a client Stetson, Jennings & Russell had organized years before, but which had recently used Samuel Untermyer—told Davis he could be the lawyer for the AP *if* he joined Stetson, Jennings & Russell. A few weeks later, the president and the chairman of the board of Standard Oil offered Davis the job of general counsel; when Davis declined, he said Standard Oil would retain him anyway if he joined Wardwell's firm. Henry Davison sent his yacht to bring the Davises to his estate on Long Island house for a round of golf and to meet other Morgan partners. Davison, too, advised Davis to go to Stetson, Jennings.[32]

In September, Davis accepted Wardwell's offer. What tipped the balance was not the amount of money Wardwell offered but instead the prospect of practicing law with men he genuinely liked. Polk already was a friend, and Davis liked and respected Wardwell. Davis found up-and-coming partner Lansing Reed friendly and gracious, but it was to the warm and charming George Gardiner that Davis took a special liking.

John and Nell Davis reveled in their final months in England. They were invited to rounds of parties and asked by the King and Queen to lunch at Buckingham Palace. In March 1921 the Davises left England aboard the *Olympic*—sister ship to the ill-fated *Titanic*. They were seen off by Foreign Secretary Curzon, the diplomatic corps, and a crowd of lords and ladies and accompanied to sea by two squadrons of British destroyers, each flying the U.S. flag.

Davis' arrival at Stetson, Jennings was an unqualified success. The firm's relations with the Morgan banks were solidified, its client list swelled, and the scope of its practice widened. By the mid-1920s, its annual profits appear to have been about $2.25 million, almost ten times what they had been a decade before.[33] On June 1, 1923, the firm name was changed to Stetson, Jennings, Russell & Davis.[34]

Davis had never lived in New York before, but he stepped easily into the life of a Wall Street lawyer. He was given the same corner office—and desk—Grover Cleveland had used 30 years before. He quickly became a director of several corporations and joined the boards of the Rockefeller Foundation and the Carnegie Endowment. Davis also achieved the financial security he had worried about since leaving Clarksburg in 1911. By the late 1920s, his annual income was $400,000.[35] The Davises bought an estate on the North Shore of Long Island, took an apartment on Fifth Avenue, and kept a cottage for the winter in South Carolina. In the summers, Davis commuted to Wall Street from Long Island on Jack Morgan's motor launch or in a chartered rail car. The Davises had an English butler, two maids, a servant, a cook, and chauffeured Pierce-Arrow. They took extended vacations to the British Isles or Europe every year. Davis enjoyed fine clothes and was always impeccably dressed.

THE PRESIDENTIAL ELECTION OF 1924

Davis could not fully escape the political limelight, and in 1924 this became an unexpected problem. On the 103rd ballot of a deadlocked Democratic convention in the sweltering Madison Square Garden, Davis reluctantly accepted his party's nomination for president. He had not sought the honor and had little enthusiasm for running. It also was common knowledge that the Republicans would win the general election, since Calvin Coolidge was popular and the Democratic Party was about to split into conservative and progressive wings.

The firm's partners must have had mixed feelings about the campaign, since the loss of Davis would have been a serious setback. Upon receiving the nomination, Davis withdrew from the partnership and resigned from a half dozen corporate boards. Nevertheless, his candidacy became a firm project. Frank Polk was one of his campaign managers, and Allen Wardwell handled finances. His young partner Edwin S.S. Sunderland traveled with Davis on the campaign trail, and various associates coordinated campaign committees and dealt with day-to-day correspondence. The outcome of the race was never seriously in doubt, and Davis lost badly. He returned to the firm in the spring of 1925 and learned it was now called Davis Polk Wardwell Gardiner & Reed.

Renaming the firm was almost certainly the work of Wardwell. Inexplicably, if not unfairly, Stetson's name was dropped. Stetson had been one of the most accomplished lawyers of his time: he had been at J. P. Morgan's side for decades, reorganized dozens of railroads, transformed corporate finance, formed the great trusts of the day, averted a financial panic, led the Democratic Party, and advised presidents. Despite this illustrious history, Stetson's name soon faded away and survived thereafter only as Davis Polk's cable address: "Stetson New York."

Frank L. Polk, 1920, as Undersecretary of the U.S. State Department. Library of Congress.

John W. Davis, September 27, 1924, Democratic candidate for U.S. president. Library of Congress.

John Foster Dulles, circa 1917, major in the U.S. Army prior to his return to Sullivan & Cromwell after World War I. Library of Congress.

Allen Welsh Dulles, circa 1920, while at the Department of State and prior to joining Sullivan & Cromwell. Library of Congress.

Russell C. Leffingwell, circa 1920, as Assistant Secretary of the Treasury prior to his return to the Cravath firm. Library of Congress.

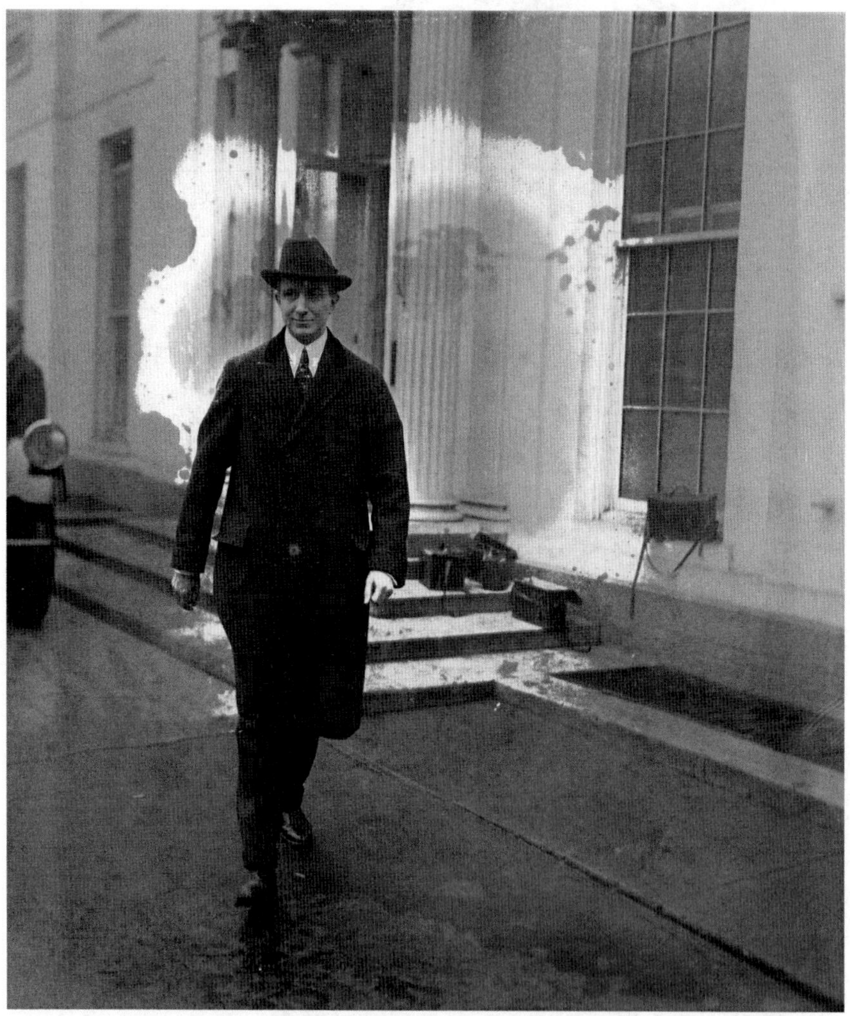

S. Parker Gilbert, January 24, 1926, while serving as Agent General for Reparations to Germany after leaving partnership at the Cravath firm. Library of Congress.

Caricature of J. P. Morgan from *Punch* magazine. Library of Congress.

J. P. Morgan, May 11, 1910, striking photographer with cane. Library of Congress.

Hjalmar Schacht, circa World War I, prior to assuming the presidency of Reichsbank in Germany. Library of Congress.

Philippe Bunau-Varilla, 1926, French citizen, who with William Nelson Cromwell was instrumental in negotiating the U.S. acquisition of the Panama Canal. Library of Congress.

Class of 1941, University of Virginia Law School (Louis Auchincloss, extreme left, front row).

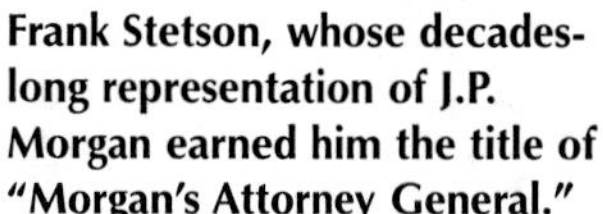

Frank Stetson, whose decades-long representation of J.P. Morgan earned him the title of "Morgan's Attorney General."

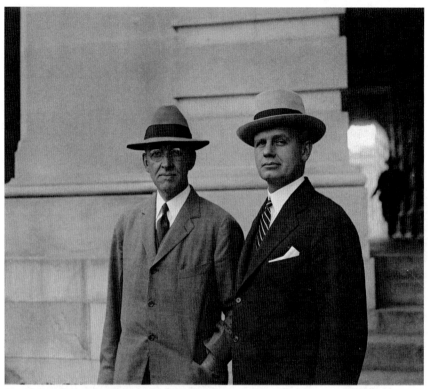

Bruce Bromley, right (with S. W. Wakeman), September 21, 1929, as young partner in the Cravath firm. Library of Congress.

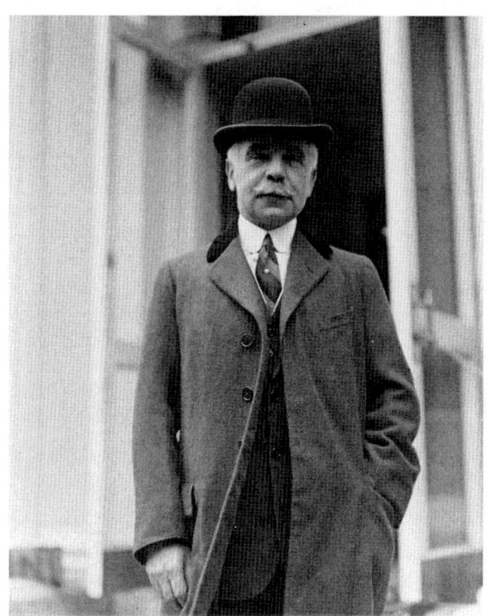

Otto Kahn, 1924, lead partner at Kuhn, Loeb & Co., major banking client of the Cravath firm, during a White House visit. Library of Congress.

Charles G. Dawes, left, circa 1920s, after whom the Dawes Plan to refinance Germany following World War I was named, en route to an official function. Library of Congress.

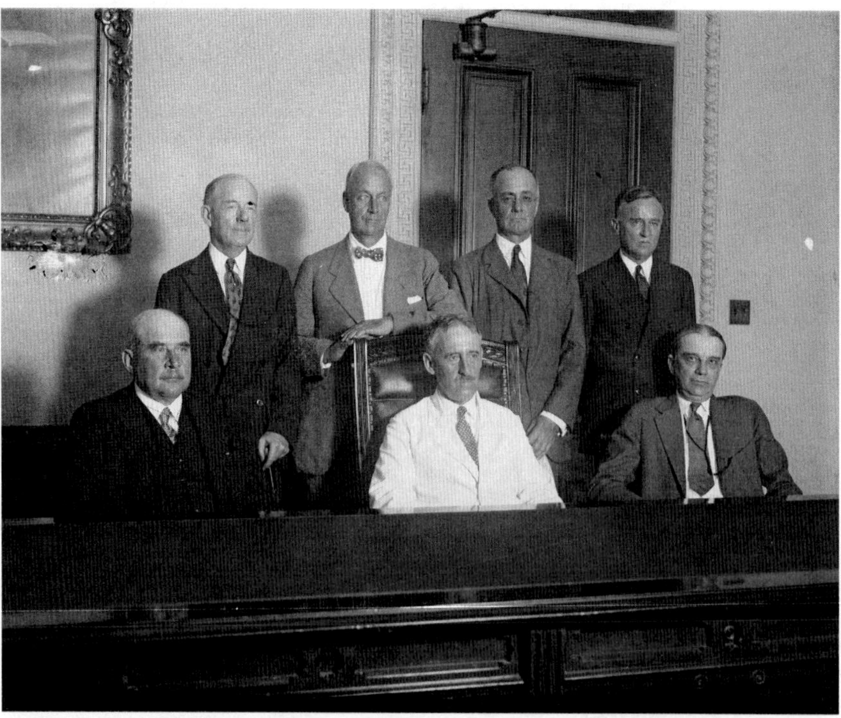

Owen D. Young, June 25, 1929 (front row, far right), and members of the American Reparations Commission, of which Young was chairman. Library of Congress.

William D. Whitney, left (a partner in the Cravath firm) and James Walter Carter, president of the Carter Coal Company, October 30, 1935, leaving court during their fight against the Guffey Coal Act. Library of Congress.

Robert Lansing, Secretary of State and uncle of John Foster Dulles and Allen W. Dulles, 1917, with Frank Polk. Library of Congress.

Allen Wardwell, who resuscitated Stetson, Jennings & Russell and created the firm of Davis Polk & Wardwell.

George Gardiner, who began work as a stenographer at Stetson, Jennings & Russell and, after graduating from night law school, became the main reason the firm retained the Morgan bank as a client during the year of Stetson's decline.

Paul D. Cravath and daughter Vera, circa 1912, at a field event. Library of Congress.

Mark Hanna, 1897, Republican senator from Ohio, being interviewed by reporters at the U.S. Capitol. Library of Congress.

Arsene Pujo, far left, 1910, congressman from Louisiana and leader of the Pujo Committee investigating Wall Street. Library of Congress.

Ferdinand Pecora (on the right), with John D. Devaney, former counsel of the Senate Banking Committee, upon election as president of the National Lawyers Guild. Library of Congress.

12

John W. Davis' Law Firm

After John W. Davis came back to the firm in 1925, Davis Polk Wardwell Gardiner & Reed returned its attention to the task of recapturing the practice it had all but lost in Frank Stetson's declining years. Davis himself maintained a pace that would have exhausted a younger man, often trying cases or arguing appeals back-to-back in different courts in different cities around the country. Polk headed the small group that handled trust and estates work. Wardwell represented the firm's anchor banking clients. Lansing Reed became one of the leading corporate lawyers in New York, and Edwin Sunderland an authority on railroad reorganizations. Several older partners retired, and new partners were made.

It was a time of great change. The war had seen huge advances in communications and aviation, creating entirely new industries. Consumers, with money in their pockets, bought cars, installed telephones, and purchased electric appliances. The entertainment industry flourished with improvements in motion pictures and establishment of hundreds of commercial radio stations. The public, having made money buying Liberty Bonds during the war, abandoned its reservations and began investing in the common stock of the new companies leading this burgeoning growth. Intact notwithstanding the war's destruction elsewhere, the United States overtook Britain, France, and Germany in international finance and commerce.

Much of the enormous growth of the U.S. economy in recent decades had been in large industrial cities of the Midwest, and those cities now had excellent law firms of their own. But the success of a law firm has historically been a function of its franchise, that is, its geographical location and historical client base, and there remained no better one than New York. It was in New York that one found the nation's largest stock exchanges and its major banks, trust companies, brokerage houses, and insurance companies, not to mention the headquarters of the giant companies assembled during the heyday of the trusts. Now that it was back on its feet, Davis

Polk had a roster of clients that included J. P. Morgan & Co., Guaranty Trust Company, U.S. Steel, International Paper Company, International Harvester, and a long list of railroads.

Two things set Davis Polk apart from other downtown firms. The first was its pervasive ties to the Morgan interests. Over time, the Morgan bank had grown more and more powerful, despite the efforts of Progressives and other reformers to rein it in. Directly and indirectly, the Morgan interests influenced broad swathes of the nation's economy. The bank's fingerprints could be found on bond issues, bank loans, corporate consolidations, and international finance, and its partners sat on countless corporate boards. Although Davis Polk remained a small law firm, it had an enviable legal practice. There were successive bond issues for AT&T, which was building out its local and national networks, financings for utilities that were expanding electrical service, and diverse legal tasks for the large corporations driving new industries. Most of this work occurred outside public notice since there were no securities laws requiring public disclosure and the Morgan bank was still a private partnership. The firm's strong ties to Morgan-controlled Guaranty Trust similarly meant abundant banking work and a vibrant trust and estate practice preparing wills, codicils, and trust instruments and administering estates. Although other law firms also represented the Morgan interests, Davis Polk got more than its share of challenging and lucrative legal work. In a well-known 1939 article in *Harper's*, the muckraker Ferdinand Lundberg described Davis Polk as "organized on factory principles" by which it ground out "standardized legal advice, documents, and services."[1] This was also a charge leveled at Cravath, Sullivan & Cromwell, and other Wall Street firms.

The second thing that distinguished the firm was the unequaled prominence of John W. Davis. Soon after Davis joined the firm, he became president of the American Bar Association and a de facto leader of the bar in New York City. Between 1923 and 1930 alone, Davis argued thirty-four cases in the Supreme Court, a number that would have been even greater had he not withdrawn from the practice of law in 1924 to run for president. There was perhaps no lawyer in the United States more continuously in the public eye in these decades than Davis. In fact, the unpublished internal history of Davis Polk refers to the institution in these years as "The Davis Law Firm."

CULTURE AND WEALTH

It was in these years that Davis Polk's patrician culture developed. John W. Davis was, by nature, reserved, conciliatory, courteous, and gently self-deprecating. With his prominence in national politics, his standing as one of the country's leading lawyers, and his diplomatic experience, Davis inspired respect. His partners were relieved by his friendliness and wit, and even his fondness for corny jokes. Davis behaved like a gentleman and required the same of everyone else. He took less money from the partnership than he could have asked for and repeatedly reduced his share of the profits unilaterally. To dispel the threat of intrigue, Davis instituted a rule—

the "open door policy"—prohibiting any partner from even shutting the door to his office. His advice, when he gave it, was often in the form of subtle suggestion. Davis insisted that all partners were equal, but his colleagues referred to him as *primus inter pares*—first among equals. Decades after Davis' death in 1955, Davis Polk partners would recount, reverentially, anecdotes about Davis or lessons he had imparted.

Davis was famous for his kind gestures. In the 1920s, he chided a young lawyer for not wearing a hat, but gave him ten dollars to buy one. Another time, learning that a promising associate wished to join a country club, Davis increased the man's salary to cover the club's initiation fee and dues. Davis made it a practice of taking young lawyers to Washington at his own expense to move their admission to the Supreme Court bar personally.[2] Associates were expected to work on Saturday mornings, but Davis softened the burden by inviting those working on his cases to come to his Locust Valley estate, where they could work from the private law library he kept there. After the morning's work was done, the young lawyers would have lunch with the Davises, then catch an afternoon train back into Manhattan.

Davis' personality became that of the firm itself. Partners were paid in lockstep and expected to stick together. Disagreements about staffing matters, acceptance of new clients, or cases and the direction of firm management were handled quietly and resolved by deference and consensus. Even during difficult times, the partnership protected its own. When Howland Auchincloss was unable to work for months at a time, incapacitated by severe bouts of depression, the firm continued to pay him his $100,000 annual draw, with no suggestion that he should resign from the partnership.[3] Like their counterparts at Cravath and Sullivan & Cromwell the Davis Polk partners were inextricably bound to each other by culture, tradition, and money. As one Davis Polk partner once said, "This business of taking a partner into one's house is almost more important than choosing a wife."[4]

Although Davis and his partners certainly were committed to making the practice of law as congenial as possible, they did not lose sight of the fact that the central purpose of the enterprise was to make money. Felix Frankfurter (in a letter to Learned Hand) chastised Davis for this. "But surely you will agree," said Frankfurter, "that it bodes ill for the state if talent and power and prestige are predominantly in the service of power." Frankfurter, then a professor at Harvard Law School, maintained "it is good neither for these lads that I see passing through this School from year to year, nor for this country. . . ."[5] But these things did not bother Davis. In a stage whisper to the Clerk of the Supreme Court, he once joked, "Tomorrow I have a date with J. P. Morgan, the day after that with Rockefeller. God, how I hate to take their money!"[6]

Dollars aside, Davis and his partners were genuinely committed to public service. Many were devoutly religious and served on the vestries and boards by which New York's churches extended their charitable work. Besides his lifelong work for the American Red Cross, Wardwell became the head of the Legal Aid Society in 1926 and held the position for ten years.[7] Davis himself was president of the Association of the New York Bar in 1931-1933; he signed innumerable petitions on behalf of persons he believed unjustly accused, and, toward the end of his career, lent his name and prestige to the defense of Robert Oppenheimer. The Episcopal Church Pension Fund was virtually an in-house project, and at one point, three of its trustees were Davis Polk senior partners.[8] William Cannon, the rare Catholic in the partnership, was a Knight of Malta and a member of the Cardinal's Committee of the Laity. It was a point of pride to sit on the boards of schools, charities, and foundations, and the firm's directory listings detailed each of these honors at great length.

There was, however, an intimate relationship between business and public service, if only because the eleemosynary institutions of the day were part and parcel of the economic hierarchy. As novelist Louis Auchincloss—the son of Davis Polk partner Howland Auchincloss and a Wall Street lawyer himself—wrote:

> In the 1920s and '30s there existed indubitably, however hard to define, a social structure called "society" that regarded itself as just that. These persons resided on the East Side of Manhattan (never west except below Fifty-ninth Street) as far south as Union Square and as far north as Ninety-sixth Street. The members (if that is the word; it doesn't seem quite right) were largely Protestants of Anglo-Saxon origins. (Note that Catholics and non-practicing Jews were not always excluded if they were rich enough.)[9]

Members of this group governed the social institutions coveted by New York's bourgeoisie. They controlled the ladies' and men's clubs, country clubs, debutante balls, exclusive private schools, the boards of charities and museums, and even the desirable churches.

Davis Polk was certainly not alone in its elitism, but the pervasiveness of its connections is startling today. When Davis joined the firm in 1921, the firm had thirteen partners, many of whom were related.[10] Charles MacVeagh was the son of former partner Wayne MacVeagh; Allen Wardwell was married to Frank Stetson's niece; Hall Park McCullough was Frederick Jennings' nephew; Howland Auchincloss' uncle was Howland Russell and his sister's father-in-law was Frederick Jennings. Charles MacVeagh would soon withdraw from the partnership to become Ambassador to Japan, but his son Ewen would join the firm in 1927 and become a partner in 1940. Allen Wardwell's son, Edward, and Polk's sons, John M. Polk and Frank L. Polk Jr., also came to the firm in the next decade and, in time, Eddie Wardwell and the younger Frank Polk each became partners.[11]

There were common academic credentials. Eight of the thirteen partners had gone to prep schools; nine had college degrees from Columbia, Harvard, or Yale, and nine had graduated from Columbia or Harvard law schools. In fact, other than George Gardiner (who may not even have graduated from high school), Davis himself was the most notable outlier. There were similar social pedigrees. Frank Polk's father had been dean of the Cornell Medical School and a pupil of Stonewall Jackson at the Virginia Military Institute, and his grandfather a Confederate general. Charles MacVeagh's father had been Attorney General and, before that, minister to the Ottoman Empire. Ogden Mills Jr. was the grandson of Darius Mills, the original owner of the eponymous Mills Building, the son of the financier Ogden Mills, and the husband of William K. Vanderbilt's stepdaughter. He left the firm after being elected to Congress, and later became Herbert Hoover's Treasury Secretary and a successful thoroughbred breeder.[12] Hall Park McCullough came from a family of independent wealth and was a Jennings to boot. Howland Auchincloss was part of an ancient New York family that had intermarried with social equals for a century. One of his great-great grandfathers had been a founder of Standard Oil, and Jacqueline Bouvier Kennedy Onassis would be a cousin.

This patina extended to the firm's associates. Despite its adoption of the merit-based Cravath system, Davis Polk had no trouble staffing its needs from the ranks of the elite. Of the dozen associates the firm hired in the 1920s who were later elevated to partnership, all but one went to college at Columbia, Harvard, Yale, or Williams, and all but one attended Columbia, Harvard, or Yale law schools. The sole outlier, Ralph M. Carson, was the exception that proved the rule: he had gone to the University of Michigan for college and law school and was a Rhodes Scholar. While the firm did hire young lawyers from such places as Fordham and St. John's, these men, if they stayed, would never become partners of the firm. In fact, over time, they were simply called "permanent" associates.

Given the fact that other downtown law partnerships were much the same as Davis Polk, it is not surprising that an understanding developed among Wall Street law firms that each would leave the others' clientele alone. One reason was that there was enough business to go around. But there was a sociological element as well. By this time, the partners of white-shoe law firms had almost become a social class of their own. Many were second- or third-generation lawyers. It was far from uncommon for a son to join the firm where his father or uncle worked and there were family ties across law firms as well.

While partners in downtown firms did not occupy the same economic or social heights as their clients, they viewed their clients with a patronization that bordered on outright condescension. Since American capitalism had few, if any, rules, it was to be expected that bankers and industrialists should try to get away with whatever they could. It was the lawyers' job to protect their clients from destroying the very system that had made them rich. As the great Elihu Root put it: "About half of the practice of a decent lawyer consists in telling would-be clients that they are damned fools and should stop."[13]

LEVERAGE

The prestige and wealth of the partners of the blue-chip law firms perpetuated their business model. The great profits firms reaped were largely due to the fact that they had far more associates than partners—which the law firms, borrowing the lexicon of their banking clients, called "leverage." Leverage ensured that the partnership would be richly profitable, since each associate would contribute far more revenue to the firm than he received as a salary. Moreover, when the time came to make a new partner, it was a buyer's market. Promotion, in other words, was not simply about talent; considerations ranging from family connections to personal friendship to client prejudices also weighed on the scale. And since partnership was for life, decisions about elevation were deeply personal.

Even for a talented associate, the odds of making partner were low and the costs—long hours, tedious work, high pressure, and lost opportunity—were high. The challenge to downtown law firms' business model was to make the bargain attractive enough to induce smart young men to take what was clearly a bet at long odds. The exclusiveness of a white-shoe law firm, of course, would automatically appeal to any young man who graduated at the top of his class at a prestigious law school. However, the deciding factor was the promise of wealth and the entitled life that would come with it.[14]

It is unlikely that Davis Polk partners earned any more than those at Cravath or Sullivan & Cromwell. However, it was more than sufficient. Even a midlevel partner like Howland Auchincloss led an enviable life. During the Depression, he had

> a modest but ample brownstone in Manhattan; a house in Long Island for weekends and summer; a rented villa in Bar Harbor, Maine, for July; four housemaids; two children's nurses; a couple to maintain the Long Island abode; a chauffeur and four cars; several social clubs; and private schools for the children.[15]

Other partners did even better. Hall Park McCullough, for example, lived with his wife and four children in a townhouse on East 82nd Street a few steps from Fifth Avenue with four live-in servants.[16] Lansing Reed, his wife, and their five daughters lived in an imposing townhouse on East 71st Street with five maids, a governess, and a nurse.[17]

MANAGEMENT

At some point in the 1920s, day-to-day leadership of the firm shifted to Lansing Reed. It would be hard to find anyone who better characterized Davis Polk. Son of a Congregational minister, Reed attended Yale, where he was tapped for Skull and Bones. Reed then went to Harvard Law School, where he was an editor of the *Law Review*. In 1911, he married Ruth Lawrence, daughter of Episcopal Bishop William Lawrence, whose family had made their fortune in the Massachusetts textile mills in the town they named after themselves. Like J. P. Morgan, Bishop Lawrence saw a direct connection between good character and wealth. "In the long run," he was quoted as saying, "it is only to the man of morality that wealth comes. . . . Godliness is in league with riches."[18] In fact, the Bishop was a good friend of Pierpont Morgan, a fact that did nothing to diminish Lansing Reed's prospects.

Reed was that indispensable combination of good breeding, high intelligence, and discreet opportunism that downtown firms esteemed, and his promise was recognized early on. In 1925, Reed was made a named partner of the firm. In 1931, *Fortune* identified him as one of the leading business lawyers in New York. "His judgment is valued, not merely because it takes the form of expertly drawn and brilliantly conceived legal opinion, but because it is his judgment."[19] Like so many of his class and upbringing, Reed was a private man and, aside from his service as a trustee of various institutions, he kept his affairs to himself. Ironically, we know much about him anyway because Reed was the model for the lawyer Henry Knox in Louis Auchincloss' novel *The Great World and Timothy Colt.* Knox, the managing partner of Sheffield, Stevens, Knox and Dale, is portrayed as warm and thoughtful, and even idealistic about the practice of law. Despite his reputation as "a tough and exacting lawyer for a tough and exacting clientele,"[20] Knox harbors doubts about the brutal demands of his corporate practice and the toll it has taken on him, his family, and his colleagues. Knox worries about the fragility of his law firm, which Knox knows was something of a recent invention anyway. Meanwhile, Knox is apprehensive about the increasing power of a manipulative, lowborn trusts and estates partner. Knox manages the firm by example and compromise, understanding that he and his partners must get along with each other, however frustrating it may be, and make sacrifices to preserve the institution, which is greater than any of them.

Perhaps one reason Reed was made the managing partner was the need to shake things up. Despite the strong economy of the 1920s, Davis Polk made only two partners in that decade, barely enough to offset retirements. It was Reed "indubitably, who had checked, almost single-handed, the rot that had set into the organization."[21] Under his guidance, the firm expanded from thirteen to twenty-one partners between 1930 and Reed's untimely death in 1937.

The firm also moved to larger quarters, albeit at the same address. By the mid-1920s the Morgan bank's headquarters at 23 Wall Street had long since spilled over to the now-dilapidated Mills Building. The bank took an 84-year lease on the site, stipulating it would be razed and replaced by a bigger structure. After two years in temporary space at 44 Wall Street, Davis Polk moved into the 17th floor of the new building—now simply known as 15 Broad Street. The physical premises were unpretentious, perhaps a signal that the firm felt no need to impress anyone.

> At a time when other firms indulged in deep-carpeted, paneled reception rooms, Davis Polk's office displayed the functional simplicity of a true law office. The central feature was its extensive library, spread with oriental rugs, old plain tables, and straight chairs in each alcove, interspersed with deep leather armchairs. It had no walls other than its bookshelves, and it opened to a windowed area that broke through a row of partners' private offices that surrounded it. The reception room seemed like an afterthought, a sort of recess behind the receptionist, a few armchairs around a table on an oriental rug overseen by a poorly lit portrait of Grover Cleveland. . . . On the other side of the entrance a handsomely curved staircase led to offices on the 17th floor.[22]

Keeping its offices at 15 Broad Street also maintained the intimate ties Davis Polk had with the Morgan bank. In fact, there was a direct elevator between Davis Polk and the bank's offices downstairs, a connection the firm's associates dubbed the "umbilical cord."[23]

THE DEPRESSION YEARS

The Great Depression was as much a shock to the legal community as to everyone else. Bread-and-butter practices such as financings and bank lending dried up. Revenues dropped substantially and the firm curtailed hiring. Partnership draws fell off correspondingly. John W. Davis reduced his share of the firm's profits from the high of about $400,000 in the late 1920s to $275,000 a few years later.[24]

Following its election in 1932, the newly installed administration of Franklin Roosevelt enacted the wide-ranging package of economic and regulatory legislation generally known as the New Deal. Although a lifelong Democrat and his party's presidential nominee in 1924, John W. Davis did little to conceal his loathing for the New Deal. He loudly complained about federal government intrusions into states' rights and the burdens of new regulations. In an October 1936 nationwide radio address, Davis charged that the Roosevelt administration had dangerously fanned the flames of class feeling, class hatred, and class cupidity.[25]

Davis considered himself a Jeffersonian Democrat, a loose term that generally meant a minimum of government regulation, respect for the sovereignty of the individual states, and exceptional deference to private property rights. Although he spent a lifetime practicing law, taught law, served as Solicitor General, and turned down several invitations to join the United States Supreme Court, Davis had a cabined view of the role of lawyers and the law itself. It was not the job of the government, much less the courts, to remedy social ills, protect the weak, or level the economic playing field. The core rights protected by the Constitution and the inherent structure of a representative democracy, he believed, were sufficient to set down rules for the country's operation. Efforts to compel individuals or companies to take steps to repair society were counterproductive, shortsighted, and probably unconstitutional. And, if any government intrusion were necessary, it should come from the states, and not from the central government.

Yet Davis resolutely believed that the system of justice itself should be protected at all costs from politics, corruption, and interference. Thus, although Davis Polk and other downtown law firms would never have thought of hiring a Jewish lawyer, Davis led the City Bar Association's campaign to protest Tammany Hall's efforts to deny Samuel Rosenman reappointment to the New York Supreme Court in 1933. When reminded that this ran afoul of the Bar Association's charter (and Davis was the Association's president at the time), Davis joined others in creating the purportedly "Independent Judges Party" (housed in the Bar Association's building) to advocate Rosenman's reappointment.[26] That same year, Davis was first on the list of fifty leading New York lawyers who publicly petitioned Secretary of State Cordell Hull to protest Adolf Hitler's purging of Jewish lawyers and judges in Germany.[27]

SUNDERLAND AND KIENDL

Davis Polk was much more than the fiefdom of John W. Davis. New partners had risen to prominence. Despite the firm's reputation as a bastion of entrenched New York society, several partners were not from New York and did not fit the expected mold. One was Edwin S.S. Sunderland, who had been born in Great Bend, Kansas, in 1887, the son of an entrepreneur who operated a barbed wire factory. His family sent him to New England for prep school and college, and he joined Stetson Jennings & Russell in 1911, evidently as a law clerk while pursuing his legal studies at night law school. Sunderland later joined the socially elite cavalry Squadron A of the New York National Guard—the press gave it the motto "Every man a millionaire and mounted on a thoroughbred"—and he served in 1916 along the Mexican border against the Mexican revolutionary Pancho Villa. Sunderland returned to the firm the next year, becoming a partner in 1921. Sunderland succeeded to Frank Stetson's practice in railroad financings and reorganizations. After the country's overused and undermaintained railroads began to fail during the Depression, Sunderland's portfolio burgeoned. Among others, he worked on the reorganization of the Illinois Central, the Chicago, Rock Island and Pacific, the Missouri Pacific, the Seaboard Air Line Railway, and the Central of Georgia.

One of Sunderland's more notable cases was his representation of a group of senior creditors in the reorganization of the New York, New Haven and Hartford Railroad Company. The New Haven, as it was known, had been a troubled company for many years, going back to the time when J. P. Morgan attempted to use it as a vehicle to control railroad service in New England. The railroad entered bankruptcy in 1935 but, because of its tangled capital structure, did not emerge for twelve years. The record of proceedings in the reorganization court was 14,000 pages, and the case spawned fourteen appeals to the Second Circuit and six trips to the Supreme Court. The case raised such abstruse issues as whether damages for breach of a 999-year lease were provable as a bankruptcy claim;[28] the relationship among the Interstate Commerce Commission, the federal courts, and the states;[29] and whether the New Haven's losses operating the leased Boston & Providence Railroad were a priority lien against the Boston & Providence estate in the latter's own bankruptcy.[30] All the while, the New Haven's dominant shareholder, the Pennsylvania Railroad, was pushing legislation through Congress to amend the bankruptcy laws to ensure that its controlling interest would be preserved, thus undermining the reorganization plan. The Pennsylvania succeeded, only to have President Truman kill the bill with a pocket veto. Sunderland, who was a historian by avocation, thought that New Haven's reorganization deserved to be memorialized, and he privately published a short history of the case.[31]

Another was the litigator Theodore Kiendl. Kiendl was a local legend in New York. He had been born to a large, financially strapped family in Brooklyn in 1890 and graduated from Boys' High School there. He attended Columbia for college, where he was a three-time all-American basketball player. Columbia's basketball team of 1909-1910 was named as the national champions and Kiendl crowned as the National Player of the Year, an honor later conferred upon Larry Bird, Michael Jordan, and Kevin Durant. Kiendl also was a baseball star, and the New York Yankees made an effort to recruit him. He rejected the Yankees' offer of a tryout, opting instead to go to Columbia Law School.[32] After graduating in 1913, Kiendl returned to Brooklyn, where he joined his father and older brother in the Brooklyn law firm of Kiendl & Sons.

Like Edwin Sunderland, Kiendl also joined the New York National Guard's elite cavalry Squadron A, and he shared a tent with Sunderland during the 1916 Pancho Villa campaign. Kiendl nursed Sunderland back to health after Sunderland collapsed from exhaustion, and the two became good friends.[33] After their return to New York, Sunderland encouraged Kiendl to join Stetson, Jennings & Russell to take over the firm's poorly handled litigation for the Erie Railroad. He was elevated to partner in 1923.

Kiendl soon became the firm's leading trial lawyer and was considered by many to be the best trial lawyer in New York City. As one of his proteges, Lawrence Walsh, remembered:

> He was a challenging person. Somehow, at least in my imagination, he never lost the stance of a star basketball player, putting his eye on his opponent as he took his place in court. At 50, with full, iron-gray hair, wearing perfectly tailored clothes, he made no pretense that he could pass unnoticed. Whether in court or in conference, whether before a judge or a jury, his self-confidence drew people to him.[34]

Kiendl was a generation younger than John W. Davis and grumbled in private about the deference the world accorded Davis. One of the few times the usually unflappable Davis lost his temper was when Kiendl pulled on Davis' coat in the middle of trial while Davis was examining a witness. "How in the world can I cross-examine with you tugging on my tail?" Davis exclaimed.[35]

Despite the national prominence of its Supreme Court cases, Davis Polk also took on routine work including personal injury lawsuits. In the early morning of July 27, 1934, for example, an unemployed ironworker named Harry Tompkins was walking along a railroad track in Hughestown, Pennsylvania, when he allegedly was knocked over by the unsecured door of a passing refrigerator car. He fell beneath the wheels of the train, costing him his right arm. His lawyers filed a negligence case against the Erie in New York. Kiendl—who suspected Tompkins had actually tripped while trying to hop a ride on the train—tried the case. Despite Kiendl's withering cross-examination of plaintiffs' witnesses, the jury awarded Tompkins $30,000, plus costs and interest.

Kiendl appealed, arguing that the district court had misapplied the law. Under Pennsylvania law, Kiendl argued, the plaintiff had been a trespasser on Erie property and the railroad thus owed him no duty of care. Prevailing law, however, reaching back to the 1842 case of *Swift v. Tyson*,[36] held that a nebulous set of rules known as federal common law governed and, under those rules, the Erie might owe a duty of care even to trespassers. The Second Circuit affirmed, and the railroad decided to file a certiorari petition with the Supreme Court. With the assistance of a summer associate—Samuel Hazard Gillespie—Kiendl obtained an emergency stay of the judgment from Justice Benjamin Cardozo, who heard Kiendl's stay motion in the parlor of his summer home in Mamaroneck, New York, dressed in a velvet jacket. Kiendl was as surprised as anyone else when the Supreme Court took the case, unaware that a number of the justices had long been unhappy with *Swift*. In his briefs on the merits, Kiendl conceded that *Swift* was good law, but maintained that the trial court should have applied Pennsylvania law anyway under *Swift*'s exception for "local customs." At oral argument, Kiendl continued to defend *Swift*, even in the face of the court's suggestions that it should hand him the victory by simply overruling *Swift*. In any event, few thought that the case was particularly important. No one bothered to order a transcript of the argument that day, and Kiendl tossed out his files on the case shortly after the Supreme Court handed down its opinion in 1938. That case, of course, was the landmark decision of *Erie Railroad Co. v. Tompkins*, which overruled *Swift*, made state law the rule of law in decision in cases based on diversity of citizenship, and gave Kiendl a sweeping victory that he had not asked for and may not have wanted.[37]

With time, Kiendl's reputation grew to rival Davis'. In 1942, the federal court assigned him to represent one of the members of the German American Bund, a group of whom had been indicted for allegedly encouraging resistance to the draft. The Bund's proceedings had been in German, and Kiendl's withering cross-examination of the FBI's translator was so effective that the Supreme Court ultimately threw out the case.[38] Later, in the 1950s, Kiendl successfully represented the State of Arizona in its longstanding litigation in the Supreme Court against California for water rights to the Colorado River.[39] Toward the end of his career, Kiendl prevailed in the seminal case of *Lartigue v. Reynolds Tobacco Co.*,[40] one of the first lawsuits seeking to impose liability upon cigarette companies for the hazards of their products.

CLOSING OUT THE DECADE

By the end of the 1930s the impending war in Europe began to overshadow all else. The economy improved as the United States began supplying war materiel to the British and French, and beginning in 1938, Congress passed legislation funding a massive, two-ocean navy. The New Deal was, by now, a fait accompli that Wall Street had learned to live with and even profit from.

Two of the firm's named partners passed away in these years. George Gardiner died of a heart attack in late 1936. Modest to the end, he told one chronicler "I never had any pull . . . and just how I got where I am is something beyond my power to tell. I suppose, however, my clients believe me reliable and industrious."[41] Lansing Reed died suddenly of pneumonia in 1937.[42] After Frank Polk's death in 1943, the firm renamed itself Davis Polk Wardwell Sunderland & Kiendl.

13

Sullivan & Cromwell and Opportunity in the Aftermath of War

The New York establishment (bankers, industrialists, and Wall Street lawyers alike) knew that a transformed world order would emerge from the wreckage of the First World War. Dulles was not alone in seeking to find advantage in postwar markets. Stetson Jennings and Cravath, whose clients included the banks and industrial combines assembled before the war, were already well positioned to prosper as "normalcy" returned to the United States (in President Harding's coinage). Dulles looked to the reconstruction of Europe, and particularly Germany, as the path to leverage, profit, and influence. He set out to capitalize on his intimate knowledge of continental economics, gained as counsel at the Peace Conference. Keenly alert to the need for reconstruction finance in prostrate Germany, Dulles was intent on pursuing European investment prospects. His service on the Reparations Committee gave him an insider's grasp of the postwar financial prospects for the shattered nations of Europe, notably Germany. Hard-working and self-aggrandizing, Dulles "projected the heavy opaqueness of a large bear." He may have been unloved by his Wall Street contemporaries, given his fixed scowl and typical costume (soot-black overcoat, homburg, wing-tip collar, and walking stick). But foreigners were impressed. To compensate for his relative youth, Dulles had developed a negotiating style combining moral superiority, technical mastery, and the cold opacity of a professional poker player. He shared with Cromwell a desire to rehabilitate Europe, Cromwell through private charity in France and Dulles through his clients' financing of German industry. Dulles' recent partnership augured a charmed life, free of the shackles of routine. Others might endure the drudgery of drafting mortgages and indentures; he would pursue his interests unhindered.[1]

Only three months after leaving, Dulles returned to Europe to promote business for firm clients and scout investment possibilities. Postwar turbulence sank his immediate hoped-for business prospects but found him in Berlin during the right-wing

Kapp putsch that threatened to destroy the Weimar Republic. There he joined forces with his brother Allen, newly assigned by the State Department as First Secretary to the American legation in Berlin. The brothers wandered the abandoned streets of that city amid machine gun fire as the revolution unfolded around them. Business offices were empty, but Allen was still able to introduce his brother to Hjalmar Horace Greeley Schacht, a minor official of the German banking authority, later to become the architect of Germany's economic resurrection and war economy. Schacht was a self-regarding bombastic windbag, but he played a significant role in Dulles' career. The two men were drawn to each other. "Of all that I met in Berlin," Dulles recalled later, "Dr. Schacht alone looked forward with hope to the future . . . and felt it worthwhile to try to save something out of the wreckage. . . . " American-born, Schacht spoke fluent English and understood U.S. business. Tall, with a Prussian haircut and high starched collar, he shared with Dulles a belief that Germany could be a bulwark against Bolshevism. Mobilizing U.S. bank loans to finance its recovery was their mutual interest. Dulles became Schacht's chosen instrument for this purpose.[2]

In an economic sense the United States was the sole victor of World War I. It had emerged from the war with enormous productive capacity but in need of export markets. Germany was Wall Street's prime international focus. Thomas Lamont, the Morgan banker, many years later recalled: "The British and ourselves regarded Germany as the economic hub of the European universe. We feared that unless Germany were rebuilt and prospered all the surrounding countries of the Continent would likewise languish." In 1920, however, rehabilitating Germany through private industry, as Dulles intended, was anything but a mainstream idea. When Dulles returned from his European trip empty-handed, Cromwell took the long view. "This kind of work," he said, "is the most effective and far-reaching in the future (as well as the present) of S & C. It is only a matter of time when you will be called to take a more active part in these great questions." Cromwell's instinct was correct.[3]

Just two years after his initial encounter Dulles met again with Schacht, who revealed the blueprint of an international system that would resurrect Germany and solve the reparations problem. "Germany must find a loan of 5 billions of marks," he said, "proceeds of which have to be handed at once to France." He contemplated formation of four giant industrial cartels, each to have a government-granted monopoly on a basic bulk commodity such as sugar, cement, or coal, and each to control its export. Together the corporations would receive cash credits from American lenders, repayable through exports in ten years. Schacht said the proposed loan would not be based on a political treaty but would instead be launched by industrial and commercial sponsors of impeccable standing. Dulles immediately forwarded Schacht's proposal to Thomas Lamont of J. P. Morgan, describing Schacht as one of the ablest and most progressive of the young German bankers. The Anglo-American banking consortium had at last found its man. Two weeks later Dulles replied: "If a period of political stability could be assured, I have no doubt that bonds issued by such monopolistic corporations as you mention would command the confidence of the investing public." In the next few years Schacht's plan was to have profound impact on German industry, reparations, international finance, Sullivan & Cromwell, and, not least, the personal careers of Messrs. Schacht and Dulles.[4]

While U.S. bankers remained diffident about lending to Germany in the face of rampant currency inflation, Dulles plunged into work at Sullivan & Cromwell and as counsel to the War Finance Corporation, which made export financing loans to American firms so they could sell their products overseas. His diverse client base included International Nickel, a major company with global interests, for which Cromwell had long worked and on whose board, thanks to his mentor, Dulles served. Dulles also cultivated a formidable array of banking clients, the most important being J. P. Morgan and Dillon Read. He continued to seek a solution to the reparations problem, opposing the Coolidge administration's hard line on repayment of war debts, urging England and France to moderate their enormous claims against Germany, and proposing a fixed indemnity that would sharply reduce those claims. In 1923 Schacht, now the head of the Reichsbank, succeeded in halting German hyperinflation through a temporary currency, the rentenmark. It seemed a miracle. The Germans awaited a new plan that would settle reparations, get the French out of the Ruhr, and extend foreign credits to underwrite their national recovery.[5]

THE RESURRECTION OF GERMANY

Schacht's financial coup triggered a prompt response. In 1923, the Morgan bank retained Dulles as special counsel to the Dawes committee, charged with resolving the reparations crisis and restoring the German economy. The following April Owen Young of General Electric and Chicago banker Charles Dawes—both close to the Morgan interests and chosen by Secretary of State Hughes—presented a stabilization plan that reduced German reparations and tied them to the country's ability to pay. Under the plan, reparations would convert into foreign exchange only if Germany had enough reserves to avoid a run on the Reichsbank. The plan also empowered the Allies (at Dulles' suggestion) to appoint a transfer agent to supervise reparation payments (many of which were funneled through the Morgan bank) and preside generally over the German economy. This effectively placed Germany in international receivership, indentured to the Allies, with its railways and central bank under foreign control.

The key to the Dawes plan was a massive bank loan, underwritten in London and New York and senior to all other claims. The Morgan bank assumed responsibility for half ($110 million). At 10 a.m. on October 14, 1924, a nationwide syndicate of 400 banks and 800 bond houses led by J. P. Morgan opened the German loan subscription books. By 10:15, the syndicate had received orders for the total American portion of the loan and had to turn away millions more. It was the first of several Dawes loans to Germany, used in part to consolidate the gigantic chemical and steel combinations of I. G. Farben and Vereinigte Stahlwerke. The Dawes loans also enabled Germany to pay reparations to France and England, which then repaid war debts to the United States. The American demand for foreign bonds continued insatiably for the rest of the decade. In the seven years that followed, Dulles and his partners at Sullivan & Cromwell arranged for another $900 million in loans to Germany, equal to more than $15 billion in twenty-first century dollars. Dulles became the preeminent promoter of German bonds in the United States.[6]

To facilitate foreign borrowing, Dulles orchestrated complex financial transactions and carefully cultivated government contacts, domestic and abroad. Newly emboldened Wall Street banks, many of them Sullivan & Cromwell clients, pursued likely foreign borrowers with loan offers. If the foreign party wished to play, it would issue high-interest bonds at wholesale to those banks, which would then retail the bonds to investors in the United States, creating a spread of several points and funding Sullivan & Cromwell's fees from the difference. Ronald W. Pruessen, Dulles' biographer, provides a catalogue of the many international financings Dulles and Sullivan & Cromwell handled in the 1920s. It is a formidable list, including diverse worldwide transactions from Argentine bonds to the German External Loan of 1924. Dulles' firm advised Dillon Read and National City Company, among many others that purchased a flood of risky foreign bonds and securities and resold them to eager American investors.

The initiative for these loans came from Dulles and his clients, not borrower supplicants. A virtual army of brokers, soliciting on behalf of American banks, besieged European borrowers, large and small. Prospecting for foreign loans was intense. "During 1925 and 1926," the Prussian Minister of Finance recalled, "not a week went by that a representative of a group of American banks did not come to see me." German municipalities, banks, utilities, and shippers like North German Lloyd shrewdly signed up for easy money as Sullivan & Cromwell arranged a non-stop offering of German bonds. The American Agent General for Reparations, Parker Gilbert, pronounced himself "constantly amazed at the recklessness of American bankers . . . " Dulles meanwhile viewed the gold rush as constructive employment of the United States' financial power. He had every reason to identify with the powerful business clients that had propelled his career as they funded German borrowers and companies, including its huge chemical and steel cartels. Apart from Dawes plan credits, U.S.-German capital flows during the decade approached $1.5 billion.[7]

"Foster Dulles became so deeply enmeshed in the lucrative revitalization of Germany," writes one historian, "that he found it difficult to separate his firm's interests from those of the rising economic, and military power. . . . "[8] At the core of that power were cartels in chemicals, steel and electric technology, each financed by U.S. loans advanced under the Dawes plan. I. G. Farben, the chemical cartel formed in 1925 out of six German chemical producers, was a massive corporate octopus with tentacles around the globe and party to thousands of cartel agreements with foreign firms including Standard Oil of New Jersey, DuPont, Alcoa, Dow Chemical, and others. I. G. Farben was in fact the second largest shareholder in Standard Oil, a

Dulles client. The steel cartel, a combination of the four largest steel producers in Germany, raised more than $100 million in bond finance from U.S. investors and eventually controlled almost all iron and steel shipped in international trade. Sullivan & Cromwell floated bonds for Krupp, the arms manufacturer, extended I. G. Farben's reach through cartelization and blocked Canada's effort to restrict steel exports to Germany.

Although cartels violated the nation's antitrust and alien property custodian laws, Dulles defended them as guarantors of economic stability and later, on behalf of clients International Nickel, Solvay & Cie. and Allied Chemical & Dye, promoted cartel schemes with global impact. In *Foreign Affairs,* an influential international periodical, Dulles contended that the cartel system, with government supervision of prices, was economically superior to the domestic concept of competition enforced by law. Nominally, bank credits enabled reparation payments. In reality Germany was rebuilding its military-industrial potential, often paying for credits with shares of German companies. The result was integration of American capital into the German economy. Standard Oil, a key Sullivan & Cromwell client, acquired a controlling stake in I. G. Farben while the Morgan bank owned shares in AEG and Siemens through General Electric and Germany's telephone network through ITT Corporation. By the early 1930s U.S. banks controlled major sectors of Germany's industry.[9]

DULLES TAKES THE HELM

Dulles' rise within Sullivan & Cromwell, propelled by a stream of profitable international bond underwritings, was dramatic. Fate spared him a tortuous climb through layers of the firm's hierarchy. In 1926 Royall Victor, Sullivan & Cromwell's managing partner, died of a heart attack while piloting his boat at a regatta at the Oyster Bay Yacht Club. He was not yet 50. Victor's death created a gaping void in the firm's management. Alfred Jaretski Sr., once the managing partner under Cromwell, had died of stomach cancer just the year before, and Henry Hill Pierce, who directed the firm's utility work, was near retirement. Cromwell chose Dulles, then 38, to fill the vacancy as part of a four-man directorate including Wilbur Cummings, Edward Green, and Eustace Seligman. Dulles was clearly the leader of the triumvirate, responsible for pay and recruitment and chosen by Cromwell to take over work for his clients, including International Nickel, American Bank Note, Cuban Cane Sugar, and the Gold Dust Corp. As mentioned, Dulles also represented an array of New York banks. He became sole managing partner in 1927 and embarked on a run of several decades as head of the law firm of choice for international clients willing to pursue profit regardless of national interest.[10]

Dulles immediately offered a place at Sullivan & Cromwell to his brother, 33 years old, a recent law school graduate but not yet a member of any bar. In the words of one commentator, "[t]his was nepotism of a high order." Allen Dulles had been five years behind his brother at Princeton, where he "sported a neat black mustache, an expression of rakish chic." His uncle, Robert Lansing, Wilson's Secretary of State, launched Allen's career at the State Department, first as a lowly secretary in the embassy in Vienna and then as an intelligence officer in Bern. Allen secured a coveted position at the Boundary Commission at the peace conference, where he and his brother had adjoining rooms at the Crillon and met many of the world's movers and shakers. After an interim posting to Berlin, Allen became chief of the State Department's division of Near Eastern affairs for four years. Between trips to the Middle East, he attended evening and early-morning classes at George Washington University Law School, graduating in 1926, the same year he resigned from the foreign service. Diplomatic life on $8,000 per year had lost its luster. His note of resignation to Secretary Kellogg mentioned financial burdens involved in the acceptance of a higher position. Other lawyers at Sullivan & Cromwell may have resented how Allen gained entrance to the firm, but his value was not measured by legal experience or skillful advocacy. He was a customer's man who brought business to the firm. During his first year as an associate, with assistance from his former State Department contacts, banks he represented made multi-million-dollar loans to Bolivia and Colombia. Allen may not have grasped the intricacies of a foreign bond prospectus, but he had an insider's access to levers of influence within the State Department.[11]

The Dulles brothers were as different as chalk and cheese. Allen Dulles possessed powers of charm and seduction. Even those who disagreed with him found him congenial and good company. It was said that he knew everyone, would meet everyone, would go anywhere. He married his hometown sweetheart, Clover Todd, but had a famously roving eye, once frequented the Sphinx, a notorious Parisian brothel, and carried on open affairs with a series of women including Wally Toscanini Castelbarco, Clare Boothe Luce, and Queen Frederika of Greece, among others, often reported in letters to his long-suffering wife. In retaliation for Allen's dalliance with a white Russian émigré on his brother's estate at Cold Spring Harbor, his wife bought an emerald at Cartier on Allen's charge account, provoking a bitter domestic crisis. New York life beckoned nonetheless—"opening nights at the Metropolitan Opera, charity balls, club dinners, squash sessions at the New York Athletic Club, tennis parties."[12] John Foster Dulles was precisely the opposite. He had no interest in music or art and came across as a rough-cut figure still bearing the imprint of northern New York. George Kennan said of him, as Secretary of State, that he had a reputation for coldness and ruthlessness. Dour, uxorious, and moralistic, he struck William O. Douglas, later an iconoclastic Supreme Court justice but then an applicant for an associate slot at the firm, as pontifical, a high churchman out to exploit someone. ". . . [W]hen he helped me on with my coat, as I was leaving the office," Douglas recalled, "I turned and gave him a quarter tip." Eleanor Dulles, the brothers' talented, Bryn Mawr-educated sister, noted how different her siblings were. Despite his cold-blooded reputation, Dulles would help anyone in the family who was in distress, even securing an abortionist if that were required. "As for Allen," she said, "when anyone was in trouble, [he] seemed always to be off somewhere, lying under a palm, getting himself fanned."[13]

Hiring his brother was not an aberration. As sole managing partner Dulles felt free to remake the firm and soon established offices in Berlin, Paris, and Buenos Aires. In New York the firm had impressive new offices on the nineteenth and twentieth floors of 48 Wall Street, complete with wall-to-wall carpeting and a winding staircase. The offices imparted to Dulles "a sense of certainty, confidence and continuity, a feeling for American power and the knowledge that he had part in it." Fueled by corporate and banking business, Sullivan & Cromwell became the world's largest law firm in the 1920s. By 1929 it had over sixty lawyers. With a handful of rivals, notably including Cravath, de Gersdorff, Swaine & Wood and Davis, Polk, Wardwell, Gardiner & Reed, the firm was at the center of a white-shoe legal elite. A sprinkling of Jewish partners made Sullivan & Cromwell unique among the three at the time and anticipated the meritocratic wave that washed over the legal profession decades later. Even during the desperate Depression years Dulles was the highest paid lawyer in the United States, with a town house in Manhattan, a retreat at Cold Spring Harbor, and a yacht he sailed across Lake Ontario. He enjoyed an unsurpassed network of influential contacts in government and the business world combined with an insider's knowledge of international finance. "Although famously unable to remember the names of junior partners," wrote one biographer, "he drew on a mind filled with legal minutiae. His appetite for work was legendary, as was his toughness in negotiation."[14]

For several years Dulles kept Allen on a short leash and saw to it that technically adept associates reviewed his work product. Allen's long suit was his insider's ability to get around government prohibitions, eventually by hiding clients' foreign-owned assets from government scrutiny. His state department credentials gave him entry to the Council on Foreign Relations, whose publication, *Foreign Affairs*, was edited by his old Princeton friend Hamilton Fish Armstrong. His reputation as an international expert also made him a frequent delegate to conferences on naval disarmament and international debt restructuring, where he combined legal and diplomatic work. Disarmament talks in Geneva introduced him to Chancellor Heinrich Bruening, Sir John Simon, and Benito Mussolini. Although he never bothered to understand the technical side of complex financial transactions, Allen became Sullivan & Cromwell's key man in Latin America and developed a nose for business deals, a talent he later employed to help the J. Henry Schroeder Bank become a global financial player. In a few short years Allen was no more his brother's lackey but emerged as powerful counsel for an inner circle of rich and influential clients. In 1930 he became a partner in Sullivan & Cromwell, immediately assigned to the firm's Paris office for a year. During the first three months, before inviting his wife and children to join him, he lived at Cromwell's palatial suite on Avenue Foch, enjoying the pleasures of the capital city. Allen's frolic and detour in Paris did nothing to divert his commitment to the companies supporting his elegant lifestyle.[15]

BOND MARKET REVERSAL AND THE BURDEN OF GERMAN POLITICAL UPHEAVAL

In the late 1920s, payment of bankers' credits and reparations created a dollar shortage in Germany, threatening the international financial structure just as the stock market boom sucked funds back to New York. "This situation cannot long continue," Dulles warned, "without a collapse which will mean the realization of the dangers that were forecast ten years ago." Continued prosperity depended on the outflow of American capital. The Dawes plan gave priority over reparation payments only to the $200 million Dawes loan itself. The flood of private loans to Germany made after 1924 was unprotected. If Germany did not have enough foreign exchange to pay reparations to the Allies, they would predictably resist making payment of their war loans to the United States. Frightened American investors would then cut off new credits to Germany. To deal with this impasse, in early 1929 a conference of experts under Owen Young proposed to reduce reparations and give payments for private loans priority, i.e., to treat reparations as junior debt. The plan also created a Bank for International Settlements to handle reparation payments and authorized a $300 million loan shared by the German government and reparations creditors. The Wall Street stock market crash intervened between the plan's proposal in 1929 and its adoption by the German government in 1930, dooming its intended prospects.[16]

No one was happy with the Young plan, least of all Hjalmar Schacht, who resigned in 1930 as president of the Reichsbank and denounced Germany's continued payment of reparations in speeches across the United States, conveniently forgetting Germany's imposition of a crushing levy on France following the Franco-Prussian War. Later that year the Foreign Policy Association invited Schacht and Dulles to speak at a dinner meeting in New York. Schacht, a man of unbridled ambition, praised the Nazi party, which had gained significantly in the most recent election, as a warning to the world. He predicted another reparations crisis, disclaimed all responsibility for the Young plan and said he had been deceived by foreign experts and his own government. Dulles, ever the optimist in German matters, thought Germany was exaggerating its economic problems to rid the country of its reparations obligations. The issue, he explained, was largely psychological.

In fact, the market crash in October 1929 had unleashed an economic tsunami that was to overwhelm the United States, Germany, and the rest of the world. Clients who had taken Sullivan & Cromwell's advice to buy German bonds risked total loss. Schacht had led Dulles and his firm to support Germany far too long. As mute evidence of the financial disaster the Union League Club, one of Dulles' occasional haunts, papered a room at the club with now worthless stock and bond certificates. Foreign securities issues, a Sullivan & Cromwell specialty, declined from $1 billion to $50 million in under three years. In 1935, speaking at the Downtown Association, Allen Dulles reviewed Sullivan & Cromwell's decisive role in managing issuance of foreign securities during the 1920s. The firm, he said, had "permitted debt to pile up too fast and too high, [taking] bad moral risk."[17]

After the Nazi party did unexpectedly well in the Reichstag elections in 1930, money flowed out of Germany, threatening an economic crisis. Solicited for advice by President Hoover, Dulles warned of economic collapse. Robert Olds, head of Sullivan & Cromwell's Paris office, reporting to Dulles on the financial crisis, predicted further advances to Germany through an international banking consortium. When Allied officials declined to stabilize German finances, the burden passed, as Olds had foreseen, to a syndicate of private bankers with an overwhelming stake in continued international lending, led by Lee, Higginson, with Dulles as counsel. The bankers persuaded Chancellor Bruening's government to accept millions in short-term credits as a bulwark against default and Hitler's control. As large as they were, the credits could not stem the crisis. "Once again," said Hjalmar Schacht, "the German government was endeavoring to conceal the true situation by piling up fresh debts abroad." Sovereign bond defaults began, first in Latin America and then in Europe. By the late 1930s almost two-thirds of European issuers' bonds and securities were in default. But Sullivan & Cromwell prospered on the downside as it had on the upside. "It was not surprising," writes his principal biographer, "that Dulles, who had been so involved with the great promotion of foreign securities in the United States during the 1920s, should soon become involved with the grand-scale defaults of the 1930s. His role as a lawyer for major American banking houses, in fact, was as great in the negative phase of the interwar period as it had been in the positive. Fees from banker clients continued to contribute substantially to the income of Sullivan & Cromwell. . . ."[18]

Dulles successfully navigated the arcane world of international debt restructuring. His firm reaped huge fees from collapse of Ivar Krueger's match king pyramid scheme and represented banks that were refinancing the debts of financially pressed borrowers. But Sullivan & Cromwell's continued prosperity was jarringly at odds with the fate of investors it had served. By early 1933, when Hitler assumed power in Germany, more than $1 billion in bonds the firm had arranged in Europe were worthless. The Nazi regime abruptly repudiated reparations. Later that year, as counsel for U.S. banks (Brown Brothers Harriman, Kuhn Loeb, and Dillon Read, among others), Dulles attended debt conferences in Berlin arranged by the Reichsbank to work out settlements with creditors and address financing of the new Hitler government. Hjalmar Schacht, now reinstalled as president of the bank, said Germany would treat creditors differently depending on trade balances, a policy that harmed Dulles' clients because Germany's imports from the United States far exceeded its exports. Schacht's policy implied selective default, a divide-and-conquer strategy to undermine creditors' unity. Although Dulles bitterly criticized Schacht's bilateralism, there was little he could do to forestall the global onset of regressive debt and trade policies—tariffs, exchange restrictions, quotas, import prohibitions, barter trade agreements, central trade clearing arrangements. Dulles instead found a way to work with Schacht, who became the Nazi Economics Minister in 1934 and helped Hitlerite Germany find financial sources in the United States. "Behind Schacht," wrote one observer, ". . . stood important segments of German absentee ownership and Anglo-Saxon finance."[19]

To handle the German end of its bond business, Sullivan & Cromwell opened a Berlin office in 1929, housed in a suite at the Esplanade Hotel, and joined forces with a Berlin firm, Albert & Westrick, as corresponding counsel. Both the Berlin office and the local firm were problematic. After the stock market crash killed Sullivan & Cromwell's bond business, the firm's Berlin office languished; its three associates, with time on their hands, watched Nazi street demonstrations as they awaited Dulles' semiannual visits. Joseph Prendergast, an associate in the Berlin office, noted its difference from New York, where the eighteen-hour day prevailed and partners' nervous tics accompanied their Park Avenue apartments and houses on Long Island. Albert & Westrick, for its part, was well connected with the resurgent Nazi movement. Its senior partner, Dr. Heinrich Albert, on assignment in New York City as privy counselor to the German Embassy during the First World War, directed a nationwide espionage ring, discovered when his briefcase was left accidentally in a New York subway. After the war he was German secretary of state and a key link to major German borrowers. Albert had worked closely with Dulles for years and was clearly someone to be cultivated, however irregular his credentials. Gerhardt Westrick, the workaholic junior partner, represented International Telephone & Telegraph in Europe, where accumulating German profits supported the Third Reich's ominous armaments economy. Sullivan & Cromwell did not let inconvenient facts inhibit promising business relations. Westrick shared odd moments with Allen Dulles, lunches at the Herrenklub in Berlin and family golf at Oberdorf. Sullivan & Cromwell maintained its relationship with Westrick's firm after Hitler took power in 1933. In that year cables from Sullivan & Cromwell's Berlin office were preceded by the salutation "Heil Hitler," as required by German law. The Berlin office had become an embarrassment, and Dulles' frequent appointments in New York with emissaries from I. G. Farben and Solvay et Cie. on cartel matters made his partners uneasy.[20]

In June 1935 Allen Dulles sailed on the *S.S. Europa* for Berlin and Budapest, representing the Council of Foreign Relations at a League of Nations conference on collective security before dealing with law firm business. Allen had burnished his international credentials as President Roosevelt's delegate to disarmament talks in Geneva culminating in a meeting with Hitler two years before. While his brother blandly viewed the rise of dictators as redress by dynamic younger powers against static imperial hangers-on, Allen, on the ground in Europe, gained a contrary impression. He heard disturbing news from the Warburgs and other Jewish clients of the need to sequester their financial assets outside the reach of the Nazi government. He feared Sullivan & Cromwell's Berlin office was nothing but an admission of the firm's support for Hitler. When Allen returned home, he urged his brother to close the Berlin office at once. Dulles was vehemently opposed, believing major corporate clients like Remington, Standard Oil, and General Motors needed German representation. Allen raised the Berlin office at a partners' meeting. Dulles resisted, saying closure would "do great harm to our prestige," but several younger partners found it morally objectionable to continue a Berlin office. Allen said the firm would suffer more if it failed to do so. Several of the partners—Edward Green, Eustace Seligman, and Arthur Jaretski—were Jewish, leading Arthur Dean to suggest the firm not represent German clients. Almost to a man, the partners voted to close the Berlin office. Dulles was said to have stalked off in tears.[21]

Closure of the Berlin office did not end Sullivan & Cromwell's work for clients with German interests. During the 1930s, after Hitler's ascension, Dulles made annual trips to Berlin and represented international steel and chemical cartels, serving as a director of Consolidated Silesian Steel Company, Poland's largest company, with co-ownership ties to Friedrich Flick, an industrial magnate and key supporter of Hitler who was later tried at Nuremberg as a war criminal. Dulles continued to use Heinrich Albert's impeccable Nazi connections to uncover lucrative business opportunities for Sullivan & Cromwell.

Of the firm's bank clients none was more important than the J. Henry Schroder Banking Corporation (Shrobanco), the U.S. affiliate of Schroeder banks in London and Germany, which soon accounted for half of Allen's legal caseload and made him a director and general counsel. Shrobanco financed Chilean manganese; engineered sophisticated dollars-for-reichsmarks swaps to stockpile strategic materials for transshipment to German producers; and was linked, according to one account, "through blood and commercial ties with . . . Baron Kurt von Schroeder, Heinrich Himmler's special angel." Von Schroeder, a radical Nazi and Cologne banker, had financed Hitler at a critical juncture in his rise to power. Another account denies any proof that Sullivan & Cromwell, or the Dulles brothers, or the London Schroder Bank ever had any ties to or dealings with von Schroeder. Nonetheless the dominating shareholder in both J. Henry Schroder offices continued to be Baron Bruno von Schroeder in London. Managing the Schroder interests in Germany were Schroder Gebruder of Hamburg and its Cologne affiliate, J. H. Stein & Co., in which Baron Kurt was a partner. In the 1930s, as trade between England and Germany grew, the Schroeder Bank became Germany's main financial agent in England. Later in both Dulles brothers' careers this tangle of associations proved a political liability. Their defenders could only argue lamely that "[any] corporation lawyer of like position will find that policies of certain of his clients are open to social criticism."[22]

GERMAN CLIENTELE AND THE IMPENDING WAR

As the Second World War drew nearer during the 1930s, Dulles remained fatalistic and viewed the impending crisis as unavoidable. He blamed the western powers for imposing oppressive peace terms on Germany and spoke of the historic struggle, as he saw it, between the dynamic and the static—the urge to acquire and the desire to retain. He supported America First, an isolationist lobby; denounced Roosevelt and Churchill as warmongers; acted once as counsel for the Franco regime; and seriously misjudged Hitler as a passing phenomenon. John J. McCloy, once a Cravath partner and later head of the World Bank and overseer of occupied Germany, looked back askance at Dulles' prewar views. "I was always puzzled," he said, "to see where Foster

Dulles stood . . . with the Nazi business and what his feeling was about the oncoming menace from Germany."[23] Dulles in fact minimized that menace, believing the allies had committed "blunders so colossal they must be paid for." His were not merely political sentiments; they reflected underlying business realities.

Both Dulles brothers were heavily engaged in representing German clients in the United States. While publicly advocating support for the British, Allen represented German corporate clients in their effort to acquire American Potash and Chemical Corporation, an important source of strategic chemicals and foreign currency. Dulles himself had longstanding German ties in the United States. In the 1920s he and Sullivan & Cromwell had represented Metallgesellschaft of Frankfurt, the world's largest nonferrous metals company, in its successful effort to regain control of American Metal Company, a U.S. subsidiary seized by the government during the war.

Almost two decades later he acted for General Aniline & Film (GAF), a U.S. subsidiary of I. G. Farben, seeking to mask its relationship with its parent, avoid Treasury regulations on foreign funds, and negate the possibility of its seizure as enemy property if war broke out. GAF was an important producer of war materials, including atabrine, magnesium, and synthetic rubber, all subject to restrictive patent agreements with I.G. Farben that were to limit domestic supply of these products during the coming war. It was no surprise when, shortly after Pearl Harbor, the government seized control of GAF. Treasury Secretary Morgenthau invaded GAF's offices and began sacking pro-German personnel. "In case anybody asks you," Morgenthau explained, "you can say that the President [says] 'Kill the son-of-a-bitch.'" Despite the seizure, Dulles' work as GAF's counsel benefited I. G. Farben, the hugely powerful chemical combine that was part of a cartel he orchestrated during the 1930s, together with Solvay and Allied Chemical & Dye. I. G. Farben became indispensable to the Nazi war machine as supplier of synthetic rubber, poison gas, explosives, and Zyklon B. Dulles' driving concern was always to protect his client base; political views were shaped accordingly. Except for discontinuing its Berlin office, his firm appeared largely unembarrassed by his Germanophile posture.[24]

Sullivan & Cromwell's work for GAF was not unusual. Several of its German clients sought to shelter their American assets from government seizure and confiscation, as had happened during the First World War, by interposing cut-outs or intermediaries to hold title. American Bosch, the subsidiary of Robert Bosch gmbh of Stuttgart, was a hugely successful company whose spark plugs and magnetos had become the industry standard and whose direct fuel injection technology for diesel engines it attempted to deny the U.S. military during the Second World War. During the First World War its German provenance had led to seizure by the Alien Property Custodian and sale of its shares to new owners. During the interwar years, following the stock market crash, Robert Bosch gmbh was able to reacquire ownership, thereafter using a series of nominal bank holders as intermediaries. The Enskilda Bank of Sweden, controlled by the Wallenberg brothers, eventually bought the

American Bosch shares in order to cloak them from government reprisal. In 1940, to perfect cloaking arrangements, Marcus Wallenberg visited the United States. Working together, he and Dulles established a voting trust on behalf of Enskilda to hold the American Bosch shares and appointed Dulles' old friend, George Murnane, as sole voting trustee.

Murnane was a logical choice, having served as chairman of the American Bosch board since 1935. During his visit, Wallenberg told Murnane that the American Bosch shares belonged outright to Enskilda, although Enskilda had in fact agreed to resell the shares to Robert Bosch gmbh after holding them during the war. Wallenberg also told the U.S. government, incorrectly, that there was no German interest in American Bosch. As war raged in Europe, the Wallenbergs acquired nominal ownership of a portion of the American Bosch shares formerly held by Enskilda and transferred them to a Delaware corporation of which Dulles was sole voting trustee. In early December 1941 the U.S. Treasury declared that American Bosch was German, Dutch, and Swedish property. After Germany declared war on the United States, Dulles took legal action to reverse the Treasury's classification. Enskilda continued to argue that American Bosch had no German ownership, but the Treasury was not persuaded.

The Alien Property Custodian seized the American Bosch shares, believing Dulles must have known it was German owned. At the end of the war in Europe, based on Robert Bosch gmbh archival material liberated by U.S. troops in Germany, the *New York Herald Tribune* alleged that Enskilda and the Wallenbergs had acted as a front for the Germans. Concerned, Dulles urged, unsuccessfully, that the Swedish government declare its support for Enskilda, which the Treasury viewed as a cloak for American Bosch's true German ownership and an implement of Axis policy.

Eventually, in 1949, the government sold the American Bosch shares to U.S. investment bank Allen & Co., for $6 million. The Wallenbergs sued to get the proceeds of sale. Complex legal proceedings ensued. Inzer Wyatt, a young Sullivan & Cromwell partner, wished to litigate, but his seniors, Dulles and Alfred Jaretski Jr. thought otherwise, and a year later Enskilda and the Alien Property Custodian settled. "Perhaps," wrote one historian, ". . . Sullivan & Cromwell and others were simply working to keep industrial assets out of Nazi hands. Their subterfuges, however, involved faking titles of ownership and management, claiming neutral rather than German control. To critics of the Wall Street mentality, it looked as though American capitalists were conniving with their German counterparts to circumvent their respective governments and the 'integrity of international capital' was taking priority over the 'national interest.'" By the end of the war, America's most important German trading partners from the inter-war years had blood under their fingernails; Dulles' international clients had attracted antitrust scrutiny; and Dulles himself was accused of collaboration with the enemy.[25]

GOLDMAN SACHS

Sullivan & Cromwell served clients in areas other than international finance. During the boom years of the 1920s, the firm organized and promoted investment trusts, leveraged and speculative industrial holding companies that mushroomed spectacularly, then crashed after 1929. Goldman Sachs, a Sullivan & Cromwell client, had come late to the investment trust game but succumbed to the entrepreneurial dynamism of Waddill Catchings, a onetime associate at Sullivan & Cromwell whom Goldman had hired immediately after the war to head its underwriting business. Talented, handsome, and well connected, Catchings offered Dulles preferential shares in and arranged for him to become a director of and counsel to Goldman Sachs Trading Company, the investment trust that fatefully tied the reputation of the bank to the fortunes of its new business, which grew exponentially in the months ahead. The Trading Company issued massive amounts of common stock and merged with another investment trust.

As its share price more than doubled, it confronted an unusual problem: where to invest so much money. Dulles had a ready answer. He introduced the Trading Company to Harrison Williams, a Sullivan & Cromwell utility client and then the richest man in the country. A powerful speculative alliance, the sponsors created two new investment trusts, Shenandoah Corporation and Blue Ridge Corporation, both heavily leveraged. Dulles became a director of each, leading one tongue-in-cheek commentator to attribute his "lack of discrimination in this instance . . . to youthful optimism."[26] In less than a month these trusts issued securities worth a quarter of a billion dollars— a scale ordinarily associated with the United States Treasury. The share prices of the Trading Company and its progeny peaked, then quickly plummeted to pennies after 1929, spawning endless litigation against Dulles individually and Goldman Sachs, which lost millions and settled with the largest plaintiffs, its reputation in tatters. Aggrieved investors filed so many suits against Goldman Sachs that brokers, legend has it, would call the firm and ask for the Litigation Department. Events during the decade of the thirties severely tested Dulles' vaunted optimism, also present in his dealings with German finance, but did not extinguish it, perhaps because Sullivan & Cromwell continued its highly profitable practice through the depths of the Depression.

THE WORLD'S LARGEST LAW FIRM

To serve its growing practice during the interwar years Sullivan & Cromwell became the world's largest law firm, described by its critics as a law factory. "Steadily," wrote Supreme Court Justice Harlan Stone, a former partner at the firm, "the best skill and capacity of the profession [have] been drawn into the exacting and highly specialized service of business and finance."[27] Sullivan & Cromwell was a notable case in point. Arthur Dean justified its size and increasing specialization by the need to "cope with the present complex network of laws and regulations . . . and the scale of American enterprise."[28] By the early thirties the firm had over sixty lawyers, including several women associates, but only fourteen partners. The women hired (including Ruth Hall, a 1929 Yale Law School graduate) knew their partnership prospects were negligible but, after having been routinely rejected by Cravath, Davis Polk, and White & Case, were grateful to have a Wall Street job. Many of the newly recruited associates stayed only a few years, forcing the firm to replace departed juniors annually.

As managing partner, Dulles was an intrepid promoter but an indifferent administrator, a man of formidable reserve, but insensitive to others' concerns. While professing interest in hiring the best and brightest law graduates, he rarely interviewed applicants and barely knew the names of most lawyers in the firm. Louis Auchincloss recounts that, while an associate lawyer at Sullivan & Cromwell, he was in a partner's office when that partner phoned Dulles to ask whether several associates could take their fiancees to an obligatory New Year's Day party at the Colony Club hosted by the firm's partners and their wives. Dulles hesitated and replied, "No. Fiancees are not wives." "A man like that," Auchincloss mused, "should never have been in charge of the State Department."[29] To fill the managerial vacuum, Cromwell, then in his 70s and often an exile in France, could on occasion be seen roaming the halls and terrorizing the young lawyers.[30]

As Cravath's Robert Swaine had predicted, Sullivan & Cromwell, among a few other peers, prospered mightily during the 1930s, a decade that framed a battleground between the clashing forces of big finance and big government. When Sullivan & Cromwell's corporate and banking clients confronted New Deal regulation, the ensuing struggle provoked legal innovation. The firm litigated and became expert in the emerging fields of shareholder derivative suits, antitrust, federal income tax law, and securities law. It remained, equally, a leader in international business transactions, the indispensable firm for investment in a rearmed Germany. Sullivan & Cromwell consciously shaped itself as a modern business law practice. Its pyramidal structure required very few partners but many associates, the latter anonymously excluded from listing on the firm's letterhead. In every visible way the firm conveyed institutional authority and became the archtypical big-business practice.

The firm's wealth flowed through to its partners. Dulles earned almost $400,000 in 1936. Allen earned about half as much, still extraordinary by the standards of the time, and was able to buy a townhouse in Manhattan and a summer retreat in Cold Spring Harbor. Weekends often found both brothers in Long Island, Dulles on his yacht and Allen partying with Archie Roosevelt, the Lindberghs, Rebecca West, and Tallulah Bankhead.

Leisure pursuits, however intriguing to Allen, did not divert Dulles from intense focus on the firm's economics. He proposed a more egalitarian financial structure, sharing firm profits relinquished by Cromwell, creating a capital base through contributions from junior partners, and limiting his own partnership share. "The only quarrels we ever had with Mr. Dulles on percentages," said one of his partners, "were that we could never get him to take enough."

Still, through the long years of the Depression, Dulles continued to earn a stupendous income and convinced Cromwell to allow the firm to invest in First Boston Corporation, thereafter a firm client. He and Cromwell also contributed $25,000 each to an investment banking partnership between George Murnane and Jean Monnet, whom Dulles had first met at the Versailles peace conference. Murnane was a legend in the investment banking business, formerly a partner in Lee, Higginson & Company, which collapsed in the Ivar Krueger scandal. Monnet & Murnane thrived in the late thirties, thanks to both partners' international connections. Murnane went on to become a partner in Lazard Freres, and Monnet was to be a principal architect of the European Economic Community. Murnane also served as a director of Allied Chemical & Dye; a voting trustee for shares of American Bosch appointed by Dulles; and the main American adviser for Belgium's great industrial family dynasties, the Solvays and the Boëls, with whom Dulles had close business connections as counsel for Solvay & Cie. Like his mentor, Cromwell, Dulles found ways to move beyond mere legal advice to reorder events as a promoter and principal.

14

The Advent of Regulation

Roosevelt's New Deal portended seismic changes at home just as Hitler's regime did in Germany. The stock market crash had devastated many investment houses, tarnishing the reputation of the financial community. New Deal legislation reshaped the nation's capital markets, affecting the business of Wall Street law firms in ways they could not have predicted.

THE PECORA INVESTIGATION

After it became apparent that the nation had entered an enduring economic depression, the Senate Banking and Currency Committee initiated an investigation into the cause of the numerous bank failures. For its chief counsel, it chose Ferdinand Pecora, a seasoned New York City prosecutor. Born in Sicily, Pecora had worked his way up through the District Attorney's office, earning such a reputation for probity that his original backers at Tammany Hall abandoned him.

Pecora began work in early 1933 under a lame-duck Republican senate. There were obvious parallels to the Pujo hearings twenty years before; in fact, Pecora's job originally had been offered to Samuel Untermyer, who had turned it down in expectation Pecora would be dismissed when the new Democratic majority was seated in the Senate and the job would then be Untermyer's for good.[1]

It is tempting to see the Pecora investigation as simply a continuation of reformists' assault on the power of the Morgan interests that had begun with the Pujo Committee and continued until resolution of the Justice Department's antitrust case against the Morgan bank and a dozen co-defendants in the 1950s. The Pujo Committee had convincingly demonstrated that, indeed, there was a "money trust" in the United States, concentrated in a few blocks of downtown New York, but laws Congress had passed had done little to control it. In fact, the creation of the Federal Reserve System may have enhanced its strength. Following the stock market crash and nationwide bank failures, it was time to bring the bankers to heel.

Like Untermyer in 1911, Pecora summoned partners from the Morgan bank—including Jack Morgan himself—as witnesses and probed the network of affiliations and hidden connections on Wall Street. Just as Frank Stetson had represented Pierpont Morgan before Samuel Untermyer, John W. Davis was counsel for Jack Morgan and his partners now.

Pecora demonstrated that the web of interlocking directorships and corporate affiliations was as pervasive as ever, and he focused on secretive Wall Street connections that had permitted shocking abuses. One of the worst cases was National City Bank, and Pecora's careful questioning of its brazen president, Charles E. Mitchell, exposed repeated examples of misconduct. These included revelations that the bank had aggressively marketed its common stock to its customers and promoted risky South American bonds and that it had dumped its holdings of Anaconda Copper while simultaneously selling Anaconda stock to unsuspecting investors.[2] The public also learned that Mitchell—who had used his office to pay himself millions—had engaged in a sham wash sale of bank stock with his wife to manufacture tax losses and used the deduction to avoid paying income taxes in 1929. Equally revealing was the fact that National City had distributed the stock of the newly created Boeing Air Transport Company to a group of select insiders (including the bank's lawyers at Shearman & Sterling) on preferential terms that ensured the insiders a windfall.[3]

Pecora found similar misdeeds at Chase National Bank. Under the leadership of its chairman, Albert H. Wiggin, Chase had ballooned in size, alternating with National City as the country's largest commercial bank. Like Mitchell, Wiggin had been richly compensated. Perhaps worse, he had speculated in Chase's stock, using his family's private corporations to participate in the trading pools Chase's securities affiliate, Chase Securities Corporation (CSC), had organized.[4] To allay concerns from officers at Chase and CSC, Wiggin installed them as directors of his family corporations, cut them in on the profits and made personal loans to them as well. Most damning of all was the revelation that Wiggin's family corporations—with money borrowed from the bank—had shorted Chase's stock at the time of the stock market crash, while Chase and CSC were buying Chase stock to buoy up the price. Thus, Wiggin netted $4 million just as the bank's small shareholders were all but wiped out.[5]

The Morgan bank considered itself above such machinations. Unlike National City and Chase, Morgan's was a private bank, a partnership owned by a handful of men. It had no small depositors, and, with as much business as it could handle, it had avoided the speculative practices of other banks. It had never issued stock nor, for that matter, been part of the boom in equities during the 1920s. It was obsessively discreet: in fact, the bank's name did not even appear on the front door of its headquarters at 23 Wall Street. Although subject to regulation by the New York state banking authorities, the Superintendent of Banking had never troubled himself to examine the bank's books because of its impeccable reputation.[6]

Davis ostensibly cooperated with Pecora, but never trusted his motives and did all he could to impede the investigation. He resisted Pecora's demands to see lists of the bank's depositors and made its voluminous correspondence files available only during business hours. Davis also used his political connections, reputation, and public standing to cloak his resistance. During the hearings, Davis interrupted Pecora's questions, openly coached witnesses, and interjected rebutting evidence whenever he could. At one point, he even put his young tax partner, Montgomery Angell, on the witness stand to show that the IRS itself had endorsed a tax position Morgan partner William Ewing had taken.[7]

Jack Morgan testified in late May 1933. The Committee chamber was crammed with reporters, photographers, and spectators as Morgan entered accompanied by Davis, the senior Thomas Lamont, and a retinue of bodyguards.[8] Morgan was 60 and had an almost legendary reputation; in fact, many confused him with his long-dead father. Indeed, he resembled his father in appearance, dress, and demeanor. He abhorred publicity, and the Pecora investigation was a rare instance that allowed the general public to see what he looked like.[9]

Davis had written Morgan's opening remarks. His strategy was to distance Morgan from the likes of Mitchell and Wiggin and stress the bank's patrician ethos, conservatism, and sound judgment. Instead Morgan's prepared statement instead came off as aloof and pompous. He intoned that his bank had intended to do "only first-class business, and that in a first-class way." "We have never been satisfied with simply keeping within the law," Morgan said, "but have constantly sought so to act that we might fully observe the professional code, and so maintain the credit and reputation which has been handed down to us from our predecessors in the firm." Morgan pointed out that private bankers like himself avoided foolish practices for the simple reason that it was their own personal wealth that they were putting on the line. Unlike lesser financiers, private bankers adhered to an unspoken code of ethics and prudence; they were, in fact, a mainstay of the economy. "To sum up, I state without hesitation that I consider the private banker a national asset and not a national danger." Echoing his father's testimony before the Pujo Committee, Jack Morgan maintained that "[a]s to the theory that he may become too powerful, it must be remembered that any power which he has comes, not from the possession of large means, but from the confidence of the people in his character and credit, and that that power, having no force to back it, would disappear at once if people thought that the character had changed or the credit had diminished—not financial credit, but that which comes from the respect and esteem of the community."[10]

Morgan's reputation and personal gravity lent credence to his restatement of banking ethics. But Pecora soon revealed that Morgan and his partners were not above cutting corners. It emerged that they had paid no income taxes at all in 1931 and 1932.[11] Worse, Thomas Lamont's son (also a Morgan partner) had engaged in the identical sham wash sale Mitchell had engineered, selling depreciated securities to his wife at a loss and then buying them back a few months later.[12] Such antics were fodder for newspapermen. Davis railed at the press for inflating these disclosures since the transactions exposed were perfectly legal.[13] But in a time of national economic distress, the fact that the immensely wealthy Jack Morgan and his partners were dodging income taxes was indefensible.

And other disclosures showed that the Morgan bank was not really the servant of the public interest after all. It turned out that the bank had a list of 500 preferred investors to whom it passed out stock at below-market prices. The list may have had innocuous beginnings: at the height of stock market speculation in 1929, the bank decided to boost its underwriting business by launching three captive holding companies, each a platform for issuing bonds that the Morgan bank could underwrite. One was the United Corporation, a holding company for electric utilities, which controlled much of the electric power distributed east of the Mississippi. Another, Standard Brands, was a food conglomerate. The third, Allegheny Corporation, owned a collection of railroads. Each company needed stockholders, but the Morgan bank had no interest in the risks or disclosures attendant to a public stock offering. Instead, the bank privately placed the companies' shares with its friends, almost guaranteeing healthy profits to the chosen few.[14] The Morgan bank, it now seemed, was no better than its competitors. It even came to light that the biggest allotment of the Boeing stock National City had distributed to insiders had gone to a partner at J. P. Morgan, who then parceled it out to others at the bank.[15]

These covert transactions revealed favoritism and self-dealing, if not insider trading, and the press had a field day. Making matters worse, the Morgan insiders list included many prominent people who should have known better. These included Senator William Gibbs McAdoo (who, for good measure, happened to sit on the Senate Banking Committee), Treasury Secretary William H. Woodin, Supreme Court Justice James Clark McReynolds, a recent chairman of the Democratic Party, and even former President Coolidge. The *New York Times* published an expose, suggesting that the scheme's purpose was to curry favor in Washington.[16]

Davis pushed back at what he deemed Pecora's excesses, his playing to the worst instincts of the press, and his smearing the names of decent, honest men.[17] He argued that the bank had not, in fact, concealed from the public the price at which shares had been sold to insiders; many of the political figures on the list were there for independent reasons; and if the mighty Morgan bank had wished to lobby Congress or the Hoover administration, it would not have done so in such an amateurish way. But Davis' credibility evaporated when it came to light that almost every single Davis Polk partner was on the Morgan insiders list and had received preferential grants of stock, with Davis benefiting more than anyone else.[18] Few believed Morgan's bromides about the integrity of private bankers or accepted downtown lawyers' assurances that they were a bulwark against the excesses of capitalism. The lawyers, it turned out, seemed to be in on it too.

THE GLASS-STEAGALL ACT AND THE SECURITIES ACT OF 1933

Just as Pecora was exposing bankers' self-dealing, stock manipulation, and tax avoidance, the Roosevelt administration contemplated legislation to reform the banking business and securities markets. The Pecora hearings—like the Pujo hearings twenty years before—had proven that banks were too big, bankers were too powerful, and Wall Street was awash in unethical practices. Finally, Wall Street must be brought to heel.

President Roosevelt had presaged reform of the securities markets in his message to Congress of March 1933 where he asked for "legislation for Federal supervision of traffic in investment securities in interstate commerce." Soon, a group led by Felix Frankfurter was drafting a bill to regulate the securities industry. This law—now known as the Securities Act of 1933—was not the product of public hearings, although it was given enormous momentum by Pecora's shocking revelations. Frankfurter's working group—his former students Benjamin V. Cohen, Thomas G. Corcoran, and James M. Landis—designed a regime that mandated public disclosure of material facts about issuers of new securities with criminal and civil liability for false or misleading statements.

Wall Street mobilized to undermine the new legislation. Dulles found himself, uncharacteristically, on the outside looking in. Sullivan & Cromwell partners, led by Dulles, Eustace Seligman, and a promising younger partner, Arthur Dean, attacked the initial draft of the Securities Act. Dean called it a "hopeless confusion of ill-assorted provisions." Seligman said that holding corporate directors responsible for the truth of registration statements was "revolutionary . . . and without precedent in Anglo-Saxon law." The objections caused Frankfurter to propose a revised draft focused on full and fair disclosure and a waiting period between registration and sale. Dulles, Dean, and other downtown lawyers were allowed to review the bill in the company of its drafters. Violently opposed to the New Deal, Dulles said the bill would undermine the nation's financial system. Dean spoke of the bill's burden on commerce and economic recovery. Having vented his rage, Dulles returned to New York while Dean stayed in Washington in an effort to improve the bill.

Unlike Dulles, Dean was not an ideologue and presciently saw the bill as a potential fount of high-paying legal work. With the face of a bulldog and rustic manners, he disarmed adversaries. "It seems hardly necessary," he advised, "to burn the house down to exterminate the vermin."[19] Restoring confidence in the stock markets would require conciliation and matching penalties to offenses. The Securities Act, as revised, reflected his influence. President Roosevelt signed it into law in May 1933.

The Securities Act was not, in fact, much of a surprise. Surveying the wreckage of the stock market in 1933, the securities industry anticipated some level of reform. In its final form, the Act had recognizable outlines. It borrowed heavily from existing state blue sky laws and the British Companies Acts of 1908 and 1929, which lawyers and financiers already were familiar with. The Act's promise to bring order to a profoundly distressed market also tempered objections.

Reform of the banking industry, however, was another matter. In the aftermath of thousands of bank failures, many Democrats demanded that the federal government provide some form of deposit insurance. Yet it was unlikely that the government would do so if the banks were still tied to their high-risk securities affiliates. Thus, any overhaul of the federal banking law would require the separation of commercial banking from investment banking. This measure—long proposed by reformists such as Louis Brandeis and Samuel Untermyer—became a centerpiece in Congress' deliberations. The final law, the 1933 Banking Act, better known as the Glass-Steagall Act after its Senate and House sponsors, gave commercial banks one year to divest themselves of their securities affiliates.

Wall Street watched the progress of the legislation intently. John W. Davis himself followed it from the Jekyll Island Club in coastal Georgia, where he was ensconced with Jack Morgan and other bankers, receiving daily dispatches from an associate he had sent to Washington. Davis and his clients viewed the bill as unnecessary, vindictive, and foolish, if not outright unconstitutional. Although some banks threw in the towel—the heads of the now-discredited National City and Chase banks already had promised to divest their banks of their securities affiliates—the banking industry as a whole predicted disaster. But the bankers had few allies now and, as one financial historian quipped, it was "that rare time when money talked and nobody listened."[20] Glass-Steagall became law in June 1933.

It is not clear what Congress believed Glass-Steagall would accomplish. Historian Ron Chernow concluded that "Glass-Steagall was as much an attempt to punish the banking industry as it was a measure to reform it."[21] Glass-Steagall embodied much of what critics resented in Roosevelt and the ascendant Democratic Party: it was thought to be punitive, class-based, and vengeful. Nor did it help matters that prominent in Roosevelt's coterie of advisers were Jews—Felix Frankfurter, Louis Brandeis, Henry Morgenthau, and Samuel Rosenman, to name just a few—an ethnic group Wall Street lawyers had long shunned and who now had the power to threaten the social order.

In fact and ironically, the new legislation did the banks a favor. By 1933, the underwriting business for stocks and bonds had dried up and the economy had not improved. The commercial banks' securities affiliates had become an economic burden and a public relations nightmare, and the banks were looking for reasons to divest them. Glass-Steagall gave banks the shotgun divorce they needed. Yet it did little to break the financial oligopoly and instead spawned a host of new investment banks, each with organic ties to the commercial bank it had parted from. Many investment banks were headed by the same executives who had run them before divestment and continued to use the same lawyers who had advised them before. The separation of commercial banking from investment banking simply handed entrenched law firms a parallel set of clients.

Even more important, the new laws also thrust Wall Street law firms into the emerging field of federal securities law. Among many other things, the Securities Act required issuers to prepare prospectuses and registration statements, conduct due diligence, and defend against litigation brought by securities holders—all to become staples of Wall Street's green goods business. When Congress enacted the Securities Exchange Act the next year, creating the Securities & Exchange Commission (with James Landis as its first chairman) and imposing broad civil penalties for fraud, it made lawyers all the more indispensable. The downtown law firms, already institutionalized in their relationships with clients, were now fixtures in the national economy. Even Arthur Dean, originally an opponent of the new law, moderated his position. The Act, he conceded, had become a permanent part of the nation's social fabric, and nothing should disturb "the very cordial relations which are being established between the SEC and the investment banking community."[22] Subsequently, Dean and partners from other downtown law firms had a major hand in the drafting of such crucial follow-on legislation as the Investment Company Act of 1940.

Enactment of the Securities Act and the Banking Act mitigated widespread anxiety about the form federal regulation of banking and securities would take, and the Securities Exchange Act of 1934 fixed several shortcomings of the Securities Act. Once these uncertainties were removed, there was a flood of new issues.[23] Despite predictions that these New Deal laws would kill capital markets, securities underwritings actually increased. In its first year of operations, after being divested by J. P. Morgan, Morgan Stanley handled $1 billion in securities issues. Davis Polk, Cravath and Sullivan & Cromwell were now busy advising their new investment banking clients about compliance with the new laws and drafting the volumes of legal documents the new laws required.

In the coming years, Congress would further regulate the securities industry with the Public Utility Holding Company Act and the Trust Indenture Act. Each of these corrected abuses, curtailed fraud, and improved public confidence in the financial markets. Since the playing field was at the same level for all banks and businesses, neither act materially hurt the clients of the downtown law firms. On the other hand, the new laws provided a gusher of work for skilled corporate lawyers. The New Deal, wrote Cravath's Robert T. Swaine, "created such demands on the profession that competent legal assistance was at a premium." Given their hold on the critical and enormously lucrative capital markets practice, Wall Street law firms were now not simply powerful but had become executors of a formidable legal specialty.

For the most part, the New Deal reforms were based on concepts of disclosure and regulation and stopped short of wholesale restructuring. Not surprisingly, the post-New Deal Wall Street resembled its old self. The same investment bankers and commercial bankers continued to do much the same work as they had before, represented in most cases by the same lawyers they had used before.

There were, of course, efforts to dislodge the Wall Street oligopoly. In the mid-1930s Morgan Stanley's hold on the lucrative bond financings for AT&T was attacked by investment banks in Chicago and Cleveland, who then joined other regional banks in a campaign before the Interstate Commerce Commission for competitive bidding in the underwriting of railroad securities.[24] In 1940, the SEC effectively vetoed the decision by Dayton Power & Light to hire Morgan Stanley for a $25 million bond underwriting on the ground it violated the Commission's rules requiring competitive bidding in situations where the underwriter was affiliated with the issuer, and its decision was upheld by a divided court of appeals over John W. Davis' vigorous attack.[25] The Temporary National Economic Committee, created in 1938 to study the concentration of economic power, also took up the subject, issuing a one-sided report in 1941 criticizing, among other things, the ongoing concentration of economic power among the New York investment banks.[26]

It was perhaps once again to assail this resilient world that in 1947 the Department of Justice filed a civil antitrust suit, *United States v. Morgan*, against seventeen investment banking firms alleging that their clubby underwriting practices violated the Sherman Act and attacking their business practices in minute detail. Tellingly, the first named defendant was Henry Sturgis Morgan, the head of Morgan Stanley and grandson of Pierpont. The case launched an epic, lengthy, and complex courtroom drama, not resolved until 1953, that engaged pillars of the Wall Street bar in defense of a business at the very core of their economic existence. It was the largest case in the immediate post-war years for Sullivan & Cromwell, Cravath and Davis Polk, requiring the service of teams of their new associates.

Cravath appeared for Kuhn Loeb and Union Securities; Davis Polk for Morgan Stanley and Harriman Ripley; and Sullivan & Cromwell for Goldman Sachs, First Boston, and Lehman Brothers. Other counsel included Shearman & Sterling for White Weld, Webster Sheffield for Kidder Peabody, and Drinker Biddle for Drexel & Co. The case pitted defenders of the old order against New Deal progressives. It consumed more than 300 courtroom days, captured in a stenographic trial transcript of almost 2,500 printed pages. If ever a single legal confrontation framed the economics, customs, and dealings of a critical business and, by implication, its defense counsel, this was it. William Dwight Whitney of Cravath and Ralph Carson of Davis Polk attracted particular notice at trial. Whitney had occupied second chair to Frederick Wood, Cravath's weapon of choice against the New Deal. Whitney spoke with a slight English accent, had once lived in London and in the late 1930s had swapped wives with Raymond Massey, the actor. He later wrote a detailed analysis of the case in the *Yale Law Journal*,[27] of course from the defendants' point of view. Carson tried cases so aggressively he made opponents hate him but lightened the tedious trial proceedings with droll literary references. The most colorful figure was Judge Harold Medina, who had a year earlier presided over the conviction of several prominent Communists for violations of the Smith Act. A handsome man of magnetism and charm, Judge Medina dressed impeccably, sported an elegant mustache, and was a master of the judicial put-down. He had once taught law at Columbia Law

School and became rich and famous from teaching the New York bar review course. He wrote a discursive opinion of more than 200 pages and granted the defendants' motion to dismiss. The core issue of the case was whether the defendant investment banking firms had engaged in any joint action, combination or conspiracy in restraint of trade. Judge Medina's decision that they had not was an absolute win for the New York investment banks and their silk-stocking counsel. It remains good law; to this day, investment banks are free to form underwriting syndicates and set the prices of new securities offerings without fear of antitrust liability.[28]

United States v. Morgan was a touchstone in the immediate postwar era, reassurance that the financial domain of Wall Street and its law firm consiglieres would continue undisturbed despite the vast social and economic changes wrought by world conflagration. The structure and social character of Wall Street defense counsel seemed for a time immutable even during the following decade. Eventually change overtook Wall Street law firms as it did Wall Street itself, but for now the old order prevailed.

15

Fighting the New Deal

As the scope and depth of the Depression ravaged the economy, public sentiment turned against Wall Street. In a speech during the 1932 election, Franklin Roosevelt foretold the essence of New Deal economic policy. "A mere builder of more industrial plants, a creator of more railroad systems, an organizer of more corporations," he said, "is as likely to be a danger as a help. The day of the great promoter or the financial Titan . . . is over. Our task now is not discovery or exploitation of natural resources, or necessarily producing more goods. It is the soberer, less dramatic business of administering resources and plants already in hand . . . of meeting the problem of underconsumption, of adjusting production to consumption, of distributing wealth and products more equitably, of adapting existing economic organizations to the service of the people. The day of enlightened administration has come."[1] These were not simply anodyne economic formulations. The president trained his sights squarely on Wall Street. "There must be an end," he declared in his first inaugural address, "to a conduct in banking and in business which too often has given to a sacred trust the likeness of callous and selfish wrongdoing." The conviction that self-serving bankers had fleeced innocent investors aroused widespread demand for reform and legislative protection. Within 100 days of his inauguration in March 1933, the Roosevelt administration pushed fifteen major pieces of legislation through Congress. Besides new banking and securities laws, these measures included the National Industry Recovery Act, the Agricultural Adjustment Act, and the Tennessee Valley Authority Act. By the end of 1934, Congress had added new income tax legislation, eliminated the gold standard, and passed the Frazier-Lemke Bankruptcy Act, which protected farmers from having their lands repossessed by creditors.

Perhaps because of the backlash inspired by the Pecora hearings, Wall Street originally took a wait-and-see attitude toward Roosevelt's prolific legislative agenda. But after a brief honeymoon, big business turned on Roosevelt and the New Deal, seen by its enemies as a lunge for power by Democratic Party politicians.

Conservative lawyers in downtown New York generally loathed Franklin Roosevelt and considered the New Deal an usurpation of power. Many, literally, would not utter Roosevelt's name, referring to him instead as "that man." In public comments, John Foster Dulles described the avalanche of legislation during the first 100 days as a hodgepodge of measures principally aimed at superficial symptoms. The federal government, he wrote in a letter to the *New York Times*, had "drained the lifeblood out of sound institutions in order to operate an extravagant public budget. . . . " Somehow ignoring the comfortable lives he and his partners lived, John W. Davis maintained that it was now almost impossible to accumulate sufficient wealth for future needs. "I don't tell my young men, because I don't want to discourage them, that with the present tax system they won't be able to put by enough to take care of their families and provide for old age. An old age pension, that's a chilling prospect."[2] Perhaps because of his broadening international role, Cravath was one of the few voices of moderation on domestic issues during the 1930s. He avoided the personal attacks on Roosevelt and supported certain progressive social initiatives such as government subsidies for low-rent housing.

Constitutional challenges to the New Deal were inevitable. As the country's preeminent appellate lawyer, Davis was soon hired to mount legal challenges to New Deal programs. Between 1931 and 1940 Davis had twenty-seven Supreme Court arguments, some of which struck at the heart of Roosevelt's legislation. In *Louisville Joint Stock Land Bank v. Radford*,[3] Davis successfully argued to the Supreme Court that the moratorium on foreclosures imposed by the Frazier-Lemke Act was an unconstitutional taking. He also attacked the Public Utility Holding Company Act in the lower courts, and challenged the National Labor Relations Act on behalf of the Associated Press to the Supreme Court in *Associated Press v. NLRB*.[4] The Cravath firm was similarly involved and between 1928 and 1944 had as much business in the Supreme Court as any other law firm. Frederick H. Wood alone made 25 arguments there.[5]

The most radical and intrusive New Deal securities law was the one aimed at public utility holding companies. When President Roosevelt took office, three superholding companies—J. P. Morgan's United Corporation, Samuel Insull's utility empire, and Electric Bond and Share—controlled nearly half the electricity generated in the United States. After the stock market crash, many utility holding company systems fell into receivership or bankruptcy. In his State of the Union address in 1935, the president urged abolition of the evil features of public utility holding companies. Translated into legislation (the Wheeler-Rayburn bill), this meant simplification of each holding company system within five years. Meanwhile holding companies had to register with the SEC and could not sell securities or acquire new businesses without SEC approval. Most importantly, the SEC could compel dissolution of any holding company that could not establish an economic reason for its existence within the five-year term—the so-called "death sentence" clause. The bill's death sentence requirement provoked a grassroots crusade fueled by moral outrage. The utility industry, led by Wendell Willkie, headed an intense lobbying campaign—of which John Foster Dulles was a prime mover—against the bill, predicting a chaos of liquidation and receiverships. The idea of a business boycott gained traction, particularly among electric utility executives, whose companies planned a rush to the courthouse to enjoin enforcement of the Act.

Congress, unpersuaded, passed the Public Utility Holding Company Act of 1935, giving the SEC plenary power to refashion the structure and business practices of the entire utility industry. The new head of the SEC, William O. Douglas, pointed out the "great financial rewards available to those who took over the job of redesigning and reorganizing these systems and floating the new securities." Among others, Dulles remained intransigent. At a meeting of utility executives at the firm's offices, he predicted the Act would not withstand a legal challenge. "The men who drafted and promoted this law," he said, "obviously do not know the law or the constitution. I can assure you that it violates basic constitutional guarantees and that the Supreme Court will strike it down. My strong advice to you, gentlemen, is to do nothing. Do not comply, resist the law with all your might, and soon everything will be all right."[6] Dulles' crystal ball ultimately proved cloudy; it took three visits to the Supreme Court before the Act's constitutionality was finally resolved in the government's favor a decade later. Meanwhile Sullivan & Cromwell earned large fees by disassembling a holding company client, American Water Works and Electric Company, into its component parts, each a major regional utility.

Eight well-coordinated cases challenged the Act's constitutionality in the first two years following its passage. Five of these were handled by Davis Polk, which had been retained by the Edison Electrical Institute to resist the new statute. One of the earliest cases became notorious.[7] In September 1935, the bankruptcy trustees of American States Public Service Company—vigorous opponents of the Act—asked the federal judge supervising the bankruptcy for his guidance on the question whether the new law required the company to register with the Securities & Exchange Commission. A group of bondholders, tepidly represented by a lawyer who was a known opponent of the new statute, informed the court that registration would be in the bondholders' interest. The federal judge—an outspoken opponent of the New Deal—avoided deciding the narrow issue and instead invited a constitutional challenge to the Act itself. Eager to have John W. Davis on their side, the trustees found a Baltimore dentist, Ferd Lautenbach, who owned $2,500 of the utility's bonds, and arranged for Lautenbach to intervene in the case with Davis as his lawyer to challenge the constitutionality of the law. The entire proceeding obviously was collusive: the trustees were supposedly neutral, but nonetheless recruited Davis and located Lautenbach; the bondholders themselves otensibly supported the Act, but were represented by a lawyer who was a known opponent; the Edison Institute apparently paid Davis' fees; and Lautenbach was unaware until the hearing on his petition who Davis was or even that Davis was his lawyer. However, by posturing the case as a dispute between bondholders and the bankruptcy trustees, the parties were able to exclude the SEC itself—the principal entity with an interest in defending the Act—from participating in the case except as an *amicus curiae* at the sufferance of the bondholders. Adding injury to insult, the district court scheduled its hearing on ten days' notice and denied the SEC's request for an extension of time to prepare its case. At the hearing on the trustees' petition, Davis spent two hours excoriating the statute, while the bondholders made little effort to defend it at all. Meanwhile, the SEC was left to attack the entire matter as procedurally improper and openly collusive. Not surprisingly, the district court agreed with Davis and issued a 60-page opinion condemning the Act. Yet it was a pyrrhic victory. On appeal, the Fourth Circuit affirmed the district court only to the extent the debtor was not engaged in interstate commerce. Otherwise, the Act stood.

Despite its flood of work for electric utilities—Electric Bond & Share Co., North American Co., Detroit Edison Company, and Western Power Company among them—Sullivan & Cromwell was largely on the sidelines during the litigation against New Deal legislation. Like several of its Wall Street peers, it still farmed out many cases headed for court. It may have had a trial partner, but it did not have a litigation department, preferring instead to hire influential barristers like Charles Evans Hughes Jr., George Medalie, and Joseph Proskauer for major matters. The New Deal's legislative avalanche demanded a more coherent response, so work went to the major competitors. Dulles tried, unsuccessfully, to lure his former partner Harlan Fiske Stone from the Supreme Court. Stone declined, observing that corporate law "has made the learned profession of an earlier day the obsequious servant of business . . . "[8] Dulles then hired John C. Higgins, a litigator in the Pacific Northwest, to lead the firm's opposition to the New Deal's assault on public utilities. Higgins wanted to force the government to prosecute all utility defendants at once, instead of sequentially, and perfected the firm's tactic of drowning its adversaries in paper. He was a workaholic, driven obsessively, with no regard for his own time or that of others. He spent day and night, weekends and holidays at the office and expected his associates to do likewise. The firm's campaign against the New Deal caused Justice Stone to disqualify himself from Sullivan & Cromwell cases if the lawyer arguing before the court had been at the firm during his time there or if the petitioner had then been a client. To channel opposition, Sullivan & Cromwell, purported to speak for the legal profession as a whole, maintaining the appearance of monolithic opposition and defining its image as the servant of power and wealth.

Cravath himself may have been averse to litigation, but his firm could not ignore the critical importance of courtroom advocacy in the epic struggle to stem the tide of government intervention in the economy. His firm, too, reached outside for its principal litigator, recruiting the talented and aggressive Frederick H. Wood.[9]

Unlike most of Cravath's partners, Wood was a product of the heartland, a graduate of the University of Kansas law school. He earned his spurs as counsel to several railroads, notably the Southern Pacific, and was constantly in motion as a litigator before diverse state courts, the Supreme Court, and the Interstate Commerce Commission. At the age of 47 in 1924 Wood joined Cravath as a rare lateral partner. There, using the firm's broader platform, he soon emerged as one of the nation's leading trial lawyers. Wood filled a gap, given Cravath's preference for transactional law and the firm's lack of a senior full-time litigator. He prepared for trial obsessively. Day after day, for a pending case, a half-dozen associates would argue points of law with him, anticipating questions from the bench or opposing counsel. Pacing around his office, Wood would work out the precise words he would later use in court. His detailed preparation gave him reassurance. He was never flustered by hostile questioning and rarely got excited in trials. For major out-of-town arguments he traveled with a retinue of assistants and would set up a virtual office at his hotel, complete with desks, filing cabinets, stenographers, and associates. So intense was his focus on the problem at hand that he would often absent-mindedly mislay needed documents. His assistants often found him about to leave for court, waving his arms and shouting, "Oh, God, where in hell are my papers!" Still, as Swaine recalled, he had a warm and winning personality and many friends in the firm, which in 1928 became Cravath, de Gersdorff, Swaine & Wood. During the New Deal years he argued before the Supreme Court multiple times in aid, it is said, of the firm's sophisticated long-term anti-New Deal litigation strategy. Two of the cases in which Wood appeared, in 1935 and 1936, on the limits of the commerce clause and the federal government's ability to regulate the national economy, were landmark setbacks for the Roosevelt administration.[10]

Through the National Industrial Recovery Act, passed in 1933, the Roosevelt administration hoped to rescue the nation's economy. The Act authorized a program of state control over the private sector—anathema to Cravath and its many corporate clients. Its basic machinery rested on industry codes of fair competition submitted by trade associations deemed representative of the trade or industry to be regulated. The Act called for minimum wages, collective bargaining for labor unions, and maximum-hour regulations to limit production and increase employment. "In lieu of competition," wrote Gene Rostow, the future dean of Yale Law School, "there was to be a kind of industrial self-government in business; competing business men would meet in committee and legislate on prices, wages, and conditions of trade."[11]

From start to finish code-making was a joint effort by industry representatives, NRA officials, and the President to prescribe binding rules of business conduct upon all members of an industry. Code rules came about through informal ad hoc hearings and negotiations. The President, riding a wave of public support, approved the first Code but could not possibly deal with thousands of trade associations. Hugh S. Johnson, a former general now heading the NRA, tried the risky strategy of first securing agreement in the ten largest industries. NRA lawyers, over-matched by corporate counsel, allowed industry leaders to dictate anticompetitive Code provisions, even price-fixing. Small businesses claimed that Codes dictated by their large competitors forced them to choose between violation and bankruptcy. Voluntary compliance did not work. Each Code therefore applied to all firms in an industry, whether they had participated in its formation or not, and was made enforceable by criminal and civil process. Cravath and other Wall Street firms attacked the Code as an example of the New Deal's overweening government intervention.[12]

The Act by its terms was due to expire in two years after passage. Although several major industries continued to support it, companies nationwide found the proliferation of NRA rules governing every aspect of their businesses unduly restrictive and challenged the Act in court. The American Liberty League, an anti-New Deal coalition of industry executives and lawyers bankrolled by the du Ponts (and including Frederick H. Wood and John W. Davis), pledged support to businesses challenging the NRA. It depicted the United States on the verge of socialism, bankruptcy, and tyranny, an opinion shared by most Wall Street lawyers, including Cravath himself.[13]

In 1935 Donald Richberg, NRA general counsel, unwisely pushed for Supreme Court review of the constitutionality of the Act in *Schechter Poultry v. United States.* The case involved a small poultry-slaughtering and poultry-retailing business in Brooklyn run by the Schechter brothers, who had appealed a lower court verdict that found them guilty of violating the wage and hour restrictions of the NRA "Live Poultry Code." Few trades in the nation were more squalid. "It was a fiercely competitive industry," wrote one historian, "dwelling on the margin of the underworld and abounding in vicious practices."[14]

The case came before the court in early May 1935 in one of its last sessions in the old Senate chamber in the Capitol. Three weeks later the Schechters' conviction, affirmed in part by the Second Circuit Court of Appeals, was reversed when the Supreme Court declared the Act unconstitutional as an unlawful delegation of legislative power to the executive branch and extension of federal authority beyond matters directly affecting commerce to purely local activity. Chief Justice Hughes read the opinion aloud. The Schechters' trial counsel, who had borne the main burden of presenting their case before the Supreme Court, was Joseph Heller. A short, stocky, and voluble Brooklyn resident, Heller practiced with his brother Jacob in small offices near the federal courthouse in Manhattan. He told the court that, although chickens sold by the Schechters came from another state, they had been purchased through a middleman in New York. His clients, he argued, were therefore engaged solely in intrastate commerce not subject to federal regulation. Although energetic and colorful, Heller was thought to be in over his head. As it turned out, he had help. The steel corporations represented by Frederick H. Wood and Cravath had grown impatient with the Act's labor provisions and seconded Wood to assist Heller with the case just weeks before it was heard. Heller's clients by proxy were thus the American Liberty League, of which Wood was a member, and the Iron and Steel Institute.[15]

Heller's earthy exposition of the details of the kosher poultry business sparked the interest of the court. Asked by Justice McReynolds, a crusty and disagreeable conservative (and onetime partner in Guthrie, Cravath & Henderson), to explain the code prohibition of "straight killing," Heller replied, "You have got to put your hand in the coop and take out whatever chicken comes to you." McReynolds asked, "And it was for that your client was convicted?" "Yes," said Heller, "and fined and given a jail sentence." He further explained that "if a customer wants half a coop of chickens, he has to take it just like it is." At this Justice Sutherland, one of the conservative Four Horsemen on the court, asked, "What if the chickens are all at one end?" The answer was lost in laughter from the bench and counsel. Heller concluded that the grant of authority in the code contained no intelligible standard and vested unrestrained discretion in the President. In his first appearance before the court he had painted the Schechter brothers as struggling small businessmen abused by an oppressive bureaucracy.

Wood's supporting role was rhetorical. He made a political argument. Carried to its logical conclusion, he said, the government's extreme interpretation of the commerce clause would lead to a "planned economy" and permit Congress to "nationalize industry" and establish "some form of national socialism—whether soviet, fascist or Nazi." Wood's policy argument, reminiscent of the American Liberty League's denunciation of the New Deal, was icing on the cake. In a severe setback for the Roosevelt administration, the court declared the Act unconstitutional. It was a warning that the New Deal's ambitious agenda would be subject to the checks and balances of traditional jurisprudence.

Roosevelt remained silent for several days but then spoke out. "Does this decision mean," he asked, "that the United States Government has no control over any national economic problem?" Answering his own question, he said, "We have been relegated to the horse-and-buggy definition of interstate commerce." It was a decision, he believed, that denied the economic interdependence of the nation. Frederick Wood thought otherwise. The decision was in his view a declaration of freedom from federal intervention.[16]

The Supreme Court's ruling in *Schechter* echoed far beyond the poultry business. By invalidating the industrial codes of fair competition, *Schechter* also ended federal regulation of the coal industry. Workers in that hard-hit business fought to preserve their rights, and Cravath again was a key player. The Bituminous Coal Code, now void, had fixed minimum prices for coal and minimum wages and also guaranteed the right to bargain collectively. The United Mine Workers and mine operators needed to avoid restoration of disastrous pre-Code competition and sought legislation that would put a floor under prices and wages.

The resulting bill, the Bituminous Coal Conservation Act (the Guffey Coal Act), imposed a heavy excise tax on the sale of coal by producers who did not agree to be bound by the Code. The bill fixed minimum prices for coal, overseen by district boards and a commission, and prohibited unfair methods of competition. It also guaranteed miners the right to bargain collectively and set binding minimum wages and maximum hours as agreed by a majority of coal producers and miners. The United Mine Workers union, the driving force behind the bill, had formed an alliance with Pennsylvania operators seeking federal approval for the high coal prices needed to offset union wages. President Roosevelt asked Congress to pass the bill, despite admitted doubts as to its constitutionality, and it became law on August 30, 1935.[17]

Wood was counsel for the Carter Coal Co., which operated mines in West Virginia, and had represented its interests under the Code and in negotiations with the United Mine Workers led by John L. Lewis, the powerful labor leader. Long before its enactment Wood had prepared to contest the constitutionality of the Guffey Coal Act through a prearranged shareholders' suit, a method first pioneered decades earlier by William D. Guthrie in his attack on federal tax law in *Pollock v. Farmers Loan & Trust.* On the day of the Guffey Coal Act's passage, Wood, assisted by William D. Whitney, convened a meeting of Carter Coal Co.'s board of directors consisting of James Carter, his father, and a company employee. Carter submitted a letter alleging unconstitutionality of the Guffey Coal Act, just passed, and demanding that the company refuse to accept the Code. His father agreed that the Guffey Coal Act was unlawful but feared the risk of having to pay an excise tax if it should be upheld. The company refused to accept the Code, a position sustained by vote of the board. Carter then filed suit in the District of Columbia against the Carter Coal Co. to enjoin it from accepting the Code and restrain government officials from enforcing the Guffey Coal Act against the company.[18]

Carter v. Carter Coal Co. resulted in a three-week trial in district court on Carter's motion for temporary injunction, at which the government produced as witnesses a procession of coal operators, the vice president of the United Mine Workers, a coal economist, the Assistant Secretary of the Treasury, and other experts to tell the checkered story of the bituminous coal industry. The court denied the motion for injunction despite vigorous arguments by Wood and Whitney. It found the Guffey Coal Act's wage and hour provisions outside the commerce power and an unlawful delegation of legislative authority, but sustained its price-fixing regulations. The trial had taxed the firm's resources. "Feelings ran high," Swaine recalled. "Heywood Broun devoted a column to a description of Whitney as an exponent of rapacious capitalism. The work on the trial required almost superhuman endurance. Everybody worked day and night." The case was immediately appealed, and the Supreme Court agreed to hear it directly without awaiting decision by the intermediate court of appeals.[19]

Wood argued the case before the Supreme Court in March 1936. The attorneys general of seven coal-producing states had filed massive briefs supporting the Guffey Coal Act. Together with briefs by Wood and government counsel, the Supreme Court had to wade through well over a thousand pages. Because the trial court had not struck down the Guffey Coal Act's price-fixing provisions, Wood contrived a novel argument that Congress had no power to impose restrictive regulations under the commerce clause. The purpose of the clause was instead to free commerce from state control, not to permit affirmative federal regulation. The court split 5-4, with the majority finding the wage-and-hour provisions unconstitutional and inseparable from the price provisions, thus condemning the entire statute. Dissenting opinions held that the price provisions could stand independently. Frederick Wood and Cravath had again prevailed in halting the New Deal in its tracks.

A year later, after the president's overwhelming victory in the 1936 election, he secured passage of a new Guffey Coal Act from which the wage-and-hour provisions had been deleted. Given the change in the Supreme Court's polarity following the election, wrote Swaine, "the Cravath firm advised its clients that an attack on the constitutionality of the price provisions of the new Act would probably fail." Swaine's advice was pragmatic recognition of political reality. Cravath's anti-New Deal litigation had succeeded only too well. *Schechter* and *Carter Coal* marked the triumph of the old order, but led to Roosevelt's political effort to pack the Supreme Court. Although the court-packing plan was not realized, the president changed the judicial views of individual justices, replaced others, and procured a court that embraced the New Deal. The reoriented Court handed down a series of decisions in 1941 and 1942 sustaining Roosevelt's legislative program, holding that the commerce clause gave Congress the power to broadly regulate labor practices, markets, and industries.[20]

The elite bar remained steadfastly opposed to the New Deal and influenced the direction of the American Bar Association and the American Liberty League. Wall Street lawyers did not merely reflect client interests. They mounted an ideological anti-New Deal crusade. Their politics, wrote one commentator, can be explained "not only in terms of servants performing for masters but also in terms of conscious experts in defense of their symbolic capital." No longer just hired hands for wealthy corporate interests, counsel had appropriated their clients' point of view to halt or divert an onrushing wave of government intervention.[21]

Litigation at Cravath embraced more, of course, than opposition to the New Deal. No one defined the firm's characteristic courtroom style more typically than Bruce Bromley. A graduate of Harvard Law School, he came to Cravath, Henderson, Leffingwell and de Gersdorff in 1923 after brief intermediate stops at Winthrop & Stimson and his own firm, there to work on a Federal Trade Commission case against Paramount Pictures Corporation challenging its business relations with theaters around the country. Bromley rapidly assumed a major role in the case, traveled widely in the course of litigation, and developed a national reputation as an antitrust lawyer. He became a partner in the firm in 1926. His practice soon broadened to include representation of magazines and newspapers in cases involving libel, rights of privacy, broadcast rights, copyright, and unfair competition. His publishing clients were diverse. Smash Magazines and Quality Comic Group shared his services with Time, Inc., whose "lively, breezy style," according to its corporate history, ". . . led to many scores of suits and threatened suits for alleged libel and invasion of the right of privacy." The Cravath litigation department boasted it had never lost a libel or privacy case, and Bromley became well known in the bar for hardball tactics. He exhausted opposing counsel by filing motion after motion and dragging out the simplest cases. Called the "Diaghilev of discovery," he once told an audience of Stanford law students that he "was born . . . to be a protractor. . . . I would take the simplest antitrust case and protract the defense almost to infinity. . . . We won that case and, as you know, my firm's meter was running all the time, every month for 14 years."[22]

Perhaps Bromley's finest hour came in defense of *Esquire Magazine* following the Postmaster General's attempt to revoke its second-class mailing privileges during the Second World War. The Postmaster General, a devout Catholic, was determined to purge sexually provocative magazines from the mails by interpreting the second-class mailing privilege as a badge of good conduct. Whether a magazine received the much cheaper second-class rate was made to depend on whether he believed it contributed to the public good. With its sexy jokes and Vargas girl color pinups, *Esquire* was a prime target for a negative ruling. Since first-class mailing rates were prohibitively expensive, *Esquire*'s loss of the second-class privilege was effectively a death sentence and a form of censorship in violation of the First Amendment. The Postmaster General's 1943 decision barring *Esquire* from second-class mails led to a massive public protest. *Esquire* hired Bromley, a "suave, dapper, seasoned litigator," as its lead counsel. He appeared at the Post Office hearing, before the District Court, on appeal to the D.C. Circuit, and before the Supreme Court, which heard oral argument before eight justices in 1946. Bromley's presentation marked the apex of his career. Justice Douglas, who sat on the panel, praised him as a great appellate advocate—with an easy, relaxed manner of presentation, a knack for "reducing a complicated case to one or two starkly simple issues," the ability to frame those issues with "homely illustrations," and "never using the full time allotted to him." The Supreme Court ruled unanimously in *Esquire*'s favor.[23]

In 1949 Governor Dewey appointed Bromley as a judge on the New York Court of Appeals to fill a vacancy during an eleven-month term. Bromley rendered his most important opinion, for the majority on a divided court, in *Dorsey v. Stuyvesant Town Corp.* Metropolitan Life Insurance Company had sponsored Stuyvesant Town, a major private housing project, under the Redevelopment Companies Law to attract private investment and offered partial tax exemption and assistance in land acquisition for redevelopment. Three Black war veterans applied for apartments in the project but were rejected on racial grounds. Their suit reached the Court of Appeals, where they argued that discrimination against them violated the Fourteenth Amendment. The project, they argued, would not have been possible without state action. Bromley was not convinced. "The State of New York," he ruled, "has consciously and deliberately refrained from imposing any requirement of nondiscrimination upon respondents as a condition to the granting of aid in the rehabilitation of substandard areas." Bromley's opinion doomed his hopes for reelection. The Jamaica branch of the NAACP said Bromley placed "property rights above human rights" and supported "the Hitlerian doctrine of racial superiority." The Republican Party, the Lawyers Committee of former City Bar Presidents, including John W. Davis, Robert E. Patterson, and Henry L. Stimson, and the *New York Times* endorsed him nonetheless. In November Bromley lost his bid for reelection by over 400,000 votes statewide. He then returned to Cravath where he practiced for many years. "Bromley the man," wrote one of his partners, "was always a joy to work with or just simply to be with. He was direct, always right on the mark, and sometimes devastatingly blunt. . . .With Bromley one never knew what was coming next. He was always a fresh breeze. When he was 80, he seemed to be one of his firm's younger partners."[24]

16

The Dulles Brothers and the Postwar World

PUBLIC SERVICE, A CAREER ENHANCEMENT

" . . . [O]ne of the satisfactions of the . . . profession of the law," wrote Arthur H. Dean in his tribute to William Nelson Cromwell, ". . . [is] that lawyers can more readily than many executives effect temporary or partial withdrawals from the daily routine to attend to public affairs. . . . "[1] Taking advantage of this liberality, both Dulles brothers pursued their long-range career interests outside the confines of Sullivan & Cromwell. Competitively courting public recognition, each saw high office within his grasp.

Allen Dulles used the Council on Foreign Relations as a springboard. The Council was a global policy pillar of the eastern establishment and a roosting place for investment bankers, corporate executives, Wall Street lawyers, public figures such as John W. Davis and Elihu Root, and leading academics with an international bent. Allen Dulles had served on the Council's board since the late 1920s and became a regular contributor to *Foreign Affairs*, its influential periodical, whose editor, Hamilton Fish Armstrong, was an old friend from Princeton days, a neighbor on Manhattan's Upper East Side, and a fellow member of the Century Association. Spurred initially by passage of the Neutrality Act, Mussolini's invasion of Ethiopia, and Hitler's remilitarization of the Rhineland, they authored two books together, *Can We Be Neutral?* and *Can America Stay Neutral?*, in which Armstrong drew on Allen's arms-control expertise and prior State Department service to project their shared Wilsonian view that America must be engaged in the world for its own good. Neutrality in their view was simply untenable. "No nation," they wrote, "can reach the position of a world power as we have done without becoming entangled in every quarter of the globe. . . ."[2]

Foreign Affairs ordinarily disdained advocacy but in the late 1930s became known for its support of American intervention in the rapidly developing war in Europe and provided classified policy memos to the State Department. Armstrong thrust Allen into the cockpit of American foreign policy debate and promoted his reputation as a moderate progressive. Allen pursued influence among a privileged elite thought to guard entry to the political game. Luminaries such as Henry Luce, Dean Acheson, and James Conant were on his side; Joseph Kennedy, Charles Lindbergh, and H. L. Mencken, stalwarts of isolation who viewed intervention in a European war as the slippery slope to perdition, were opposed.

Allen cultivated a friendship with William Donovan, a combat hero of the First World War, winner of the Congressional Medal of Honor, and founder of an international Wall Street law firm that competed with Sullivan & Cromwell. A pugnacious man, full of Irish charm, Donovan "knew everybody from Dwight Morrow to Bernie Gimbel," wrote one observer, "and both his Georgetown townhouse and his Manhattan duplex on Beekman Place became watering spots for movie stars, and diplomats, European financiers and U.S. labor leaders, and women of virtually every background." Widely traveled, he became an arch proponent of U.S. intervention and monthly visitor to the Room, an unmarked apartment on East Sixty-Second Street in Manhattan, where representatives of the British secret service met with a group of New York anglophiles, including Vincent Astor, Kermit Roosevelt, Nelson Doubleday, Winthrop Aldrich, and David Bruce. Allen also became a frequent attendee and the first of the Dulles brothers to leave the firm for war service.[3]

While Allen saw America's fate intertwined with Europe's, John Foster Dulles believed the nation was succumbing to war hysteria. "Only hysteria," he said in 1937, "entertains the idea that Germany, Italy, or Japan contemplates war upon us."[4] Dulles remained complacent in the face of naked aggression, urging instead caution and impartiality. Allen could not understand his brother's lack of concern, which stood in sharp contrast to impressions gathered in his own travels abroad. The rise of Hitler, he believed, meant war. Dulles, for his part, saw no reason why the United States, as a status quo power, should enter into a European quarrel.

On the weekends, at Cold Spring Harbor, Allen attacked his brother's indifference to Hitler's persecution of the Jews and threats against Germany's neighbors. Their arguments grew heated. "How can you call yourself a Christian and ignore what is happening in Germany?" Allen shouted. "Why don't you go over and see what is happening there? It is terrible." In fact, Dulles did sail for Europe shortly after, taking his wife and son Avery with him, to participate in a seminar in Paris on Peaceful Change and then in a meeting of the World Council of Churches at Oxford. Dulles later wrote a book, *War, Peace and Change*, based on his experience.

The road to peace, he argued, lay in avoiding confrontation with Germany, Japan and Italy, all members of the future wartime axis. The book was little more than an apology for ignoring naked aggression in Asia and Europe, where the Nazis had overrun Austria and were mounting a campaign of violent racial terror. In a speech given shortly after Germany had invaded Poland to start the Second World War, Dulles saw no reason for the United States to become a participant. He made common cause with Charles Lindbergh, a strident leader in the America First movement.

Dulles' biographer contends he was not a pro-fascist but was instead an observer determined to remain above the fray.

His partners at Sullivan & Cromwell did not suggest that Dulles bore antipathy toward the Jews by ignoring Hitler's vicious repression of them, but they opposed his decision to represent German (now Nazi) clients as before simply because they paid large fees. Eustace Seligman, one of Dulles' few Jewish partners, was moved to send him a remarkable memo. "I regret very much," Seligman wrote, "to find myself for the first time in our long years of association, in fundamental disagreement. . . . [You] apparently take the view that Germany's position is morally superior to that of the Allies. . . ." Dulles was not apologetic. He opposed President Roosevelt's growing efforts to have the nation join the conflict and signaled his support for any Republican candidate capable of undermining those efforts. To promote his views he became a prolific pamphleteer, writing articles for *Life* and *Reader's Digest* as well as *Foreign Affairs, The New Republic,* and *Harpers.* He was seen as a foreign policy sage who harbored ambitions for high public office.[5]

Dulles' political entrée arose unexpectedly. In 1937 he offered a promising young lawyer, Thomas E. Dewey, a guaranteed $150,000 a year to head Sullivan & Cromwell's litigation department, then embroiled in scorched earth opposition to the New Deal. The offer was tempting, but Dewey declined, choosing instead to run for (and win) election as district attorney in New York, thereafter scoring high-profile convictions against Lucky Luciano, Legs Diamond, and Jimmy Hines of Murder, Inc. A year later he became the Republican nominee for governor of New York. Although he lost, his campaign electrified the party. Now a rising star in an era unfriendly to Republican candidates, he assembled a group of elder statesmen for guidance. In 1939 Dulles helped plan Dewey's presidential run, initially with 1940 in mind.

Japan's unprovoked attack on Pearl Harbor in 1941 utterly changed domestic politics. Isolationism vanished as a viable political stance, and Dulles had to adjust. His indifference to England's life-and-death struggle against Hitler gave way to advocacy of restructured international relations under the aegis of the United Nations. Dulles reverted to his Wilsonian roots, eventually formulating "Six Pillars of Peace," a synthesis of theology and philosophy that called for international collaboration but caused Sir Alexander Cadogan (later Britain's permanent representative to the United Nations Security Council) to dismiss its author as "the wooliest type of useless pontificating American."[6] Dulles nonetheless became Dewey's mentor in foreign affairs and found an interventionist path to the political mainstream. Relying on Dulles' advice, Dewey called for abandonment of selfish nationalism. Just a few years earlier, Republican politicians in the isolationist Midwest would have dismissed such rhetoric as heresy. But the political climate had changed. In 1942 Dewey won the governorship of New York and, guided by Dulles, was the Republican presidential candidate in the 1944 election. It quickly became clear that Senator Taft and other mandarins of the GOP would not buy his internationalist platform without modification. Party leaders asked Senator Arthur Vandenberg to prepare a policy statement acceptable to both sides. Dewey asked Vandenberg to consult with

Dulles. Together they crafted a compromise that pledged GOP support for postwar cooperative government but also committed to sovereign rights and self-government. The party convention approved the statement, and Dewey won the nomination on the first ballot. Although he lost to Roosevelt, he did well enough to enhance his prospects for 1948. Dulles emerged postelection as a leading proponent of bipartisan foreign policy with credibility among Republican party power brokers and the inner councils of the Protestant church. In 1945, aided by Vandenberg's support but over Roosevelt's objection, Dulles served as an adviser to the U.S. delegation to the conference drafting the United Nations charter. Dulles' advisory work established him as a principal Republican voice on foreign policy. He was also Thomas Dewey's shadow Secretary of State.[7]

Allen was at the same time plotting his next move. "He was a strong interventionist by then," wrote William Bundy, "but I think he had the feeling that Foster and the German clients of the firm had pulled his coat tails."[8] In 1940 Allen and his brother attended the Republican National Convention in Philadelphia. Allen was a delegate and a Wendell Willkie supporter, having enhanced his Republican gravitas in an unsuccessful run for Congress two years before. After the final vote nominating Willkie, William Donovan, also a delegate, pulled Allen aside in the crowded hotel lobby and invited him for a drink. Donovan had just returned from London on a private mission for President Roosevelt where he had met with Prime Minister Churchill and studied the organization of British intelligence. Convinced that America's military planning would depend on intelligence, Donovan proposed reorganizing the nation's intelligence system, then fragmented among multiple government departments, and was recruiting candidates for a central intelligence agency that did not yet exist. Donovan anticipated war. "We'll be in it before the end of 1941," he said, "and when we are, there are certain preparations which should already have been made. That's where you come in." With his State Department and Wall Street credentials, Allen was an obvious target and immediately receptive.

In June 1941 Donovan presented President Roosevelt with a proposal for an American intelligence program. A week later the president ordered creation of a new $100 million agency, the Coordinator of Information (COI), with Donovan as its founding director. A few weeks after Pearl Harbor Donovan offered Allen a position at COI. Allen accepted immediately and by early the following year had left Sullivan & Cromwell to become chief of the COI in New York on the sixth floor of Rockefeller Center, bringing with him an eclectic array of would-be agents. Allen embarked at once on a plan to create an intelligence network within Nazi Germany. Later that year President Roosevelt transformed the COI from an agency that merely gathered intelligence into one empowered to conduct covert and paramilitary operations, renamed the Office of Strategic Services (OSS), which quickly opened secret training camps for agents of diverse talents. OSS management, said columnist Drew Pearson, comprised "one of the fanciest groups of dilettante diplomats, Wall Street bankers, and amateur detectives ever seen in Washington," including many who later achieved fame and influence—Richard Helms, William Colby, Arthur Schlesinger

Jr., Stewart Alsop, Walt Rostow, and Douglas Dillon among them. Radio Berlin dismissed the OSS collective as "fifty professors, twenty monkeys, ten goats, twelve guinea pigs, and a staff of Jewish scribblers." In November 1942 Allen left New York for Bern in neutral Switzerland, there to pursue espionage activities until the end of the war.[9]

The outbreak of war meant that many others at Sullivan & Cromwell also had to withdraw from daily routine. One partner, Rogers Lamont, impatient to serve, resigned his partnership and joined the British army as an officer, only to die fighting in France in 1940. After Pearl Harbor, more than half the firm's lawyers enlisted, many as officers in the intelligence service. Inzer Wyatt became expert at penetrating German and Japanese secret codes at Bletchley Park in England; other partners held sensitive positions at the Pentagon and SHAEF headquarters in Europe.

Dulles faced a delicate policy question whether to guarantee the departing associates places upon their return from military service. The firm's main competitors had no hesitation in offering postwar employment, but Dulles equivocated. "[We] cannot assure," he said, ". . . at the termination of their government service [that associates will] resume their relationship with us where they left off." Dulles' decision, deeply resented at the time, resurfaced as a political issue during his 1949 senatorial race. Joseph Broderick, a one-time Sullivan & Cromwell associate who managed the Democrats' downstate campaign, used Dulles' failure to offer a guarantee to firm lawyers returning from military service as a point of political attack.

In one respect, however, the wartime exodus of lawyers foretold a more inclusive future many decades hence. During the war Sullivan & Cromwell hired nine women as general corporate, securities, and trust and estate associates. All left after several years, none having achieved partnership, as their male counterparts returned. Constance Cook, one of the first women hired by a competitor, Shearman & Sterling, recalled that "[w]omen with marvelous qualifications had been graduating from law school for seventy-five years, and they never took any of them. There's no question. They were desperate for help."[10] The firm's treatment of women reflected a profession-wide bias. President Conant of Harvard, asked about the welfare of the university's law school during the war, said, "[It's] not as bad as we thought. . . . We have 75 students, and we haven't had to admit any women." Harvard Law School remained single sex until 1950.[11]

AFTER THE WAR: NEW DIRECTIONS

The lawyers who returned to Sullivan & Cromwell and its peers after the war confronted a world transformed. Four years of total mobilization had recast the economy, the role of women, race relations, and the importance of the United States as a guarantor of the international order. But within the hushed precincts of most Wall Street law firms very little had changed. The eastern establishment continued in charge—a select group of prominent men who, like Allen Dulles, had been interventionists before the war when the nation was still isolationist. Such ornaments of the bar as Henry Stimson, John McCloy, and Dean Acheson had pushed for American engagement and later containment of Soviet aggression. Their social and class credentials, which informed the ethos of the firms they led, had been forged in elite private schools, then at Ivy League colleges and the best clubs within those colleges (Porcellian and the Fly at Harvard, Skull and Bones and Scroll and Key at Yale, and Ivy, Cottage, and Cap and Gown at Princeton). As presiding partners they defined establishment manners and mores, absorbed unblinkingly by most associates, whose greatest virtue may have been the absence of sharp edges.

As described by David Halberstam in *Vanity Fair*, "The bloodlines were tested, the values confirmed early on. The legatees knew who had 'the right stuff' and who, conversely, would never pass muster; they knew what was to be discussed only in private. They knew—and this was perhaps the most elemental rule of all—that they were not to take credit for anything, even if the credit was rightfully theirs. They tended to be self-deprecating and detached, stoic. (Many were uneasy with John Foster Dulles not just because of his slowness to perceive the danger of Hitler but also because he was considered too partisan and vainglorious.)"[12] Only decades later, as old-line Wall Street firms displaced uniform WASP social origins in favor of talent wherever located, did the interior life of Sullivan & Cromwell and others like it undergo real change. In the immediate postwar era there were only a few exceptions. Paul Weiss, founded in the nineteenth century, claimed to be the first major New York City firm to break down the barrier of Jews practicing with Gentiles. In 1946 the firm recruited two prominent (non-Jewish) government lawyers: Randolph Paul (former General Counsel of the Treasury Department) and Lloyd Garrison (former head of the War Labor Board). Both became name partners, a recruiting coup that, according to the firm history, thrust it into the ranks of the city's first-tier legal powerhouses. Another postwar exception was Cleary Gottlieb, formed by four former partners at Root Clark Buckner & Ballantine, George Cleary, Leo Gottlieb, Henry Friendly and Mel Steen, and three prominent government lawyers, Hugh Cox, Fowler Hamilton and George Ball. Sullivan & Cromwell, Cravath and Davis Polk may not have realized it at the time, but Paul Weiss and Cleary Gottlieb portended fundamental change.[13]

The Dulles brothers, drawn by the freewheeling excitement of high public office, seemed little concerned with the mundane realities of post-war law practice and pursued their international interests outside Sullivan & Cromwell. Dulles enhanced his bipartisan foreign policy credentials in a Democratic era. In 1946 he became a member of the U.S. delegation to the United Nations General Assembly in London; assisted Secretary of State Byrnes at an early Council of Foreign Ministers meeting; published a two-part article in *Life*, "Thoughts on Soviet Foreign Policy and What to Do About It"; and received an honorary degree from Princeton as "a man . . . trained and sharpened in the conduct of important affairs, yet tempered by a strong religious belief and a passion for world peace."

Dulles saw the emerging Cold War in Manichean terms and made common cause with Richard Nixon, then a politically ambitious anti-communist congressman from

California. Yet his views and those of George Kennan, author of the nation's containment policy toward the Soviet Union, were initially similar. Although a principal Republican foreign policy spokesman, Dulles became for a time part of the Democratic policy apparatus. He attended almost every Council of Foreign Ministers meeting and worked with the United Nations Security Council and General Assembly. Dulles' diligent attendance at these postwar conferences kept his name before the public and exposed him first-hand to Russian intransigence. The government consulted him on major issues (the Marshall Plan, North Atlantic Treaty Organization, Berlin blockade, and Korean War). He negotiated the peace treaty with Japan and served as U.S. ambassador-at-large. As Dewey's chief adviser on international affairs during the 1948 presidential campaign, he was assumed by all to be the next Secretary of State.

After his candidate's unexpected defeat, Dulles returned to New York from Paris, where he had been attending yet another conference, and reluctantly resumed law practice at Sullivan & Cromwell. But his return to private life was short. Dewey was still governor of New York. In 1949, when Senator Robert F. Wagner resigned his senate seat because of ill health, Dewey appointed Dulles to complete the final six weeks of Wagner's term. Dulles resigned from Sullivan & Cromwell and was sworn in as senator from New York on the same day. He ran against former Governor Herbert H. Lehman in the fall, narrowly losing despite the aid of Dewey's own staff. The Democrats noted his work for the Schroder Bank and other German-based clients. Dulles campaigned as a hard-core anti-communist, positioning himself for the 1952 election, the last chance to fulfill his legacy and become Secretary of State.

The likely candidate was General Dwight Eisenhower, then in Paris as supreme Allied commander. Dulles arranged to meet him there and to leave the text of an article, "A Policy of Boldness," just written for *Life*, that charged Democrats with merely seeking to contain Communism rather than securing the liberation of captive nations. It was a transparent ploy to distance his recent thinking from one-time support for President Truman's foreign policy and George Kennan's advocacy of containment. Eisenhower won the election in a landslide, and Dulles became Secretary of State. The Senate confirmed his nomination by voice vote as he took his place seamlessly among the captains of industry and finance dominating Eisenhower's cabinet. Still, there were pointed dissenters. "It is fortunate for this country, Western Europe and China," wrote I.F. Stone, the liberal journalist, "that he was not at the helm of foreign policy before the war. It is unfortunate that he should be now."[14]

In 1945, following the defeat of Germany and Japan, President Truman disbanded the OSS, accused in a report commissioned by President Roosevelt of "poor security, incompetence, waste, nepotism, inadequate training, extravagance, corruption, alcoholism, orgies, foreign penetration. . . ." Allen, then working for the OSS in Germany, returned to civilian life, where he resumed his partnership at Sullivan & Cromwell. Joined by other OSS veterans like William Donovan, Richard Helms, and Frank Wisner, he longed to relive his espionage adventures and envisioned an intelligence vehicle for the dawning age of the Cold War. His wartime credentials as a spymaster lent him credibility in the contested field of intelligence.

To burnish those credentials, he got himself elected president of the Council on Foreign Relations and, several years later, was asked by the Senate Armed Services Committee to submit the blueprint for a centralized intelligence agency. Allen proposed an entirely new intelligence organization with separate funding, freedom from military oversight, and direct access to the president—all features of the Central Intelligence Agency established by the National Security Act in July 1947. He was convinced the Soviets were an implacable enemy and found a sympathetic ear in James V. Forrestal, Truman's defense secretary, a former investment banker at Dillon Read, and a contemporary from Allen's days at Princeton.

In 1948, as the Dewey campaign gained momentum, Forrestal persuaded Truman to appoint Allen to a committee to study the CIA. The result was a massive report that proposed a wholesale reorganization of the fledgling agency, including clear-cut separation of its research and clandestine functions. But the CIA's initial director, opposed to covert activities, utterly failed to anticipate key international events. In 1950 Truman replaced him with Walter Bedell ("Beedle") Smith, a lieutenant general and once Eisenhower's chief of staff. "Bringing in a shit-stirrer like Beedle," wrote one chronicler, "reflected the Truman administration decision to militarize U.S. policy." Smith hired Allen, the primary author of the CIA report, first as a consultant and later as Deputy Director, where he presided over a single overseas clandestine service with a single chain of command and a single set of administrative procedures. Eisenhower's election as president in 1952 reshuffled the CIA. Smith became Under Secretary of State, and Allen moved up to Director of Central Intelligence. Allen and his brother now occupied the most powerful seats in the nation's foreign policy establishment with license to wield power globally, "enforced by nuclear terror and cloak-and-dagger brutality." Each had achieved his position over decades of persistent calculated effort, both inside government and at Sullivan & Cromwell. Now, expanding the playbook of their mentor, William Nelson Cromwell, they exerted unparalleled influence in the halls of government. Their law firm had once again served as an escalator for the personal and political ambition of its partners.[15]

Cromwell, age 94, died in 1948, a date far removed from his heyday in the early twentieth century. Many Sullivan & Cromwell partners served as pallbearers at his elaborate funeral at St. Bartholomew's Church where 500 were in attendance. He left a fortune of almost $19 million, many bequests to bar associations, law societies, and universities and one to his reputed mistress for $35,000. He died without direct descendants. By instinct an entrepreneur and risk taker, Cromwell built a world-class institutional law firm. Unlike Paul Cravath, himself an entrepreneur and law firm architect, Cromwell was not primarily concerned with the methodology of law firm development. That task devolved on others. He seemed instead forever focused on the main chance—how to insert himself and his firm strategically, at great profit, in the ongoing battles that characterized the business world of unrestrained capitalism before the First World War. He was both an obsessive legal technician and a barely disguised principal who shaped events to his advantage. He enabled railroads, banks, and manufacturing companies to defeat government regulation; devised novel techniques of corporate reorganization and bankruptcy finance; and was centrally involved in the political and diplomatic machinations that resulted in the Panama Canal. His driving concern was personal gain, and he took advantage of the porous ethical and legal standards of the time to advance his cause. His political nemesis, Senator Morgan of Alabama, called him a "professional revolutionist and . . . one of the most accomplished lobbyists this country has ever produced." Cromwell might have regarded this as grudging praise from an adversary. Even a nostalgic view from the distance of many decades does not soften the harsh contours of his personality. He was preeminently a product of his age and lived long enough to see his legacy, the Sullivan & Cromwell law firm, become a pillar of the legal establishment.[16]

17

Tradition and Reform at Davis Polk

As the 1930s drew to a close, John W. Davis and Allen Wardwell were increasingly troubled by the aggressions of Germany, Italy, and Japan. John W. Davis, particularly, was deeply Anglophphilic, and his innate dislike of involvement in foreign wars slowly gave way to the realization that America might have no alternative but to intercede in the coming European war to rescue Britain. There were few lawyers better known than Davis, here or abroad, in diplomatic circles. With Paul Cravath, Davis was one of the founders of the Council on Foreign Relations, and he had served as its first president from 1921 to 1933. He was, in addition, a board member of the Carnegie Endowment, the American Foundation, and the League of Nations Association. Although reluctant to advocate war, by the spring of 1940, Davis concluded that Britain's war was America's war and came out in support of rearmament, renewal of the draft, and the Lend-Lease program.[1]

Notwithstanding his mixed experiences with the Soviets during his Red Cross mission twenty years earlier, Wardwell had continued his involvement with Russia, advocating closer economic and political ties with the Communist regime. After Germany invaded Russia in 1941, Averell Harriman asked Wardwell to join his emergency mission to Moscow to meet with Britain's Lord Beaverbrook and Russian Foreign Minister Molotov. The conference resulted in a commitment to provide Russia with tens of thousands of tanks, aircraft, and trucks to resist the Nazi invasion. A few months later, Wardwell took over leadership of the Russian War Relief Fund, which provided humanitarian support for Russian citizens in areas devastated by war.[2]

After Pearl Harbor, there was a rush to join the war effort. Soon, almost eighty of the firm's partners, associates, and clerks, including over half of the firm's lawyers, had entered the armed or civilian services.[3] Davis Polk issued periodic bulletins to its alumni in the service to report news from the office, dispatches from Washington, and updates from the various theaters of the war.[4] John W. Davis made the bulletin his personal medium, authoring articles.

Partners who served in military or senior civilian posts had desk jobs on military staffs, in civilian affairs units, or in legal or financial roles. Partner George H. Brownell was put in charge of developing 52 airfield and seaplane bases around the world, along with associated housing for crews and facilities for aircraft. By the war's end, he had been elevated to the rank of Brigadier General.[5] Charles M. Spofford, another Brigadier General, was Assistant Chief of Staff for Intelligence in the Mediterranean theater and subsequently held the rank of Ambassador to the North Atlantic Council.[6] Porter Chandler became a Lieutenant Colonel, serving in military intelligence in Egypt, Libya, and Tunisia, followed by a stint at the Pentagon.[7] Others served in acquisition of war material, military intelligence, legal staffs, or military government.Two were involved with the Nuremberg trials, and one worked on the investigation of the Japanese attack on Pearl Harbor. Associates and law clerks were young enough to serve in combat. One was a B-24 pilot in Europe, another rose from private to captain in the Marine Corps and survived the battle of Iwo Jima, and two were infantry captains, fighting their way from Normandy through the Ardennes and into Germany. Several served on destroyers or assault craft, and one was a gunnery officer on the *USS San Diego*, a light cruiser that fought in eighteen engagements and became one of the most decorated ships in the United States Navy during the war. Three young lawyers did not come back, having been killed in action.[8]

By 1946, most of the lawyers who had left Davis Polk for the war returned to work. Intervening events had brought irreversible changes to the nation and the law profession. The social barricades of the past were beginning to give, and it seemed only a matter of time before Wall Street itself would yield.

ADJUSTMENT

Davis Polk was still tradition-bound. Customarily, it hired three or four new associates each year, invariably from Harvard, Yale, and Columbia. Robert Fiske remembered that he and Samuel F. Pryor III, who came to the firm in the mid-fifties from the universities Michigan and Pennsylvania law schools, respectively, "were the first two really out of that mold."[9] Fiske discovered that two of the senior partners who had attended Oxford occasionally communicated back and forth in Latin. Sam Pryor recalled that "[t]he seventeenth floor on the Wall Street side of the building consisted of four double-size offices. These were occupied by elderly gentlemen who arrived around 10:00 a.m. and could be seen through the glass wall facing the corridor, reading the morning newspapers before starting on their mail. They would leave for lunch when they finished with the mail."[10]

The life of associates continued largely unchanged. Their annual starting salary in the early 1950s was about $4,200, barely enough to live on.[11] There were rigid rules of dress and decorum. According to Pryor,

> George Brownell was the partner in charge of associates. He was of the "old school" and very strict about all aspects of our life. Soon after the new associates arrived, he called us in to his corner office to inform us of the rules. He expected us to wear conservative suits with vests, wear hats outside, and wear full-length overcoats in winter. Hours were 9:30 a.m. to 5:30 pm and the firm expected us to work in the evenings, if necessary. Saturday hours were 9:30 a.m. to 12:00 pm.[12]

Social differences also were enforced. Pryor recalled that Brownell came close to firing him and a fellow associate when he found they had fraternized with the staff during a farewell party for one of the firm's receptionists.[13] Brownell relented because he personally knew their fathers. Their fathers, of course, happened to be wealthy, socially connected, and powerful.[14] Davis Polk's social propriety was well known, evoking humorous commentary for Cravath associates in the same building at 15 Broad Street.

JOHN W. DAVIS' FINAL ARGUMENTS

John W. Davis was still the titular head of the firm and venerated by his partners. Although few lawyers have had a longer or more interesting career than Davis, he is remembered today for the last two Supreme Court cases. One is considered a landmark decision against the abuse of presidential authority. The other is infamous as a defense of segregation.

The *Steel Seizure* Cases

Davis argued the seminal case of *Youngstown Sheet & Tube v. Sawyer*[15] in May 1952 before an overflowing crowd in the Supreme Court. The matter had arisen from a labor dispute between steel companies and steelworkers during the Korean War. Steelworkers considered themselves underpaid, but steel companies were unwilling to raise wages unless the government's Office of Price Stabilization allowed them to increase the price of steel. The Truman administration was unsympathetic to the companies, whose profits had soared since the end of World War II. After negotiations bogged down, the union prepared for a strike. Since steel was a raw ingredient of war, Truman felt compelled to avert a shutdown. He could have invoked the emergency provisions of the Taft-Hartley Act to forestall the strike but was reluctant to do so given his political support from the steelworkers union. Instead, relying on a flimsy analysis from the Department of Justice, Truman resolved to take over the steel industry itself. In April 1952, he issued Executive Order 10340, instructing the Secretary of Commerce to seize and operate the plants of the major steel companies. It was expected that eventually the companies would retrieve their assets, and meanwhile the executive order let them keep their profits, pay dividends on their stock, continue to service their debt, and otherwise abide. But the companies feared a provision of the order that seemed to empower the Secretary to increase wages, impose a closed shop, and make other concessions to the union that the companies might have to live with for years to come.

Davis Polk's client was U.S. Steel, which immediately sued. Ted Kiendl handled the first round of hearings in the district court, asking for no more than a preliminary injunction against changing the terms and conditions of the steelworkers' employment. The district court judge rejected Kiendl's restrained approach and instead went directly to the merits of the case, finding Truman's order illegal and ordering the mills returned to the steel companies. On the following day the court of appeals stayed the district court's order. The Supreme Court then reinstituted the injunction and granted certiorari.

The crux of the case was whether the president had the inherent authority in times of emergency to seize private property without an express delegation of that power by the Congress. Davis maintained that Truman's executive order violated the Constitution's separation of powers; the government, represented by Solicitor General Philip B. Perlman, contended that the president's powers were sufficiently broad in times of war or national emergency to take control of strategic property.

The Court heard the case on May 12, allotting five hours for argument. It was Davis' 138th argument there, and by all accounts he was at his best. The Justices rarely interrupted him, although Felix Frankfurter could not pass up the opportunity to question Davis about the argument he had made in 1915—when Davis was Solicitor General—that President Taft had the power to remove public lands from public entry even without an act of Congress. Perlman had a harder job, bedeviled by Justices Frankfurter, Black, Douglas, Jackson, and Reed. When the time came for Davis to offer his rebuttal, he used only a few of the sixty minutes he had reserved.

The Court issued its opinion a few weeks later, holding that Truman's executive order was unconstitutional. Justice Black's majority opinion, not eight pages long, was almost devoid of citations or rigorous analysis. There were four concurring opinions, each expressing some reservation, with one justice, Tom Clark, concurring in the result, but not in the majority opinion. There was a vigorous dissent by Chief Justice Vinson, a Truman appointee, joined by the remaining justices. Accolades poured in for Davis' performance in *Youngstown*, hailed as a landmark decision constraining the powers of the president. Although gratified, Davis shrugged them off; he complained that the decision should have been unanimous.[16]

Brown v. Board of Education

Davis today is best remembered for his advocacy of school segregation in *Brown v. Board of Education*.[17] His defenders and apologists maintain that his role in the case was misunderstood or that his arguments are properly seen as a realistic appraisal of the then-state of racial relations rather than that he genuinely believed in racial segregation.

Such apologies and explanations are unpersuasive. Davis was a deeply conservative man, born eight years after the Civil War in a place that—until the Civil War—had countenanced slavery. Davis expressed no reservations about taking the case when asked to do so by South Carolina's governor James F. Byrnes, even though Byrnes was an admitted segregationist and had threatened to close all the public schools in South Carolina if the courts ever ordered them integrated.[18] While Davis had, for years, relied upon his younger partners and his associates to write his briefs, he did much of his own work in *Brown*.[19] He ignored suggestions from several of his partners, friends, and even his own daughter to withdraw from the case.[20] Instead he represented South Carolina *pro bono*, refusing the offer of a fee.[21] When a joint session of the South Carolina legislature thanked Davis for his service and presented him with a silver tea set, he had it displayed prominently in the firm's library.[22]

The background of *Brown* is intriguing. Since the Supreme Court's 1896 opinion in *Plessy v. Ferguson*,[23] it had generally been accepted that the equal protection clause of the Fourteenth Amendment permitted states to segregate public facilities by race so long as those separate facilities were of equal quality. In fact, such separate facilities were anything but equal. Black schools, in particular, suffered from chronic underfunding, overcrowding, outdated textbooks, and underpaid teachers. By the 1940s, civil rights plaintiffs had won a series of cases by demonstrating this inequality of treatment, and the federal courts now seemed disposed to view *Plessy* with a critical eye. With this in mind, the NAACP brought suit in May 1950 on behalf of a child named Harry Briggs to compel South Carolina to bring its desperately inadequate Black schools to the same level as white ones.[24]

The case was assigned to Judge J. Waties Waring, who at great personal cost had recently decided two civil rights cases in favor of Black plaintiffs.[25] At a pretrial hearing, Waring encouraged the NAACP's lawyer, Thurgood Marshall, to expand his suit to address *Plessy* head-on and to challenge the principle of segregation itself. Judge Waring's suggestion was especially shrewd. South Carolina had inserted in its constitution and its statute books provisions that explicitly required the segregation of Blacks and whites in public schools.[26] Under the then-prevailing procedural rules, any lawsuit for an order to enjoin enforcement of these state laws as unconstitutional must be heard by a three-judge panel of the district court.[27] Any ensuing decision that granted or denied such an injunction could be appealed as of right to the Supreme Court itself.[28] In this way the NAACP's challenge to South Carolina's regime of school segregation would automatically get a hearing before the highest court.

South Carolina's legal strategy was largely driven by its newly installed governor, James F. Byrnes, who had achieved one of the most extraordinary political careers in American history.[29] He had been a Supreme Court Justice and thus appreciated the threat posed by the NAACP's lawsuit. Fully aware that *Plessy* required that segregated facilities should be equal, Byrnes tried to forestall the lawsuit, but preserve segregation, by having the legislature undertake a massive spending program to bring Black schools to the same level as white ones.[30] This it did, feverishly building new school buildings, raising the salaries of Black teachers, buying new furniture and equipment, and creating a school bus system for Black children.[31] Byrnes also knew that the NAACP had framed its case in a way that would lead directly to the Supreme Court, and he therefore took the precaution of engaging John W. Davis to represent the state on appeal.[32]

At trial, a divided three-judge district court found that Black schools were still unequal, if improving, but that segregation itself was constitutional. The NAACP took its direct appeal to the Supreme Court, which remanded the case to the District Court for a report on the progress of equalization.[33] After the District Court found that "substantial equality" indeed had been achieved, the NAACP took its second appeal to the Supreme Court to challenge the segregationist provisions of South Carolina's constitution and laws.[34]

Davis thought the case bordered on frivolous. He was a stalwart defender of states' rights, and there was ample precedent holding that the decision to segregate public facilities was one firmly within the power of a state. He put great stock in *Plessy*'s dictum that "if one race be inferior to the other socially, the Constitution of the United States cannot put them on the same plane."[35] And it seemed axiomatic that there could be no violation of the equal protection clause if different races were treated equally, albeit separately.

Davis, now almost 80, seemed oblivious to the vast changes that had overtaken the nation. His briefs rested on ample precedent and, in his view, sound constitutional learning. He was appalled by the NAACP's papers and those of some *amici curiae*, which cited recent sociological studies showing that segregated schools—even if putatively equal in resources—resulted in profound and lasting injury to Black students. Such speculation, Davis fumed, had no place in a brief, much less in a courtroom. The law, he believed, was simply a set of rules, whose interaction led, ineluctably, to logical results.

The case was argued twice, with Davis facing Thurgood Marshall each time. At the first argument, in December 1952, the Court peppered Marshall with questions, many about the practical implications of banning segregation. The Court listened respectfully to Davis, whose argument was learned and eloquent. Uncharacteristically, he used almost all of his allotted argument time.

Davis left the Court that day sure that he had won and, in fact, he almost had.[36] As the Court ruminated on the case, though, at least two justices began to harbor misgivings, and in June the Court ordered reargument on the Fourteenth Amendment's legislative history and other issues.[37] After another round of briefing, and more remonstrances from Davis about the NAACP's misleading and sloppy briefs, the second argument occurred on the second week of December 1953. This time, Davis was more emotional than before, clearly frustrated by the Court's willingness to entertain the sociological theories the NAACP offered up and angry that the Justice Department—specifically invited by the Court to participate in the reargument—took the NAACP's side. The Court was again deferential to Davis, but now it was out of respect, not agreement. His age showed; even Thurgood Marshall, an unabashed admirer of Davis, thought "[h]e was over the hill."[38]

Chief Justice Earl Warren delivered the Supreme Court's unanimous decision in May 1954. The Court decided that the Fourteenth Amendment should be construed in the context of current realities, and it accepted the conclusions of the sociological studies and authorities the NAACP had collected. Segregated schools violated the equal protection clause. The Court simply dismissed *Plessy*, holding that "[s]eparate educational facilities are inherently unequal."[39] Davis was stunned by the opinion in *Brown* and never fully recovered from it. His straightforward, if not mechanistic, view of the law was now unmoored and his Jeffersonian certitudes ignored. He died ten months later; one of his partners said *Brown* had killed him.[40]

ENTROPY

Once again, Davis Polk had succumbed to complacency. We can only speculate on the causes. Perhaps it arose from the firm's entrenched position with respect to the Morgan banks or its reliance on the stature of John W. Davis. In any event, Davis Polk seemed to be coasting. Even when business was slow, the firm seemed to see no reason to seek new clients or expand into new areas. In fact, when Sam Pryor—still an associate—was asked by Daniel Lufkin to help him organize his new investment bank, Donaldson, Lufkin & Jenrette, a senior partner snapped: "Don't spend your time on them. You're supposed to work on firm clients."[41]

There had been little growth. Davis Polk had a net gain of only four partners during the 1940s, and the partnership was not much bigger in 1954 than it had been in 1937. In fact, during those years, more and more of its business was in the field of trusts and estates. The head of that department, Walter D. Fletcher, had come to work with Frank Polk in 1922 and displaced him by the mid-1930s. When J. P. Morgan & Co. decided in 1940 to incorporate itself as a New York bank with trust powers, Fletcher established its trust department and became its counsel. With the generational passing of fortunes amassed during the heyday of robber barons and industrial trusts, demand for this work soared and Fletcher became increasingly powerful within the firm.

Fletcher was a difficult partner. He was overbearing, gratuitously insulting, given to exaggerating his credentials, and a thoroughly unpleasant colleague. He spent much of his time on his estate in Virginia, where he enjoyed fox hunting with his wealthy clients. Fletcher resented the greater prestige enjoyed by the banking and securities practices and seems to have gone out of his way to be difficult.

This led to internal friction, which Louis Auchincloss chronicled in one of his novels where Fletcher is depicted as the thinly disguised character Sheldon Dale, a crass man given to three-martini lunches, unctuous fawning on dowagers, and resentment of his more patrician colleagues.[42] Of the eight partners elevated between 1949 and 1956, three were in the trust and estates department, while only one partner was made in each of the firms other core practices.

Davis Polk was slow to correct the imbalance. In 1957 the firm admitted a group of five—two tax lawyers and three banking and securities lawyers—to the partnership, but then took on no more partners for the next four years.

Real reform did not come until 1961. Davis Polk eliminated fraternal restrictions on firm membership such as race, religion, and gender.[43] The firm then admitted an unusually large group of eight partners. Those men, along with their cohort from 1957, were to sustain its practice for the next thirty years. One was Bruce Nichols, a banking lawyer of unsurpassed talents who became the principal advisor of Morgan Guaranty Trust, probably the firm's largest client. There were two new corporate lawyers—Sam Pryor and the uniquely brilliant Peter Bator[44] and tax lawyer John Carroll, credited as the inventor of the foreign currency swap.[45]

Davis Polk also took the unusual step of bringing in a lateral partner. This was Lawrence E. Walsh, who had worked briefly as an associate in 1941–1942, before leaving to join the staff of New York Governor Thomas Dewey. Walsh ultimately became counsel to the Governor and and a manager of Dewey's 1948 presidential campaign. In 1953, Walsh became the first director of the commission created to rid the New York waterfront of organized crime, then was appointed a federal judge and Deputy United States Attorney General. Walsh would go on to further achievements, including service as the United States Ambassador to the Paris Peace Talks in 1969 and president of the American Bar Association in 1975–1976. Walsh's final turn at public service was his appointment in 1986 as the Independent Counsel to investigate the Iran/Contra scandal.

One of the new partners was a young litigator named Henry L. King, born Henry L. Katz in Brooklyn in 1928. His grandparents on both sides had been Jewish immigrants from Russia. He had long aspired to be a lawyer—his high school yearbook joked about it saying that "He'll be keen competition for Attorney-General Biddle."[46] He attended Columbia College and Yale Law School, changing his name in his early twenties to avoid discrimination. Still, King's background was generally known, and he became Davis Polk's first partner of overt Jewish extraction. Years later, he would become managing partner of the firm. Another three years passed before the firm hired its first female associate, tax lawyer Lydia Kess, who later became its first woman partner.

In 1962, after 70 years at 15 Broad Street, the firm moved up the street to a new skyscraper at One Chase Manhattan Plaza.[47] Its offices had grown to twice the previous size. The spacious reception area on the forty-fourth floor enjoyed a commanding view of New York Harbor. Mimicking 15 Broad Street, there was a grand spiral staircase leading to the lower floor and a doorway to the large law library. On the west side of the reception area, a hallway led to the long row of oversized offices reaching halfway around the building and occupied by the firm's senior partners, a corridor jokingly referred to as the "Gold Coast."[48] The partners also resolved to change the name of the firm one last time and thereafter keep it unchanged.[49] It became Davis Polk & Wardwell, and so has remained.

18

Back to the Future

At war's end, in 1946, inner circle Wall Street law firms entered a period of peace and prosperity. Despite the lingering aftereffects of total mobilization, the law business—at least as practiced by Cravath, Sullivan & Cromwell and Davis Polk—continued for a time without radical change. To come were several decades of accelerated economic growth and social upheaval; but, well into the postwar era, the exclusionary practices of the legal *ancien regime* persisted.

Milton S. Gould, a veteran New York litigator, described the symbolic one-time chasm between the downtown and uptown segments of the bar. Downtown, in a tight little enclave around Wall Street, were the offices of the elite law firms, near the banks and brokerage firms that supported, in Gould's description, a "lucrative no-risk monopoly." Cravath, Sullivan & Cromwell and Davis Polk, the inner sanctum of the Wall Street bar, could be found at 15 Broad Street and 48 Wall Street. In those days "uptown lawyer" was virtually an insult. "An address on Forty Second Street, or in midtown Manhattan," Gould recalled, "stamped a firm as professional *canaille*. The lawyers who inhabited these offices were criminal lawyers or negligence lawyers or labor lawyers, or they served the needs of the despised garment industry."[1]

The real gulf that divided the New York bar, however, was not simple locational snobbery. It was instead, in Gould's recollection, "religious bigotry, xenophobia, anti-Semitism and every other form of 'elitism.'" Corporate and financial business was the province of a handful of Wall Street firms that resisted all efforts to reform their hiring policies and were, almost without exception, WASP bastions. Ethnic and religious discrimination bore most heavily on Jewish lawyers, who were a large percentage of the New York bar. Although a few outliers were admitted and became partners, most of the Jews—and Irish and Italians—employed by elite firms remained permanent associates, managing dockets, practicing real estate law, or keeping tabs on the bankruptcy work their firms farmed it out to specialized, firms.

Anti-Semitism, in particular, was a long-accepted prejudice. Harlan F. Stone, a former Sullivan & Cromwell partner and later Chief Justice of the United States Supreme Court, once dismissed Jewish lawyers as exhibiting "racial tendencies toward study by memorization." Notwithstanding his decades of enlightened public service, Elihu Root expressed concern about "tens of thousands" of immigrants seeking to become lawyers. William D. Guthrie, head of the New York State Bar Association in 1921-1922 and once a partner of Paul Cravath, condemned compulsory bar membership as an attempt at democratization that threatened admission of a "teeming population of recent immigrants and their progeny." The result, he said, would be "public calamity." Other legal luminaries said the profession was attracting the "undesirable and the unfit." This prejudice was enduring: in the early sixties Alan Dershowitz, soon to be editor in chief of the *Yale Law Journal*, applied to some thirty Wall Street law firms for a summer job and was rejected by all of them—notably by Cravath, Swaine & Moore, where he badly wanted to work.[2]

The Depression and the Second World War, both cataclysmic events, set in motion changes that would eventually force white-shoe firms to open their doors to Jews, Catholics, women and people of color, if only as a matter of self-preservation. As products of the WASP ascendancy, these firms eventually learned the distinction between an aristocracy, which allows new members to enter its ranks, however carefully, and a caste system, like apartheid, which seeks to maintain power and influence through exclusion.[3]

MERITOCRACY REVISITED

Speaking at Harvard Law School in 1920, Paul Cravath advised his audience that for success at the New York bar "family influence, social friendships and wealth count for little." He mentioned the many prominent lawyers who had come to New York from small places and "worked up from the bottom of the ladder without having any advantage or position or acquaintance." Arthur Dean of Sullivan & Cromwell offered similar advice. "In today's larger legal partnerships," he wrote three decades later, "advancement is by and large by competence alone." Cravath and Dean were apostles of meritocracy as they saw it. The Cravath system, eventually adopted by most large law firms, purported to put aside as irrelevant applicants' religious affiliation, ethnicity, and social status. In doing so, it anointed a new professional elite and convinced both winners and losers they deserved their fate.[4]

In fact, however meritocratic they purported to be, Cravath, Sullivan & Cromwell, Davis Polk, and other peer Wall Street law firms had, and traded on, an explicit religious and cultural identity. Well into the 1950s, these firms were almost entirely populated by WASP men drawn from a handful of elite law schools and eastern colleges. In addition to academic credentials, successful applicants were expected to possess "warmth, force of personality and physical stamina"—dog-whistle characteristics sometimes meant to exclude women, Jews, Catholics and, certainly, persons of color.

One has only to read Robert T. Swaine's detailed biographies of Cravath partners to perceive the embrace of WASP social and religious norms. Virtually every Cravath partner from the time the master took charge until the firm's history was written in 1948 was a white upper-class Protestant. Sullivan & Cromwell and Davis Polk were similar. Indeed most of the Davis Polk partners in that era were listed in the Social Register, and the few who were not usually had rejected such a listing as beneath them. While professing meritocracy, Wall Street law firms incorporated normative WASP values as key elements of their elevated professional status. As establishment institutions they believed diversity (a latter-day term they would not have used) conflicted with their vision of WASP culture.[5]

Once again, Louis Auchincloss wrote about this perceptively. In his novel, *The Scarlet Letters*, set in 1953, he explored establishment social values in the context of a merger between a prototypical WASP law firm with a Jewish firm engaged in hostile corporate takeovers and celebrity divorces, a practice reviled by the WASP firm's patrician founder. The partner proposing the merger accused the founder of objecting to the merger because the target was largely Jewish. "What are you getting at?" the founder asked. "That I'm anti-Semitic? Nonsense! I have the greatest liking and respect for the considerable number of my Jewish friends. But when you're putting together an institution of a certain type of manners and morals, it makes sense to go in for a certain quantity of homogeneity. The particular trademark of [my firm] is an old Yankee tradition of integrity, courage and gentlemanly behavior. Indeed, you can't mistake it. Now I'm not saying for a minute that Jews and Moslems and Chinamen and blacks are lacking in any of these virtues, but it so happens that they put them together in a different showcase."[6]

Wall Street firms, notably including Cravath, Sullivan & Cromwell and Davis Polk, attracted high-end legal business and the right law graduates to service that business as associate labor, notwithstanding their reputation as heartless law factories. These firms and their academic suppliers of WASP talent entered into an implicit bargain. " . . . [T]he leading law schools produced lawyers for the leading firms; the firms in turn made the schools prosperous by donations." For years large Wall Street firms, enjoying a virtual monopoly over legal services to wealthy corporate clients, rejected lawyers whose values and appearance were unwelcome in an elite enterprise.

THE CHALLENGE OF JEWISH LAW FIRMS IN NEW YORK

The Cravath system replaced idiosyncratic office habits with rational client-oriented firm administration but, strangely, did not promote competition for legal services among its peers. Instead, the best Wall Street firms formed a de facto cartel that preferred lockstep compensation (except for the founders) and eschewed unseemly competition, building instead on a network of intertwined social connections and white-shoe solidarity to maintain their professional standing. In disdaining overt competition among themselves, such firms ensured their financial success. Using their exclusive social and religious patina, they distinguished themselves from that of lower elements of the bar, invaded by foreign-born, lawyers from eastern Europe often educated in night law schools.[7]

At the same time those firms served large corporate interests that demanded ever more sophisticated legal services than those available from only a few sources. By combining a meritocracy of the well-born with the social identity of a gentlemen's club, they dominated a profession of which they were, numerically, but a tiny fraction.[8]

By the mid-1960s, the tensions between the increasing demands of sophisticated legal practice and the exclusionary hiring and elevation policies of downtown law firms had become irreconcilable. Unless the establishment Wall Street law firms broadened their talent pool and expanded their practices, they were in danger of being pushed to the margins of the profession.

Social prejudices aside, one root of the problem was Paul Cravath's vision of the practice of corporate law. The Cravath system placed greatest value on the office lawyer, whose domain was the conference room. Except for opposing the intrusive reach of the federal government, elite firms did not see litigation as a strategic tool. Instead, it was the unfortunate sequel to a transaction gone bad, to be avoided at any reasonable price. By stigmatizing certain practice areas, the elite bar created attractive opportunities for new competitors willing to explore new practice areas and compete for the clients Wall Street firms had long taken for granted.

The rising Jewish firms in particular became expert in those areas.[9] Joe Flom, the legendary takeover partner at Skadden Arps, said he got involved in mergers and acquisitions because "that was the business that was available." Marty Lipton, creator of the poison pill defense against hostile takeovers, used it to establish his firm's reputation and easily moved on to represent blue-chip corporate clients generally. Together Skadden Arps and Wachtel Lipton came to dominate the corporate takeover business and, from there, they captured a significant share of the dynamic, high-profit M&A business. Other prominent counsel were Milton Handler and Jules Berman of Kaye Scholer and Ira Millstein of Weil Gotshal, who followed pioneers such as Leo Gottlieb of Cleary Gottlieb, Ed Weisl of Simpson Thacher, and Louis Loeb of Lord, Day & Lord. And once these aggressive law firms had caught clients' attention, they did not confine themselves simply to litigation, corporate takeovers, M&A work, or real estate. Instead, they began to encroach on downtown law firms almost sacrosanct hold on corporate finance, banking, and strategic legal advice. "[T]he decision by the WASP firms to stay out of certain areas of practice," wrote Eli Wald in the *Stanford Law Review*, "was costly in terms of allowing Jewish firms to have a near monopoly in these areas, but also allowed the Jewish firms to compete for clients in the WASP firms' practice areas."[10]

The rise of the Jewish firms was facilitated by an ever-growing number of talented young lawyers. In the postwar era elite law schools abandoned discriminatory admission policies and admitted Jewish applicants previously excluded. This shift created a pool of highly qualified Jewish lawyers ignored by WASP firms but easily recruited by their Jewish rivals—an infusion of talent that drove their growth and competitive standing. WASP firms' pattern of discrimination thus enabled Jewish law firms to expand more rapidly with little competitive restraint. By 1980 Jewish firms accounted for four of the ten largest firms in New York City.[11]

Discrimination against talent was not the only factor inhibiting WASP firms' growth. The elite bar's insistence on fixed partner-to-associate ratios, eight- to ten-year partnership waiting periods, and rejection of lateral hiring all prevented firms from growing fast enough to meet client demand. Many of the hide-bound WASP firms clung to traditional metrics and white-shoe values even as these eroded their market dominance. Jewish firms, not similarly constrained, recruited many new lawyers and aggressively pursued lateral hiring from downtown law firms. The very same stereotypes that had barred Jewish lawyers' entry into WASP firms—"smarts, wealth maximizing, manipulative on behalf of clients, and instrumental, not to say conniving"—became advantages in the newly competitive world of law emerging in the late 1960s and beyond.[12]

THE WASP ASCENDANCY ADJUSTS

The downtown law firms soon realized that, for everything to stay the same, everything would have to change. The case for elite law firms' reconsideration of their WASP identity became compelling. Large law firms could no longer count on steady fees from dependable anchor corporate clients, tethered by traditional old-boy loyalty. The market for legal services, even the most sophisticated, grew increasingly competitive. In place of unblinking adherence to white-shoe values, WASP firms invoked meritocracy as part of an ideological transformation and began regularly to hire and promote Jewish lawyers. The success of Jewish lawyers became so pronounced that one critic actually complained they were vastly over-represented among leading firms in New York City. The high-end law practice repurposed itself as a for-profit service industry, resting on market competition, efficiency, and cost effectiveness. With built-in advantages of scale and embedded expertise in their core legal specialties, Wall Street firms actively promoted their functional reinvention, hoping to preserve elite professional status by relaxing discriminatory standards that no longer served their interests. They fell back on meritocratic standards as if those standards had been, all along, the only benchmark for hiring and promotion. White-shoe affinities eventually gave way to the aggressive lawyering that had given these firms their prominence a century before.[13]

WOMEN LAWYERS: ONCE A DISFAVORED MINORITY

Another group disfavored by Wall Street law firms were women lawyers, virtually boycotted by major law firms until they entered the profession in force in the 1970s.

Cravath, Swaine & Moore hired two women associates in the 1950s, but neither made partner and both left after a short time. For years women had accepted their lot as second-class citizens. That changed in 1975 when Diane Blank, an associate at Sullivan & Cromwell, and several others filed a sex-discrimination suit against the firm in a case before Judge Constance Baker Motley, a noted civil rights activist and the first African American woman appointed as a federal judge. She took her seat following delayed Senate confirmation, occasioned by Senator Eastland's racial prejudice and her work as a civil rights lawyer. Critics assumed Judge Motley would not rule from the bench objectively. The plaintiffs claimed Sullivan & Cromwell refused to hire well-qualified female attorneys; subjected women associates to less favorable working conditions than men; paid women lower salaries than men; excluded or marginalized female associates in firm culture; and relegated women to legal specialties, such as trusts and estates, rather than assigning them to high-profile litigation. It was the first case testing the antidiscrimination principles of Title VII of the Civil Rights Act of 1964.[14]

Sullivan & Cromwell's lawyer, Ephraim London, first in correspondence and then by motion, asked Judge Motley to recuse herself, arguing that, as an African American and a woman, she had experienced workplace discrimination and would therefore identify with the plaintiffs. Later in the proceeding, when Judge Motley certified the case as a class action, London formally petitioned the court of appeals to reverse the certification, contending she should have disqualified herself. Judge Motley declined to do so. "It is beyond dispute," she wrote, "that for much of my legal career I worked on behalf of blacks who suffered race discrimination. . . . [I] am a woman, and before being elevated to the bench, was a woman lawyer. . . . [I]f background or sex or race of each judge were, by definition, sufficient grounds for removal, no judge on this court could hear this case." In the wake of Judge Motley's ruling Sullivan & Cromwell settled, agreeing to reach out to women applicants and confine interview questions to qualifications for work (as opposed to personal questions about ability to travel and work long hours). The firm also agreed to offer women associate positions comparable to the percentage of applications received from them, pay women fairly, and support their professional development. A watershed event, the settlement confirmed the impact of the Civil Rights Act on private law practice and was thought to have encouraged greater acceptance of women lawyers.[15]

Women poured into the legal profession. In the decade following 1970 the number of women lawyers increased fivefold, and the percentage of women in large law firms more than tripled. But a journalistic expose revealed that Sullivan & Cromwell still had no female partners and its peer firms only a few. Women associates at Sullivan & Cromwell thought the lawsuit had diminished their accomplishment, polarized lawyers within the firm after a momentary hiatus, hurt the firm's recruitment of women, and failed to achieve lasting change because it was not effectively monitored by plaintiffs' counsel. Lawsuits alone, defense counsel replied, could not change attitudes. One former Sullivan & Cromwell female associate said that "when a woman partner . . . conforms to the male stereotype personally and professionally . . .

that's not social progress. To me, that's discrimination." Former women associates at the firm reported "largely unarticulated, cryptic promotional criteria developed and refined by men for more than a century," women associates' inability to find mentors who could relate to them, older partners' discomfort at working with women, and difficulty in getting challenging assignments, especially in litigation. "Neglecting families is a traditionally male role," said another former associate, citing the case of a managing partner at the firm who once boasted he had missed the birth of a child to complete an important deal—something, she said cheekily, that is harder for women to do. As a result, she concluded, the firm viewed women as less committed, less competent, and less promising partnership material than men—a belief that became a self-fulfilling prophecy.[16]

Although women today are the majority of law school graduates, their share of law firm equity partnerships remains at less than 20 percent and has not increased in recent years. In response to Diane Blank's suit Sullivan & Cromwell made behavioral changes but was not subject to monetary damages. The remedy for gender bias now has a price tag. Women lawyers have upped the ante through lawsuits seeking dollar compensation. Three former women partners, claiming gender-based pay disparity, recently sued a major law firm for $100 million. In an earlier era such litigation would have been unthinkable. Acts that today would bring swift legal retribution were previously ignored or quietly managed. At Cravath in the 1970s a male litigation partner routinely assigned an associate to tasks requiring him to remain over night at out-of-town locations. One day, enroute to LaGuardia Airport, the associate decided to detour to his apartment. There he found his wife in bed, alone. He next looked in the bathroom, pulled the shower curtain aside, and confronted the nude partner, who said, "What are you doing here?" The incident became Wall Street legend. The partner was quietly asked to leave, took a high government position, and later served as a partner in other white-shoe law firms.[17]

BLACK LAWYERS

Of all the minorities rejected by Wall Street firms, none has had a harder time gaining acceptance than Black lawyers. " . . . [R]acial discrimination permeated both public policy and private decision-making throughout the nation," wrote William T. Coleman, who once served as Secretary of Transportation under President Ford. In 1946 Coleman graduated first in his class from Harvard Law School and then clerked on the Third Circuit Court of Appeals and the U.S. Supreme Court for Justice Frankfurter, the first Black lawyer to do so. "I nevertheless pounded the pavement," he recalled, "in my hometown of Philadelphia, in Boston, in Washington, and on Wall Street in search of a job. I had no offers and was rarely granted an interview. . . . In those days, many Wall Street firms did not accept any minorities, including women, Latinos, and Jews and in some cases even Catholics."[18]

With a wife and two children to support, Coleman placed a call to Louis Weiss of Paul, Weiss, Wharton & Garrison in New York, was granted an interview and was hired on the spot. "This may well have been the first time ever," he wrote, "a major law firm in any U.S. city had hired a person of color as an associate." Coleman's case was, lamentably, proof of an exclusionary system. In the 1940s and 1950s there simply were no Black lawyers in corporate law firms like Cravath, Sullivan & Cromwell and Davis Polk. In fact, there were only a handful of Black lawyers in the entire country, typically employed in low-level government jobs or by small law firms. Segregation characterized the American legal profession. For many years leaders of the bar had fought to maintain its purity as a WASP institution in which Blacks, like other minorities, were denied membership. Even when nominally progressive, leading lawyers rarely considered the hiring practices of their own firms. Paul Cravath, chairman of the board of trustees of Fisk University, the Negro college founded by his father, ran a lily-white law firm whose partners shared a similar appearance, outlook, and social background. Cravath believed recruitment of such lawyers essential for representation of firm clients with similar demographics. To advance, young lawyers had to fit into the firm's rigid social structure. Fitting in was almost as important as hours worked or business developed. In an era where homogeneity ruled and diversity seemed an alien concept, it was little wonder Black lawyers were often nowhere to be seen. In the unlikely event Black lawyers were hired at all, big law firms did nothing special to include them in their social and cultural fabric. To survive, Black lawyers had to be functionally indistinguishable from the white lawyers these institutions had always hired. Assimilation was essential. Law firms rightly feared that corporate clients, slow to integrate their managerial or professional ranks, would not wish to be represented by a Black lawyer.[19]

If one were to measure the percentage of Black enrolment at law schools, Black associates at law firms, and Black equity partners at law firms as points on a graph, they would describe a sharply downward sloping line. "The profession . . . ," writes one former Black woman partner at a large Chicago law firm, "is top-heavy with white male aristocrats, bulging around the middle with white women and some lawyers of color, and chock full of the latter at the entry level." Black lawyers constitute only a small fraction of the associate ranks and only a small fraction of law firm partners in New York City, figures that have not budged in recent years. Much of the growth in minority hiring and promotion is instead attributable to Asian lawyers. Although many elite law firms actively recruit minorities, Black lawyers, unhappy with the terms of engagement, often leave for more secure jobs elsewhere. Attrition is an endemic problem. Only a few Black lawyers persevere on the tortuous path to partnership.[20]

"If there's a pattern," said one observer of color familiar with the problem, "it is that a minority associate gets good reviews, but deficiencies are brought up when the conversation turns to partnership." Black lawyers face obstacles in recruiting new clients, getting internal referrals, and commanding dedicated service from skilled associates. Those who stay often seek out or are steered into areas thought to be of relative advantage: defending discrimination cases, litigation in front of urban jury pools with significant minority presence, and municipal bond practice (where Black city officials often control the work). Law firms once were opposed to hiring minorities in deference to the prejudices of corporate clients. Now such clients, often more diverse than the firms representing them, seek proof of diversity when soliciting formal bids for legal work. Several years ago Shell Oil's general counsel set a precedent by demanding that outside law firms increase engagement of women and minorities on Shell's legal work and later cutting dozens of firms, including Baker & Botts, from the company's roster. More recently, Walmart, DuPont, General Mills, and Verizon have formed a program, Engage Excellence, to encourage other companies to require diversity. Despite public acclaim, such efforts have not yet had decisive impact. Large law firms remain dense pockets of culture, resistant to change, without much inclination to rethink the core ideas governing how they deliver and evaluate legal work.

ACCOMMODATION AND SURVIVAL

Since the end of the golden era of the 1950s, Wall Street law firms have nonetheless had to accommodate both continuity and change. The basic structure of a pyramidal partnership dictated a century ago, with equity partners at the apex supported by numerous associates vying for admission, is still recognizable, but the environment within which firms operate has been transformed. "Today," write Marc Galanter and Thomas Palay, astute analysts of the legal profession, "we are in another era of restructuring of business, the complexity of which is compounded by transnational flows of capital and new information technologies. As the demand for legal services changes, with more complex deals and more use of litigation as a business strategy, there is an expansion of services provided by lawyers. We can observe a volatility and organizational innovation that have been absent from the legal scene for generations."[21]

Big law firms are now global, rich, often huge by historic standards, seriously competitive, and run as cut-throat service businesses with onerous billable-hour requirements and professional managers. Kirkland & Ellis, a Chicago firm whose metrics exceed those of its New York competitors, earned $3.76 billion in 2018, has fifteen offices worldwide, and pays its equity partners as much as $15 million annually. It has poached partners from more conservative counterparts and embraced a two-tier partner system. Only the equity partners split the firm's profits. In the reign of the dollar, it is not surprising that firm breakups, mergers, and acquisitions are commonplace as are lateral hiring and proliferation of lawyer categories (e.g., contract, temporary, staff attorneys, nonequity partners). Firms have reluctantly had to reconsider the very concept of partnership, no longer a passport to lifetime tenure, as the law has morphed from a learned profession into a service industry. They have also demanded, as an indispensable predicate of success, lawyers' willingness to sacrifice themselves by allowing professional identity to overtake and consume personal life.

This has meant an unwavering focus on the financial bottom-line, long hours, and unlimited client-centered representation.[22]

Nowhere are these factors better illustrated than in Cravath, Swaine & Moore's defense of IBM in the government's thirteen-year antitrust suit (*U.S. v. IBM*) commenced against it in 1969. The suit triggered the paradigmatic bet-your-company litigation, recounted in detail by James Stewart in his book, *The Partners*. The case generated 66 million pages of documents, thousands of exhibits, and hundreds of depositions and was the first to use computers to organize and search all of that paper. In 1982 the government withdrew the case "without merit." Cravath conducted "the most brilliant and sustained legal representation in history at a cost that is staggering both in financial and human terms," wrote Stewart. "IBM . . . so taxed the institution of the corporate law firm that neither Cravath nor any other firm like it will ever be the same again." Cravath's defense in the IBM case became the model for complex litigation at other major firms—a scorched earth, no-holds-barred legal war that ultimately resulted in an unqualified victory. "There is no job I would rather have had, nothing I would rather have done," said Tom Barr, the principal Cravath lawyer on the case. "I'm sure my partners feel the same way. This has been the biggest and most important case in the country." Nonetheless the IBM litigation took a personal toll on the firm and its lawyers, measured in a high divorce rate among firm lawyers and massive associate defections. Not everyone bought into Barr's philosophy of unlimited commitment, but few doubted it was here to stay.[23]

AVE ATQUE VALE

For each of Cravath, Sullivan & Cromwell and Davis Polk social, racial, ethnic, and gender discrimination is an ancient, receding memory, leading one journalistic observer to recall the passing of an era. "I was close to the generation of Wall Street Wasps who are dying now," writes Robert Armstrong in *Financial Times*. "They were fantastically snobby and had unearned privilege shoveled on them from the moment the sterling silver christening gifts rolled in."[24] Whatever the accuracy of such recollection, Cravath's presiding partner is now a woman, and each firm has been or is presently led by a Jewish partner. Women lawyers are a major presence in each partnership. Although challenged by many rivals in the expanding law firm universe, each firm is today—as it was years ago—highly profitable, preeminent, and recognizable as the heir to its unique history. Associate slots are still coveted by the best law graduates. In a profession driven by talent, each firm has been able to shed outmoded prejudice, however grudgingly, in time to catch the next wave washing over the law business. At the highest level the law is a bespoke professional undertaking that requires custom tailoring of services supported by organizational and managerial capacity. It is not a commodity enterprise. Each firm has survived and prospered over the years by its ability to provide solutions to the most difficult and arcane legal problems, often at the intersection of policy and politics.

Notes

INTRODUCTION

1. *The Trow City Directory Company's Copartnership and Corporation Directory of New York City* (New York 1889), pp. 19, 243, 259.
2. *Hubbell's Legal Directory for Lawyers and Businessmen 1892* (New York 1892), pp. 1038, 1041, 1043-45.
3. Larissa MacFarquhar, East Side Story, *The New Yorker,* February 25, 2008.
4. "The term 'white shoe' comes from the footwear style 'white bucks,' the casual, carefully scuffed buckskin shoes with red rubber soles and heels worn by generations of college men at Ivy League schools." William Safire, On Language: Gimme the Ol' White Shoe, *New York Times,* November 9, 1997, Section 6, p. 28.
5. Robert T. Swaine, *The Cravath Firm,* Vol. II, p. 465. Hereinafter Swaine II.
6. *Id.* at p. 463.
7. Jan Hoffman, Oldest Law Firm Is Courtly, Loyal and Defunct, *The New York Times,* October 2, 1994, p. 33 (quoting Gordon J. Davis).
8. James B. Stewart, A Law Firm Where Money Seemed Secondary, *The New York Times,* September 24, 2012, p. F8.

CHAPTER 1

1. Lexis-Nexis Online History.
2. Kai Bird, *The Chairman* (New York: Simon & Schuster, 1992), p. 62.
3. Swaine II, pp. 256, 360–61, 658–59. Other Cravath alumni served as Assistant Secretary of War (John McCloy), directed Army intelligence (Al McCormack), and bore responsibility for distributing Magic and Ultra intercepts (Ben Shute).

4. Priscilla Roberts, Paul D. Cravath, the First World War and the Anglophile Internationalist Tradition, *Australian Journal of Politics and History*, Vol. 51 (June 2005), pp. 194, 198. Hereinafter Roberts I.

5. Swaine II, p. 256.

6. Wayne K. Hobson, *The American Legal Profession and the Organizational Society, 1900–1930* (New York: Garland Publishing, 1986), pp. 196–97.

7. George W. Alger, Review of The Cravath Firm and Its Predecessors: 1819–1947, *American Bar Association Journal*, Vol. I, No. 5 (May 1947), p. 481.

8. Milton Mackaye, Public Man, *The New Yorker*, January 2, 1932, p. 23.

9. Quoted in Wayne K. Hobson, *op. cit.*, p. 192.

10. Beryl H. Levy, *Corporation Lawyer—Saint or Sinner? The New Role of the Lawyer in Modern Society*, Chilton (1961), p. 88.

11. Milton Mackaye, Public Man, *The New Yorker*, January 2, 1932, p. 22; Robert T. Swaine, *The Cravath Firm*, Vol. I, p. 572. Hereinafter, Swaine I.

12. Swaine II, pp. 573–74.

13. See note 16.

14. Tom McNichol, *AC/DC: The Savage Tale of the First Standards War* (San Francisco: Jossey-Bass, 2006), p. 120. See also note 16.

15. See following note.

16. Jill Jonnes, *Empires of Light* (New York: Random House, 2003), *passim*; Swaine I, p. 650; Lori J. Alvey, The War of the Currents: Examining the History Behind *The Last Days of Night, Kentucky Bar Association* (June 14, 2018); Robert L. Bradley Jr., *Edison to Enron* (Beverly, MA: Scrivener Publishing, 2011), pp. 48–59; Steven W. Usselman, From Novelty to Utility: George Westinghouse and the Business of Innovation During the Age of Edison, *The Business History Review*, Vol. 66, No. 2 (Summer 1993), pp. 251–304.

17. Patrick McGuire, Money and Power; Financiers and the Electric Manufacturing Industry, 1876–1896; *Social Science Quarterly*, Vol. 71, No. 3 (September 1990), pp. 510–30; Tom McNichol, *op. cit.*, pp. 135–38; Graham Moore, *The Last Days of Night* (New York: Random House, 2016), pp. 294–95.

18. Swaine II, pp. 32–43.

19. The Cravath firm has two historical roots: one in New York City dating from 1819 with Richard M. Blatchford as its founder and the other in Auburn, New York, where in 1823 William H. Seward began practice as Miller & Seward, with former Judge Elijah Miller and later Samuel Blatchford. The two branches united in 1854 when William H. Seward became United States Senator, later the contender against Abraham Lincoln for the Republican nomination for the presidency and Secretary of State in the Lincoln Cabinet. His nephew, Clarence A. Seward, with Samuel Blatchford and another Auburn lawyer, then united in New York with Richard M. Blatchford to form Blatchford, Seward & Griswold, which was known as the Blatchford firm until 1885 and thereafter for sixteen years as the Seward firm with Clarence A. Seward as senior partner and William D. Guthrie rising in its ranks. When Paul D. Cravath joined, the firm became Guthrie, Cravath & Henderson until 1906, when Mr. Guthrie withdrew.

20. 57 U.S. 429 (1895); Swaine I, pp. 381–84, 472, 475; George W. Alger, The Cravath Firm and Its Predecessors, Volume I, *American Bar Association Journal*, Vol. 31, No. 5 (May 1947), pp. 480–82.

21. See following note.

22. See following note. Swaine I, p. 452.

23. Swaine I, pp. 477–79.

24. Wayne K. Hobson, *op. cit.*, pp. 197–98; Swaine I, pp. 572–73, 650–75, 704–9.

25. Milton Mackaye, *op. cit.*, p. 23.

26. Swaine II, p. 658; Wayne K. Hobson, *op. cit.*, p. 198.

27. Milton Mackaye, *op. cit.*, p. 22; Swaine I, p. 575.

28. Wayne K. Hobson, *op. cit.*, pp. 199–200.

29. Berle, Review of Beryl Harold Levy's "Corporation Lawyer . . . Saint or Sinner? The New Role of the Lawyer in Modern Society," *Harvard Law Review* Vol. 76, No. 432 (1962).

30. Swaine II, pp. 464–65.

31. Edward G. Burrows and Mike Wallace, *Gotham.* (Oxford, UK: Oxford University Press, 1999), p. 1047.

32. John Oller, *White Shoe.* (New York: Dutton, 2019), pp. 137–44; Swaine I, pp. 722–34; Swaine II, pp. 45–69.

CHAPTER 2

1. Matt Fleischer, Sullivan & Cromwell v. Cravath: There Was That 1861 Case . . . . *The Observer*, April 26, 1999.

2. Dog Eat Dog: The Laws of War in American History, https://erenow.com/ww/lincolnscode the laws of war in American history.

3. Arthur H. Dean, *William Nelson Cromwell, 1854–1948* (New York: Ad Press, 1957), p. 25.

4. Nancy Lisagor and Frank Lipsius, *A Law Unto Itself: The Untold Story of the Law Firm Sullivan and Cromwell* (St. Paul, MN: Paragon House, 1988) (hereafter L & L), pp. 19–20; https://erenow.com/ww/lincolns code the laws of war in American history.

5. Bernard A. Weisberger, The Strange Affair of the Taking of the Panama Canal Zone, *American Heritage*, Issue 27, No. 6 (October 1976).

6. David McCullough, *The Path Between the Seas* (New York: Simon & Schuster, 1977), pp. 271–72; Arthur H. Dean, *op cit.*, p. 58; Ronald W. Pruessen, *John Foster Dulles, The Road to Power* (New York: The Free Press, 1982), p. 15.

7. Edwin G. Burrows and Mike Wallace, *op. cit.*, p. 1047; David A. Skeel Jr., *Debt's Dominion* (Princeton, NJ: Princeton University Press, 2001), p. 69; Arthur Dean, *op. cit.*, pp. 52–53; Ron Chernow, *The House of Morgan* (New York: Grove Press, 1990), pp. 48, 66–67.

8. Robert W. Gordon, Money! Power! Ambition! *Legal Affairs*, March/April 2006.

9. Edwin G. Burrows and Mike Wallace, *op. cit.*; David A. Skeel Jr., *op. cit.*

10. Otto E. Koegel, *Walter S. Carter* (New York: Round Table Press, 1953), p. 7; L & L, p. 32.

11. L & L, p. 32.

12. *Ibid.*, p. 33.

13. *Ibid.*, pp. 28; Edwin Wildman, Romance of Success, William Nelson Cromwell, the Man Behind the Panama Canal, *The Omaha Sunday Bee*, December 13, 1908; Arthur H. Dean, *op. cit*, p. 116.

CHAPTER 3

1. Herbert L. Satterlee, *J. Pierpont Morgan: An Intimate Portrait 1837–1913* (New York: MacMillan & Co., 1939), pp. 135–36.

2. Samuel Hand's son and nephew were the famous judges Learned Hand (1872–1961) and Augustus Hand (1869–1954).

3. Herbert L. Satterlee, *op. cit.*, pp. 140–42.

4. Vincent P. Caruso, *The Morgans: Private International Bankers* (Cambridge, MA: Harvard University Press, 1987), p. 242.

5. *Ibid.*, pp. 242–44.

6. Jean Strouse, *Morgan: American Financier* (New York: Harper Perennial 2000), p. 131.

7. A substantial amount of the South Pennsylvania Railroad had been built by the time the peace treaty took effect. The track bed and tunnels lay fallow for decades until the Commonwealth of Pennsylvania incorporated them into the new Pennsylvania Turnpike in the 1930s.

8. F. L. Stetson and Samuel J. Tilden, *The Great Democrat*, p. 7. Address delivered to the Tilden Centennial Committee, February 10, 1914.

9. Ralph Carson, *Davis Polk Wardwell Sunderland & Kiendl, A Background with Figures* (privately published, 1965), p. 11.

10. F. L. Stetson, *op. cit.* p. 12.

11. Ralph Carson, *op. cit.*, p. 12.

12. Joseph Auerbach, *The Bar of Other Days* (New York: Harper & Brothers, 1940), 30-31.

13. *Ibid.*

14. *Hubbell's Legal Directory for Lawyers & Business Men 1882* (New York, 1883), p. 826.

15. Association of the Bar of the City of New York, *18th Annual Report* (1888), pp. 80-85.

16. Ralph Carson, *op. cit.*, p. 7.

17. *Ibid.*, p. 108.

18. *Ibid.*, p. 17; Jean Strouse, *op. cit.*, p. 442n.

19. *Ibid.*, p. 23. The Manhattan cocktail was invented at the Manhattan Club by one Dr. Iain Marshall for a banquet hosted by Jennie Jerome, now remembered as the mother of Winston Churchill.

20. John Oller, *White Shoe: How A New Breed of Wall Street Lawyers Changed Big Business and the American Century* (New York: Dutton, 2019), p. 21.

21. *Ibid.*, pp. 21-22.

22. Allen Wardwell, *Memorial of Francis Lynde Stetson, New York County Lawyers' Association, Year Book 1921* (New York: J. Little & Ives Company, 1921), p. 226.

23. Ralph Carson, *op. cit.*, pp. 22–23.

24. *Ibid.*, pp. 108.

25. See Otto E. Koegel, *op.cit.*, pp. 4–5.

26. Charles Howland Russell, *Charles Howland Russell 1851–1921* (privately published, 1935), pp. 58, 61.

27. *The Trow City Directory Company's Copartnership and Corporation Directory of New York City 1895* (New York, 1895), p. 316. Although Francis S. Bangs returned to the practice of law a dozen years later, he did not come back to Stetson's firm. He instead partnered with Paul D. Cravath's former partner William Guthrie in the firm of Guthrie, Bangs & Van Sinderen. See Howard Van Sinderen, Memorial of Francis Sedgwick Bangs, *New York County Lawyers Association Yearbook 1918* (New York, 1918, p. 232).

28. Charles Howland Russell, *op. cit.*, p. 13.

29. *Ibid.*, p. 24; *Obituary Record of the Society of Alumni, Williams College 1919–1920* (Williamstown, Massachusetts, April 1921), pp. 94-95.
30. Lyman Horace Weeks, *Prominent Families of New York* (New York, 1898), p. 391.
31. Charles Howland Russell, *op. cit.*, pp. 8n1.
32. *Ibid.,* p. 32n1.
33. John Oller, *op. cit.*, p. 21.
34. Ralph Carson, *op. cit.*, p. 18.
35. *Ibid.*, p. 26.
36. John A. Dolan, *Hale and Dorr: Background & Styles* (Boston: Hale and Dorr, 1993), p. 305.
37. And, oddly, for a small fee the U.S. Treasury would mint gold coins for anyone who showed up at the mint with a bag of gold.
38. Jean Strouse, *op. cit.*, pp. 340–41.
39. *Ibid.*, p. 343.
40. Herbert J. Satterlee, *op. cit.*, p. 291; Jean Strouse, *op. cit.*, p. 343.
41. Rexford Guy Tugwell, *Grover Cleveland* (New York: Macmillan, 1968), pp. 258–59.
42. *Ibid.*
43. Jean Strouse, *op. cit.*, p. 346.
44. Ralph Carson, *op. cit.*, p. 28.

CHAPTER 4

1. Susan Berfield, *The Hour of Fate: Theodore Roosevelt, J.P. Morgan and the Battle to Transform American Capitalism* (Bloomsbury, NY: Tin House Books, 2020), p. 22.
2. Vincent P. Carosso, *op. cit.*, 1987), p. 219.
3. See John F. Meck and John E. Masten, Railroad Leases and Reorganization: I, 49 *Yale Law Journal,* Vol. 1, No. 49 (1940), p. 626.
4. See following note.
5. David A. Skeel Jr., Competing Narratives in Corporate Bankruptcy: Debtor in Control vs. No Time to Spare, *Michigan State Law Review*, Vol. 2009–4 (Winter), pp. 1190–93; Troy A. McKenzie, Bankruptcy and the Future of Aggregate Litigation: The Past as Prologue, *Washington University Law Review*, Vol. 90, No. 3 (2013), pp. 849–51; Swaine II, pp. 167–68.
6. Swaine I, pp. 379, 721; Swaine II, p. 168; Ron Chernow, *op. cit.*, p. 68; David A. Skeel Jr., *Debt's Dominion* (Princeton, NJ: Princeton University Press, 2014), pp. 65–69, 102.
7. Stuart Daggett, Railroad Reorganization, *Harvard Economic Studies*, Vol. IV, 69 (New York: Houghton, Mifflin & Co. 1908).
8. Thurman Arnold, *The Folklore of Capitalism* (New Haven, CT: Yale University Press, 1957), p. 258.
9. John Moody, *The Truth About Trusts: A Description and Analysis of the American Trust Movement* (Chicago: Moody Publishing Company 1904), pp. 429–43, 492–93.
10. See following note.
11. L & L, p. 30.
12. *The Albany Journal*, September 16, 1887.
13. William Nelson Cromwell to Henry Villard, November 15, 1885, Henry Villard Papers, Box 23, Folder 198, Harvard Business School, Baker Library Historical Collections.
14. See following note.

15. Swaine I, pp. 496–97; L & L, p. 31.

16. Stuart Daggett, *op. cit.*, pp. 289–92; Northern Pacific: Two Receivers Resign, *The New York Times*, January 10, 1896, p. 15.

17. Stuart Daggett, *op. cit.,* p. 307.

18. Victor Morawetz had been born in Baltimore in 1859, the son of a Jewish doctor who had immigrated from Austria. He was educated in Europe, spoke several languages, was a skilled violinist, and loved fox hunting. After serving on the side of the Carlists in the Third Carlist War, Morawetz returned to the United States in 1876 to enter Harvard Law School. He joined the Illinois bar in 1880 at age 21. Too young to attract clients, Morawetz spent his idle time writing a treatise, *The Law of Private Corporations*, which became the definitive treatment of the field. In 1882, Morawetz moved to New York, hoping to make a living on referrals from other lawyers. Soon, he was summoned to meet Andrew Carnegie, who hired him to handle a railroad matter and then made Morawetz his personal attorney. Morawetz developed a close working relationship with Seward, Da Costa & Guthrie, which resulted in his becoming a member of the partnership in 1887. Morawetz worked on the reorganization of the Atchison, Topeka & Santa Fe Railroad when it entered receivership in 1893 and then became its outside counsel and, ultimately, its president, resigning from the Seward firm in 1896.

19. Jean Strouse, *op. cit.*, p. 419n.

20. *Ibid.*, p. 419.

21. Stuart Daggett, *op. cit.*, pp. 301-8; Future of Union Pacific, *The New York Times*, November 28, 1893, p. 8.

22. *Northern Pacific Railway Co. v. Boyd*, 228 U.S. 482 (1913).

23. F. L. Stetson et al., *Some Legal Phases of Corporate Financing, Reorganization, and Regulation* (New York: MacMillan Co. 1917), pp. 17-27.

CHAPTER 5

1. Thomas K. McCraw, *Prophets of Regulation* (Cambridge, MA: Belknap Press, 1984), p. 77.

2. Edwin G. Burrows and Mike Wallace, *op. cit.*, p. 1045.

3. L & L, p. 31; Ron Chernow, *op. cit.*, p. 82.

4. L & L, p. 27-29; Thomas K. McCraw, *op. cit.*, p. 79; Edwin G. Burrows and Mike Wallace, *op. cit.*, p. 1046.

5. *State v. Standard Oil Co.*, 49 Oh. St. 137 (1892).

6. Susan Berfield, *op. cit.* p. 49.

7. Despite Brooks' later boasting, it is unlikely that he can take complete credit for conceiving the idea of legalizing corporate holding companies. New York, among other states, had for years permitted certain categories of corporations to invest in and hold securities of other companies. See Fred Freedland, History of Holding Company Legislation in New York State: Some Doubts as to the "New Jersey First" Tradition, 24 *Fordham Law Review*, Vol. 24, 369 (1955).

8. L & L, pp. 26–27; Jeremiah D. Lambert, *The Power Brokers* (Cambridge, MA: MIT Press, 2015), pp. 28–29.

9. Daniel Crane, The Dissociation of Incorporation and Regulation in the Progressive Era and the New Deal, in *Corporations and American Democracy*, Naomi Lamoreaux and William

J. Novak, eds. (Cambridge, MA: Harvard University Press, 2017), p. 112-14; L & L, p. 27; Edwin G. Burrows and Mike Wallace, *op cit.*, p. 1045.

10. Arthur Weinberg and Lila Shaffer (eds.). *The Muckrakers* (Minneapolis: University of Minnesota Press, 2001), p. 69.

11. Edwin G. Burrows and Mike Wallace, *op. cit.*, p. 1045.

12. Arthur H. Dean, *op. cit.*, pp. 105-6; L & L, pp. 33-35.

13. United States House of Representatives, The Paper Trust, 58th Congress, 2d Sess., *Hearings Before the Committee on the Judiciary*, pp. 65-8 (April 5, 1904); Jean Strouse, *op. cit.*, p. 469-70; Vincent P. Carosso, *op. cit.*, p. 481; William H. Harbaugh, *Lawyer's Lawyer: The Life of John W. Davis* (Oxford, UK: Oxford University Press, 1973), p. 186; *Company History of International Nickel*, found at http://www.fundinguniverse.com/company-histories/inco-limited-history; Fred V. Carstensen, *George W. Perkins and the International Harvester Steel Properties*, found at https://www.thebhc.org/sites/default/files/beh/BEHprint/v009/p0087-p0102.pdf.

14. Jean Strouse, *op. cit.*, pp. 400-1.

15. *Ibid.*, pp. 402-3.

16. Ralph Caruso, *op. cit.*, pp. 471.

17. The mortgage was the linchpin of the deal because Morgan and Carnegie agreed that most of the consideration to Carnegie would be paid in bonds of the new company. In fact, each was betting against the other. Morgan did not want Carnegie to have a big equity position in U.S. Steel lest Carnegie decide to meddle in the new enterprise. Herbert J. Satterlee *op cit.*, p. 347. Carnegie, for his part, doubted that U.S. Steel would succeed and thought the entire company would fall in his lap if he held the senior debt.

18. Theron George Strong, *Landmarks of a Lawyer's Lifetime* (New York: Dodd, Mead 1914), p. 463.

19. Jean Strouse, *op. cit.*, pp. 418-19; Maury Klein, *Union Pacific: 1894–1969* (Minneapolis: University of Minnesota Press, 2006), p. 76.

20. Ralph Carson, *op cit.*, p. 34n46; Jean Strouse, *op cit.*, p. 427.

21. Jean Strouse, *op. cit.*, p. 441.

22. Balthasar Henry Meyer, A History of the Northern Securities Case, Vol. 1, *Bulletin of the University of Wisconsin* (Madison: University of Wisconsin 1906), p. 263.

23. *Ibid.*, p. 274.

24. Herbert J. Satterlee, *op. cit*, p. 401.

25. *Northern Securities Co. v. United States*, 193 U.S. 197 (1904).

26. Yet there is no need to pity Harriman. He soon sold his stock for a profit of $58 million and turned to other matters. Susan Berfield, *op. cit.*, p. 250.

27. The Rockefellers had made their fortune refining and selling oil for kerosene lamps. (The automobile was not yet much more than a curiosity.) Morgan became concerned about the Rockefellers' increasing wealth and influence, and there is speculation that one reason for Morgan's financing of Thomas Edison's incandescent light bulb was to confront the Rockefellers' monopoly on illumination.

28. Herbert J. Satterlee, *op. cit.*, pp. 456-57.

29. Jean Strouse, *op. cit.*, p. 597.

30. *Ibid.*, p. 603.

31. Louis D. Brandeis, *Other People's Money* (Frederick A. Stokes Co., 1914), p. 201.

32. Block Sheehan Revolt Grows, *The New York Times*, January 18, 1911, p. 1; Sheehan's Forces Dwindling Away, The New York Times, January 22, 1911, p. 1.

33. Michael Perino, *The Hellhound of Wall Street: How Ferdinand Pecora's Investigation of the Great Crash Forever Changed American Finance* (Penguin Press, 2010), p. 52.

34. Jean Strouse, *op. cit.*, p. 660.

35. *Ibid.*

36. Declares Stetson Backs Insurgents, *The New York Times*, March 17, 1911, p. 1; Charge that Morgan Defeated Sheehan, *The New York Times*, May 31, 1911, p. 6.

37. Jean Strouse, *op. cit.*, p. 659.

38. Herbert J. Satterlee, *op. cit.*, pp. 556–57.

39. *Ibid.*, p. 557.

40. Jean Strouse, *op. cit.*, p. 55.

CHAPTER 6

1. Arthur H. Dean, *op. cit.*, p. 1.

2. L & L, p. 37.

3. David McCullough, *op. cit.*, p. 234; J. M. Carlisle, *op. cit.*, p. 60; Ovidio D. Espino, *How Wall Street Created a Nation, Four Walls Eight Windows* (New York: Four Walls, Eight Windows, 2001), p. 12.

4. J. M. Carlisle, o*p. cit.*, p. 62.

5. *Ibid.*

6. Stephen Kinzer, *The Brothers* (New York: St. Martin's Griffin, 2013), p. 19.

7. *Ibid.*, pp. 64–67; David McCullough, *op. cit.*, p. 273.

8. J. M. Carlisle, *op. cit.*, pp. 64–67; Gerard Helferich, *J. P. Morgan, and the Improbable Partnership that Remade American Business* (Lanham, MD: Rowman & Littlefield (2015), p. 105; Ovidio D. Espino, *op. cit.*, pp. 17–18.

9. David McCullough, *op. cit.*, p. 273.

10. *Ibid.*, pp. 273–91; Gerard Helferich, *op. cit.*, p. 106; J. M. Carlisle, *op. cit.*, pp. 69–79; Ovidio D. Espino, *op. cit.*, pp. 14–15.

11. Gerard Helferich, *op. cit.*, pp. 106–7; David McCullough, *op. cit.*, p. 292.

12. Gerard Helferich, *op. cit.*, pp. 18–20; Charles D. Ameringer, The Panama Canal Lobby of Philippe Bunau-Varilla and William Nelson Cromwell, *The American Historical Review*, Vol. 68, No. 2 (January 1963), pp. 346–63; David McCullough, *op. cit.*, p. 278.

13. J. M. Carlisle, *op. cit.*, pp. 132–34; Ovidio D. Espino, *op. cit.*, pp. 23–28; David Mc-Cullough, *op. cit.*, p. 294; Bernard A. Weisberger, The Strange Affair of the Taking of the Panama Canal Zone, *American Heritage*, Vol. 27, Issue 6 (October 1976).

14. Ovidio D. Espino, *op. cit.*, p. 33; Edwin Wildman, *op. cit.*

15. *Ibid.*, pp. 27–29; J. M. Carlisle, *op cit.*, pp. 148–55; David McCullough, *op. cit.*, p. 326.

16. David McCullough, *op. cit.*, p. 324.

17. *Ibid.*, p. 322; Ovidio D. Espino, *op. cit.*, p. 33; Gerard Helferich, *op. cit.*, p. 109; J. M. Carlisle, *op. cit.*, pp. 161–66; Bernard A. Weisberger, *op. cit.*

18. Bernard A. Weisberger, *op. cit.*; Ovidio D. Espino, *op. cit.*, pp. 38–42; Gerard Helf-erich, *op. cit.*, pp. 109–11; David McCullough, *op. cit.*, p. 332.

19. David McCullough, *op. cit.*, pp. 336–37; Ovidio D. Espino, *op. cit.*, p. 45; J. M. Car-lisle, *op. cit.*, pp. 176–77.

20. Matthew Parker, *Panama Forever: The Epic Story of the Building of the Panama Canal* (London: Palgrave MacMillan, 2009), p. 228; Gerard Helferich, *op. cit.*, pp. 110–13; Ovidio D. Espino, *op. cit.*, pp. 46–47.

21. America's Devious Dream: Roosevelt and the Panama Canal, *BBC History Magazine*, November 2006; Gerard Helferich, *op. cit.*, pp. 114–16; Ovidio D. Espino, *op. cit.*, pp. 58–91; J. M. Carlisle, *op. cit.*, pp. 179–83; Charles D. Ameringer, Philippe Bunau-Varilla: New Light on the Panama Canal Treaty, *The Hispanic American History Review*, Vol. 46, No. 1 (February 1966), p. 32; David McCullough, *op. cit.*, pp. 345–46; Denis Brian, *Pulitzer: A Life* (New York: Wiley, 2007), p. 345.

22. Charles D. Ameringer, *op. cit.*, passim; Ovidio D. Espino, *op. cit.*, pp. 119–62; David McCullough, *op. cit.*, p. 400.

23. Ronald E. Pawoski, *American Presidential Statecraft: From Isolationism to Internationalism* (London: Palgrave McMillan, 2017), pp. 43–44; Denis Brian, *op. cit.*, pp. 343–48.

24. Ronald E. Pawoski, *ibid.*; Ovidio D. Espino, *ibid.*; Carol Gelderman, *Louis Auchincloss, A Writer's Life* (New York: Random House, 1993), p. 87; Ronald W. Preussen, *John Foster Dulles: The Road to Power* (New York: The Free Press, 1982), p. 16.

CHAPTER 7

1. Peter Grose, *Gentleman Spy* (Boston: Houghton Mifflin, 1994), p. 90.

2. L & L, pp. 57–58.

3. *Ibid.*, p. 61; Townsend Hoopes, *op. cit.*, pp. 3, 25; Burton Hersh, *The Old Boys: The American Elite and the Origins of the CIA* (Online: Tree Farm Books, 1992), p. 21; Arthur Dean and John Foster Dulles, *op. cit.*, pp. ii-iii.

4. L & L, pp. 58–60; Peter Grose, *op. cit.*, p. 90.

5. Burton Hersh, *op. cit.*, pp. 20–21; Ronald W. Pruessen, *op. cit.*, p. 17; Richard Gould-Adams, *John Foster Dulles: A Reappraisal* (New York: Appleton-Century-Crofts, 1962), p. 6; L & L, pp. 63–64.

6. L & L, pp. 64–67; Ronald W. Preussen, *op. cit.*, pp. 17–22; Stephen Kinzer, *op. cit.*, p. 24.

7. Ronald W. Preussen, *op. cit.*, pp. 22–23; Stephen Kinzer, *op. cit.*, p. 25; David Talbot, *The Devil's Chessboard* (New York: Harper-Collins, 2015), p. 4; Townsend Hoopes, *op. cit.*, pp. 26–28; *I.F. Stone Weekly*, April 22, 1957.

8. Burton Hersh, *op. cit.*, p. 22; Gaddis Smith, Reconsideration of the Cold War: The Shadow of John Foster Dulles, *Foreign Affairs*, January 1974; Richard H. Immerman, *John Foster Dulles* (Wilmington, DE: Scholarly Resources, 1999), p. 7; Stephen Kinzer, *op. cit.*, pp. 26–27; Ronald W. Preussen, Woodrow Wilson to John Foster Dulles: A Legacy, *Princeton University Library Chronicle*, Vol. 34, No. 2 (Winter 1973); L & L, p. 72.

9. Richard H. Immerman, *op. cit.*, pp. 7–10; Townsend Hoopes, *op. cit.*, pp. 28–31; Ronald W. Pruessen, *op. cit.*, pp. 36–44; Amos S. Hershey, German Reparations, *The American Journal of International Law*, Vol. 15, No 3 (July 1921), p. 412.

10. Townsend Hoopes, *op. cit.*, pp. 31–33; L & L, pp. 72–75; Ronald W. Pruessen, *op. cit.*, p. 52; Stephen Kinzer, *op. cit.*, p. 33.

CHAPTER 8

1. Swaine II, pp. 4–5.
2. *Ibid.*, p. 5; see generally pp. 1–5.
3. *Ibid.*, p. 6.
4. *Ibid.*
5. Marc Galanter and Thomas Palay, *Tournament of Lawyers* (Chicago: University of Chicago Press, 1991), p. 10.
6. Swaine II, p. 7.
7. *Ibid.*, pp. 8–9.
8. *Ibid.*, p. 9.
9. *Ibid.*, p. 465 (quoting *Fortune Magazine,* January 1931).
10. See Eli Wald, The Rise and Fall of the WASP and Jewish Law Firms, *Stanford Law Review,* Vol. 60 (2008), p. 1803 *et seq.*
11. *Time Magazine*, July 8, 1940, p. 58.
12. Milton Mackaye, *op. cit.*, p. 24; Swaine II, pp. 645–46.
13. Swaine II, pp. 124–25.
14. *Ibid.*, p. 125.
15. See following note.
16. Swaine II, pp. 204–7, 256; Patricia Roberts, Paul D. Cravath, The First World War, and the Anglophile Internationalist Tradition, *Australian Journal of Politics and History*, Vol. 51, No. 2 (2005), pp. 194–215.
17. *Ibid.*, pp. 202–3; Swaine II, pp. 210–11; Otto Koegel, *op. cit.*, pp. 384–85.
18. Roberts I, p. 204; Swaine II, pp. 212–17.
19. Swaine II, p. 219; Roberts I, p. 204.
20. Roberts I, p. 202.
21. Otto Koegel, *op. cit.*, p. 385.
22. See note 23.
23. Dean Acheson, *Fragments of My Fleece* (New York: George J. McLeod, 1971), p. 206.
24. Roberts I, pp. 205–9; Swaine, II, pp. 267; Priscilla Roberts, The Anglo-American Theme: American Visions of an Atlantic Alliance, *Diplomatic History*, Vol. 21, No. 3 (Summer 1997), p. 356.

CHAPTER 9

1. See following note.
2. Ron Chernow, *op. cit.*, pp. 381, 489; Swaine II, pp. 17–18, 130–32, 141, 209–10, 255, 315–16.
3. See following note.
4. Ajay K. Mehrotra, Lawyers, Guns and Public Monies: the U.S. Treasury, World War I and the Administration of the Modern State, *Law and History Review*, Vol. 28, No. 1 (February 2010), pp. 173–225; Russell C. Leffingwell, Prices, Wages and Inflation, *Proceedings of the Academy of Political Science*, Vol. 23, No. 1 (May, 1948), pp. 65–68.
5. See following note.
6. Ajay K. Mehrotra, *op. cit.*, p. 221; Swaine II, pp. 255, 315; Stephen A. Schuker, Review of Selected Letters of R. C. Leffingwell by R. C. Leffingwell and Edward Pulling, *The Business*

and History Review, Vol. 54, No. 2 (Summer 1980), pp. 260–62; Liaquat Ahamed, *Lords of Finance* (New York: The Penguin Press, 2009), pp. 462–63; Michael Hiltzik, *The New Deal* (New York: The Free Press, 2011), pp. 173–74; Ron Chernow, *op. cit.*, p. 379.

7. See following note.

8. Liaquat Ahamed, *op. cit.*, pp. 207–8; Swaine II, pp. 324–25; Ron Chernow, *op. cit.*, pp. 249–51.

9. See following note.

10. Kenneth Paul Jones, Discord and Collaboration: Choosing an Agent General for Reparations, *Diplomatic History*, Vol. 1, No. 2 (Spring 1977), pp. 118–39; Ron Chernow, *op. cit.*, pp. 250–53, 310–12, 421; Swaine II, pp. 324–26; Liaquat Ahamed, *op. cit.*, pp. 326–37.

11. See following note.

12. See following note.

13. Kai Bird, *op. cit.*, pp. 57–77; Walter Isaacson and Evan Thomas, *The Wise Men* (Simon & Schuster, 1986), pp. 119–23; Swaine II, pp. 467–69.

14. See note 17.

15. See following note.

16. See following note.

17. Max Holland, Review of Citizen McCloy, *The Wilson Quarterly*, Vol. 15, No. 4 (Autumn 1991), pp. 22–42; Swaine II, pp. 468–69, 636–44, Walter Isaacson and Evan Thomas, *op. cit.*, pp. 123–25, 182; Kai Bird, *op. cit.*, pp. 77–95, 240–68.

18. See following note.

19. Swaine II, pp. 656–67; Max Holland, *op. cit.*, *passim*; Walter Isaacson and Evan Thomas, *op. cit.*, pp. 191–209, 293–98; Kai Bird, *op. cit.*, p. 662.

20. The following narrative is based on an article by the author, Return of the Prodigals, in *Legal Times*, January 15, 1996; see also *D.C. Bar Report*, October/November 1997.

21. Swaine II, p. 722.

CHAPTER 10

1. Swaine II, p. 164.

2. Swaine II, pp. 163–64; David A. Skeel Jr., *op. cit.*, p. 102; Robert T. Swaine, Corporate Reorganization—An Amendment to the Bankruptcy Act—A Symposium, *Virginia Law Review*, Vol. 19, No. 317 (1933); Robert K. Rasmussen and Douglas Baird, Boyd's Legacy and Blackstone's Ghost, *Vanderbilt University Law School Joe C. Davis Working Paper Series, Working Paper Number 99–8*, December 15, 1999, pp. 22–23, 24, 32; Robert T. Swaine, Reorganization—The Next Step: A Reply to Mr. James N. Rosenberg, *Columbia Law Review*, Vol. 22, No. 2 (February 1922), p. 131; Robert T. Swaine, Reorganization of Corporations: Certain Developments of the Last Decade, *Columbia Law Review*, Vol. 27 (1927), pp. 901, 912–13; David A. Skeel Jr., *op. cit.*, pp. 66–67.

3. Swaine II, pp. 167–75; David A. Skeel Jr., *op. cit.*, pp. 67–68.

4. See following note.

5. Kai Bird, *The Chairman* (New York: Simon & Schuster, 1992), p. 65.

6. Swaine II, pp. 418–21, 430–31, 523n1; Kai Bird, *op. cit.*, pp. 64–67; Gardiner C. Means, Review of The Investor Pays, *The New York Times*, June 25, 1933; Kai Bird, *op. cit.*, p. 67; *United States et al. v. Chicago, Milwaukee & St. Paul Railroad Co.*, 282 U.S. 311 (1931).

7. See note 9.

8. See following note.

9. Securities and Exchange Commission, *Report on the Study and Investigation of the Work, Activities, Personnel and Functions of Protective and Reorganization Committees*, Part I-VIII (1937–1940) (written under the direction of William 0. Douglas); Douglas G. Baird and Robert K. Rasmussen, Boyd's Legacy and Blackstone's Ghost, *Sup. Ct. Rev.* (1999), pp. 393, 401–8; David A. Skeel Jr., *op. cit.*, pp. 121–27; William W. Bratton and David A. Skeel Jr., Bankruptcy's New and Old Frontiers, *University of Pennsylvania Law Review*, Vol. 166, No. 7 (June 2008), pp. 1576–79; Thurman W. Arnold, *op. cit.*, pp. 258–59; *Case v. Los Angeles Lumber Products,* 308 U.S. 106 (1939).

10. Swaine II, pp. 140–44.

11. *United States v. Johnson,* 65 F. Supp. 42 (M.D. Pa. 1946); Joseph Borkin, *The Corrupt Judge* (New York: Clarkson N. Potter, Inc., 1962), pp. 168–86; John T. Noonan, The Lawyer Who Overidentifies with His Client, *Notre Dame Law Review*, Vol. 76, April 1, 2001, pp. 834–42; George Edwards, Commentary on Judicial Ethics, *Fordham Law Review*, Vol. 38, Issue 2 (1969), pp. 269–70.

CHAPTER 11

1. Raymond, Rice and Albert J. Harno, Shares with No Par Value, *Minnesota Law Review*, Vol. 5, p. 493 (1921).

2. William H. Harbaugh, *op. cit.*, p. 186.

3. Henry Collins Brown, *Glimpses of Old New York* (New York: Lent & Graff Company, 1917), p. 94.

4. Ralph Carson, *op. cit.*, 105.

5. *Ibid.*, p. 38.

6. *Ibid.*, p. 105.

7. Henry Sprague had a checkered career as a lawyer, politician, and entrepreneur. He seems to have spent much of his time at Stetson, Jennings & Russell promoting business deals, and he resigned from the firm soon after becoming embroiled in a lawsuit with a member of the Vanderbilt family over a business deal that an appellate court determined was "illegal and immoral." See Seward Webb Wins in Suit for $243,213, *The New York Times*, June 19, 1915, p. 18. Sprague is remembered today as an historical footnote, because it was in a letter to Sprague that Teddy Roosevelt used his famous phrase "Speak softly and carry a big stick." See January 26, 1900, letter from Theodore Roosevelt to Henry Sprague, Library of Congress Manuscript Division, gift of the heirs of Theodore Roosevelt, Jr. (52A).

8. Charles Howland Russell, *op. cit.*, p. 58; *The Lawyers' List* 1915 (New York: Hubert R. Brown), p. 207.

9. William H. Harbaugh, *op. cit.*, pp. 186–87.

10. Albert Shaw (ed.), *The American Review of Reviews*, Vol. 43 (New York, 1911), p. 162.

11. Ralph Carson, *op. cit.*, p. 93.

12. *Ibid.*, p. 24.

13. *Ibid.*, p. 26.

14. See, for example, *The Living Church*, Vol. 106, No. 16 (April 18, 1943) (Morehouse-Goreham Co. 1943), p. 4.

15. See George F. Kennan, *The Decision to Intervene* (Princeton, NJ: Princeton University Press, 1958).

16. R. H. Bruce Lockhart, *Memoirs of a British Agent* (New York: Putnam 1932), pp. 340-41.

17. Shows Cruelty of Bolsheviki; Newspaper Correspondent Imprisoned and Suffers Tortures with Thousands of Others, *Indianapolis Star*, November 24, 1918, p. 24.

18. Wardwell Diary quoted in *Columbia Library Columns*, Vol. XXX, No. 1 (November 1982), p. 27.

19. William H. Harbaugh, *op. cit.*, p. 182. Except as otherwise noted, the biographical information about John W. Davis is taken from Harbaugh's definitive biography of Davis.

20. William H. Harbaugh, *op. cit.*, p. 146.

21. *Ibid.*, p. 122.

22. Davis similarly took a fatherly interest in the children of his Clarksburg cousin (and former campaign manager) Carl Vance. When Carl died prematurely in 1922, Davis became a mentor to his two young sons (William H. Harbaugh, *op. cit.*, pp. 389–90). One of the sons, Cyrus Vance, went on to become Secretary of State, among many other achievements.

23. William H. Harbaugh, *op. cit.*, pp. 186–87.

24. There was speculation at the time that Stetson also would leave his fortune—which amounted to $3 million—to Miss Lee. He did not. Instead, after various life estates were resolved, Williams College received about half of the estate. See *Williams College Bulletin*, Series 20, No. 3 (October 1922), pp. 15–16. A long list of other charities and causes received the balance of Stetson's estate. It is said that Ms. Lee was left a trust fund of $300,000.

25. *Ibid.*, p. 106; Ralph Carson, *op. cit.*, pp. 40.

26. William H. Harbaugh, *op. cit.*, pp. 186–87.

27. *Ibid.*; Ralph Carson, p. 106.

28. Ralph Carson, *op. cit*, pp. 44. The firm also lost another partner at this time. This was Winfred Thaxter Denison, who had served as an Assistant Attorney General and as the Secretary of the Interior of the Philippines. He joined Stetson, Jennings & Russell in 1916 and was made partner in 1917 (Ralph Carson, *op. cit.*, p. 41). Denison evidently contracted a tropical disease while in the Philippines, though, and was increasingly despondent about his health. He withdrew from the partnership in August 1919 and committed suicide a few months later when he jumped before a subway train at Pennsylvania Station.

29. William H. Harbaugh, *op. cit.*, p. 183.

30. *Ibid.*, p. 183.

31. *Ibid.*, pp. 183–84.

32. *Ibid.*, p. 184.

33. Extrapolation from Davis' income from William H. Harbaugh, *op. cit.*, p. 259.

34. Ralph Carson, *op. cit.*, p. 48.

35. William H. Harbaugh, *op. cit.*, p. 259.

CHAPTER 12

1. See Fernand Lundberg, The Law Factories, *Harper's Magazine* (July 1939).

2. William H. Harbaugh, *op. cit.*, pp. 257–62.

3. Louis Auchincloss, *A Voice from Old New York* (Boston: Houghton Mifflin, 2010), pp. 3–5.

4. William H. Harbaugh, *op. cit.*, p. 255.

5. George Martin, *CCB: The Life and Century of Charles C. Burlingham, New York's First Citizen, 1858–1969* (New York: Farrar, Straus and Giroux, 2005), pp. 252–53.

6. William H. Harbaugh, *op. cit.*, p. 260.

7. Ralph Carson, *op. cit.*, p. 51.

8. Samuel F. Pryor, III, *My Interesting Life* (self-published, 2014), p. 91.

9. Louis Auchincloss, *op. cit.*, pp. 17–18.

10. They were Charles MacVeagh, Frank Polk, Edward R. Greene, Allen Wardwell, George Gardiner, Lansing P. Reed, Hall Park McCullough, William C. Cannon, Ogden L. Mills Jr., Joseph Howland Auchincloss, Edwin S. S. Sunderland, Thomas Garret Jr., and Lee McCanliss.

11. Ralph Carson, *op. cit.*, pp. 136, 138.

12. After inheriting their father's fortune, Mills and his sister became two of the country's greatest thoroughbred breeders. Seabiscuit and Bold Ruler were among their horses.

13. G. C. Hazard and A. Dondi, *Legal Ethics: A Comparative Study* (Stanford, CA: Stanford University Press, 2004), p. 158.

14. However, not all associates stood on their bets, and many of them left to start their own law forms. These included Chauncey Belknap (Patterson, Belknap & Webb); Eli Whitney Debevoise and, later, Marvin Lyons (Debevoise, Plimpton, Lyons & Gates), Morris Hadley (Milbank, Tweed, Hadley & McCloy), and Frederick Sheffield (Webster, Sheffield, Fleischmann, Hitchcock & Chrystie). In 1958, associate William Meagher left the firm to join the law office that became the legal juggernaut, Skadden, Arps, Slate, Meagher & Flom. Ralph Carson, *op. cit.*, pp. 128–39.

15. Louis Auchincloss, *op. cit.*, p. 4.

16. 1930 Federal Census, New York County, New York, Manhattan Enumeration District 31–0547, Sheet No. 16B.

17. 1930 Federal Census, New York County, New York, Manhattan Enumeration District 31–556, Sheet No. 3A.

18. *The Relation of Wealth to Morals*, The World's Work, Vol. 1 (New York: Doubleday, 1901), p. 287.

19. *The Diamond of Psi Upsilon*, Vol. 24, Issue 2 (New York Psi Upsilon Fraternity, January 1938), p. 100.

20. Louis Auchincloss, *The Great World and Timothy Colt* (Boston: Houghton Mifflin, 1957), p. 47; see Carol Gelderman , *op. cit.*, pp. 164–65.

21. *Ibid.*, p. 42.

22. Lawrence E. Walsh, *The Gift of Insecurity: A Lawyer's Life* (Washington, DC: American Bar Association, 2003), p. 88.

23. Samuel F. Pryor, *op. cit.*, p. 49.

24. William H. Harbaugh, *op. cit.*, pp. 259, 261.

25. *Ibid.*, pp. 354–55. The feeling was mutual. In a letter about judicial appointments to prominent New York lawyer Charles C. Burlingham, Roosevelt wrote: "Dig me up fifteen to twenty youthful Abraham Lincolns from Manhattan or the Bronx to choose from. They must be liberal from belief and not by lip service. They must have inherent contempt both for the John W. Davises and the Max Steuers. They must know what life in a tenement means. They must have no social ambition." George Martin, *op. cit.*, pp. 483–84.

26. *Ibid.*, p. 293–94.

27. *Ibid.*, p. 436.

28. This issue alone went up to the Supreme Court twice. *See Palmer v. Connecticut Railway & Lighting Company*, 311 U.S. 544 (1941); *Connecticut Railway & Lighting Company v. Palmer*, 305 U.S. 493 (1939).

29. The so-called *88 Stations* case, *Palmer v. Massachusetts*, 308 U.S. 79 (1939).

30. *Warren v. Palmer*, 310 U.S. 132 (1940).

31. *See* Charles Alan Wright, Review of A Brief History of the Reorganization of the New York, New Haven & Hartford Railroad Company, *Yale Law Journal*, Vol. 59, No. 6, 1191 (1950). Sunderland also wrote and privately published a history of the reorganization of the Illinois Central Railroad, Abraham Lincoln's involvement in the Illinois Central Railroad, and the Congregational Church of Cornwall, Vermont.

32. Lawrence E. Walsh, *op. cit.*, p. 88.

33. *Ibid.*

34. *Ibid., p.* 89.

35. William H. Harbaugh, *op. cit.*, p. 257.

36. 41 U.S. 1 (1846).

37. 304 U.S. 64 (1938). For a fascinating account of the background of *Erie v. Tompkins*, see Brian L. Frye, The Ballad of Harry James Tompkins, *Akron Law Review*, Vol. 52, Issue 2, Article 12 (2019). Frye suggests that Kiendl defended this position because the Erie itself, which had operations in several states, generally benefited from the regime of federal common law. *Ibid.*, pp. 576-77.

38. Lawrence E. Walsh, *op cit.*, pp. 93–94.

39. Ralph Carson, *op cit.*, p. 97.

40. 317 F.2d 19 (5th Cir. 1963).

41. Ralph Carson, *op. cit.,* pp. 78–79.

42. *Ibid.*, p. 79.

CHAPTER 13

1. Burton Hersh, *op. cit.*, p. 41; Townsend Hoopes, *op. cit.*, pp. 35–36; L & L. pp. 78–81; Peter Grose, *op. cit.*, p. 91; Townsend Hoopes, God and John Foster Dulles, *Foreign Policy*, No. 13 (Winter 1973–1974), p. 162.

2. Ron Chernow, *op. cit.*, p. 250; Stephen Kinzer, *op. cit.*, p. 51; L & L, pp. 81–83.

3. Frank C. Castigliola, Anglo-American Rivalry in the 1920s, *The Journal of Economic History*, Vol. 37, No. 4 (December 1977), p. 914; Ron Chernow, *op. cit.*, p. 248; L & L, p. 87.

4. William F. Wertz Jr., The Plot Against FDR: A Model for Bush's Pinochet Plan Today, *EIR History*, Vol. 32, No. 3 (January 21, 2005), pp. 21–22; Guido G. Preparata, *Conjuring Hitler* (London: Pluto Press, 2005), pp. 160–61.

5. Frank Costigliola, The United States and the Reconstruction of Germany in the 1920s, *The Business History Review*, Vol. 50, No. 4 (Winter 1976), p. 476; Ronald W. Pruessen, *op. cit.*, pp. 61–67.

6. Frank Costigliola, *op. cit.*, p. 495; L & L, pp. 90–91; Ron Chernow, *op. cit.*, p. 249; Stephen Kinzer, *op. cit.*, pp. 49–50.

7. Burton Hersh, *op. cit.*, pp. 42–43; L & L, pp. 92–94; Ronald W. Pruessen, *op. cit.*, pp. 65–72; David Talbot, *The Devil's Chessboard* (New York: Harper Perennial, 2015), pp. 18–19; Christopher Simpson, *Splendid Blond Beast* (London: Grove Press, 1993), p. 41; Stephen Kinzer, *op. cit.*, p. 38; Guido Preparata, *op. cit.*, p. 166.

8. David Talbot, *The Devil's Chessboard* (New York: Harper Collins, 2016).

9. Ronald W. Pruessen, *op. cit.*, pp. 126–31; David Talbot, *op. cit.*, p. 19; Antony C. Sutton, *Wall Street and the Rise of Hitler* (San Pedro, CA: GSG & Associates, 2002), pp. 34–35; William F. Wertz Jr., *op. cit.*, p. 22; Stephen Kinzer, *op. cit.*, pp. 50–51; John F. Dulles, Our Foreign Loan Policy, *Foreign Affairs (*October 1926); Olga Chetverikova, *Oriental Review*,

Secret Run to World II: The Responsibility of the West, April 13, 2010; Glen Yeadon, *The Nazi Hydra in America* (York, PA: Progressive, 2008), p. 116.

10. Stephen Kinzer, *op. cit.*, p. 37; L & L, pp. 99–101; Ronald W. Preussen, *op. cit.*, p. 73.

11. Leonard Mosley, *A Biography of Eleanor, Allen and John Foster Dulles and Their Family Network* (New York: The Dial Press, (1978), pp. 39–61, 76–77; Stephen Kinzer, *op. cit.*, pp. 39–40; Peter Grose, *op. cit.*, pp. 16, 88–93; Burton Hersh, *op. cit.*, pp. 44–45; Stephen Kinzer, *op. cit.*, pp. 38–39.

12. David Talbot, *The Devil's Chessboard* (New York: Harper Collins, 2016).

13. Stephen Kinzer, *op. cit.*, p. 42.

14. Leonard Mosley, *op. cit.*, pp. 60, 76; Burton Hersh, *op. cit.*, pp. 23, 45–46; Peter Grose, *op. cit.*, p. 15; Stephen Kinzer, *op. cit.*, pp. 43–44; Robin Winks, The Wise Man of Intelligence: Uncovering the Life of Allen Dulles, *Foreign Affairs*, Vol. 73, No. 6 (November-December 1994), p. 147; Anthony C. Sutton, *op. cit.*, pp. 81–82; Townsend Hoopes, *op. cit.*, p. 40; George F. Kennan, *Memoirs 1950–1963* (New York: Pantheon Books, 1972), p. 183; David Talbot, *op. cit.*, p. 126.

15. L & L, pp. 106–7; Stephen Kinzer, *op. cit.*, pp. 42–43; Leonard Mosley, *op. cit.*, p. 80; Richard Goolde-Adams, *John Foster Dulles: A Reappraisal* (New York: Appleton-Century-Crofts, 1962), p. 29; David Talbot, *op. cit.*, p. 126.

16. Stephen Kinzer, *op. cit.*, pp. 40–41; Peter Grose, *op. cit.*, pp. 96–102; David Talbot, *op. cit.*, pp. 3–4; James Srodes, *Allen Dulles Master of Spies* (Washington, DC: Regnery Publishing, Inc., 1999), p. 167; Burton Hersh, *op. cit.*, p. 46.

17. Ronald W. Pruessen, *op. cit.*, p. 135; Frank Costigliola, *op. cit.*, pp. 499–500; Charles P. Kindelberger, *The World in Depression* (Berkeley: University of California Press, 1986), p. 68.

18. Ronald W. Pruessen, *op. cit.*, pp. 106–7; Adam Lebor, *Tower of Basel: The Shadowy History of the Bank that Rules the World* (New York: Hachette, 2013), p. 24; Stephen Kinzer, *op. cit.*, pp. 51–52; Zara Steiner, *The Lights That Failed* (Oxford, UK: Oxford University Press, 2005), pp. 472–73; Peter Grose, *op. cit.*, p. 120.

19. Ronald Pruessen, *op. cit.*, pp. 107–10; Stephen Kinzer, *op. cit.*, p. 50; Harold James, The Causes of the German Banking Crisis of 1931, *The Economic History Review*, Vol. 37, No. 1 (February 1984), p. 69; Beth A. Simmons, Why Innovate? Funding the Bank for International Settlements, *World Politics*, Vol. 45, No. 3 (April 1993), p. 359; L & L, p. 120.

20. Stephen Kinzer, *op. cit.*, p. 51; Ronald W. Pruessen, *op. cit.*, pp. 148–50; L & L, pp. 122–23; Guido G. Preparata, *op. cit.*, p. 214; Ron Chernow, *op. cit.*, p. 395; William F. Wertz Jr., *op. cit.*, p. 25.

21. Burton Hersh, *op. cit.*, pp. 64–65; L & L, pp. 95, 107, 132; William F. Wertz Jr., *op. cit.*, p. 31; Peter Grose, *op. cit.*, p. 122.

22. L & L, pp. 133–34; Burton Hersh, *op. cit.*, p. 65; James Srodes, *op. cit.*, p. 185; Ronald W. Pruessen, *op. cit.*, p. 125;

23. Burton Hersh, *op. cit.*, pp. 66–67; Guido Preparata, *op. cit.*, p. 200; James Srodes, *op. cit.*, p. 163; Martin Ehrman, *Building the Kingdom of God on Earth: The Churches' Contribution to Marshall Public Support for World Order and Peace, 1919–1945* (Eugene, OR: Wipf and Stock Publishers, 2005), pp. 91–93; Arthur M. Schlesinger Jr., *The Crisis of the Old Order* (Boston: Houghton-Mifflin, 2002), p. 7; Vincent P. Carosso, A Financial Elite: New York's German-Jewish Investment Bankers, *American Jewish History Quarterly*, Vol. 66, No. 1 (September 1976), p. 85; Ronald W. Pruessen, *op. cit.*, pp. 125–26.

24. Walter Isaacson and Evan Thomas, *The Wise Men* (New York: Simon & Schuster, 1986), p. 560.

25. Christopher Simpson, *op. cit.*, pp. 55–56; Stephen Kinzer, *op. cit.*, p. 50; Anthony C. Sutton, *op. cit.*, pp. 153–54; Glen Yeadon and John Hawkins, *The Nazi Hydra in America* (Online: Progressive, 2008), p. 117; Townsend Hoopes, *op. cit.*, pp. 46–47; Ronald W. Pruessen, *op. cit.*, pp. 122–32; L & L, p. 139.

26. Peter Grose, *op. cit.*, pp. 134–35; Glen Yeadon and John Hawkins, *op. cit.*, pp. 118–19; Gerhard Aalders and Cees Wiebes, Stockholm's Enskilda Bank, German Bosch and I.G. Farben. A Short History of Cloaking, *Scandinavian Economic History*, Vol. 33, No. 1 (1985), pp. 33–34; Ulf Olsson, Stockholm's Enskilda Bank and the Bosch Group, 1939–50, *Banking and Enterprise* No. 1, Stockholm, 1998, *passim*; Christopher Simpson, *op. cit.*, p. 57; L & L, pp. 146–59; David Talbot, *op. cit.*, p. 29.

27. John Kenneth Galbraith, *The Affluent Society* (New York: The Library of America, 2010), p. 235.

28. *Legal History Blog*, June 13, 2008.

29. Arthur H. Dean, *William Nelson Cromwell*, 1854-1948, (Middleton, WI: Ad Press, Ltd., 1957), p. 83.

30. Carol Gelderman, *op. cit.*, p. 93.

CHAPTER 14

1. This, of course, did not happen, infuriating Untermyer, who thereafter lobbied to unseat Pecora. Michael Perino, *Hellhound of Wall Street* (London: Penguin 2010), pp. 52–53, 282–83.

2. Arthur E. Wilmarth, Jr., Prelude to Glass-Steagall: Abusive Securities Practices by National City Bank and Chase National Bank in the Roaring Twenties, *Tulane Law Review*, Vol. 90 (2016), pp, 1306-20; Michael Perino, *op. cit.*, pp. 165-66, 180–81.

3. Michael Perino, *op. cit.*, pp. 232–33, 165–66, 180–81, 147, 153–54, 192–83, 274–75; Arthur E. Wilmarth, *op. cit.*, p. 1324.

4. Arthur E. Wilmarth, *op. cit.*, pp. 1325-26.

5. *Ibid.*

6. Hearings Before the Senate Committee on Banking & Currency on S. Res 84 and S. Res. 56, United States Senate, 73rd Cong., 1st Sess., Part 1, p. 25 (Leffingwell) (May 23, 1933).

7. Hearings Before the Senate Committee on Banking & Currency on S. Res 84 and S. Res. 56, United States Senate, 73rd Cong., 1st Sess., Part 2., p. 819 (Montgomery Angell) (June 9, 1933).

8. William H. Harbaugh, *op. cit.*, pp. 323–24.

9. However, Morgan became the victim of a publicity stunt that quietly infuriated him. On the eve of Jack Morgan's testimony, aged Virginia Senator Carter Glass criticized Pecora, snapping, "We are having a circus, and the only things lacking now are peanuts and colored lemonade" (Michael Perino, *op. cit.*, p. 286). This was too good a chance for any authentic circus to pass up; and, a week later, a promoter from Ringling Brothers brought a 27-inch female dwarf, Lya Graf, to the hearings. Graf shook hands with Jack Morgan and then jumped into his lap. This happened in the presence of a prearranged battery of photographers, whose images made Morgan seem a kindly old man smiling at a little girl. This angered the committee, embarrassed Morgan, and delighted the general public. But the result was tragic for Graf. Tired of persistent joking about the episode, she returned to her native Germany. There, being a dwarf and half-Jewish, she was deemed a "useless person" by the Nazi regime and murdered in the gas chambers of Auschwitz. *Ibid.*

10. Hearings Before the Senate Committee on Banking & Currency on S. Res 84 and S. Res. 56, United States Senate, 73rd Cong., 1st Sess., Part 1, pp. 3–6 (J. P. Morgan) (May 23, 1933).

11. *Ibid.*, pp. 71–72.

12. William H. Harbaugh, *op. cit.*, p. 328–29.

13. Although, in fact, it was not. The IRS subsequently ordered Lamont to pay back taxes, plus interest. William H. Harbaugh, *op. cit.*, p. 330.

14. *Ibid.*, pp. 330–31.

15. Michael Perino, *op. cit.*, p. 274.

16. William H. Harbaugh, *op. cit.*, pp. 331, and note 37.

17. *Ibid.*, pp. 331-32.

18. Hearings Before the Senate Committee on Banking & Currency on S. Res 84 and S. Res. 56, United States Senate, 73rd Cong., 1st Sess., Part 1, pp. 138–39 (May 24, 1933) (Allegheny Corporation), 220–21 (May 25, 1933) (Standard Brands); William H. Harbaugh, *op. cit.*, p. 331.

19. John H. Wood, Who Governs: Legislatures, Bureaucracies or Markets, *Palgrave Studies in American History* (2020), p. 111.

20. Michael Perino, *op. cit.*, p. 290, quoting Joel Seligman.

21. Ron Chernow, *op. cit.*, p. 375.

22. Daniel R. Ernst, *Lawyers, Bureaucratic Autonomy and Securities Regulation During the New Deal* (Washington, DC: Georgetown University Press, 2009), p. 6.

23. Ralph Carson, *op. cit.*, p. 75.

24. *Ibid.*, pp. 75-76.

25. *Morgan Stanley & Co. v. Securities Exchange Com'n*, 126 F.2d 325 (2d Cir. 1942).

26. Ralph Carson, *op. cit.*, p. 76.

27. William D. Whitney, The Investment Bankers Case, *Yale Law Journal*, Vol. 64, 873 (1955).

28. *United States v. Morgan,* 118 F. Supp. 621, 829 (S.D.N.Y. 1953); Victor A. Kramer, The Trial of the Investment Banking Case, *Litigation,* Vol. 14, No. 4 (Summer 1985), pp. 43–46, 59–60; Swaine II, p. 735; Carol Gelderman, *op. cit.*, p. 104; William D. Whitney, The Investment Bankers' Case Including a Reply to Professor Steffen, *Yale Law Journal*, Vol. 64, Issue 3, pp. 319–44.

CHAPTER 15

1. Swaine II, pp. 326–30, 449–50; David M. Kennedy, What the New Deal Did, *Political Science Quarterly*, Vol. 124, no. 2 (Summer 2009), pp. 261–62.

2. William H. Harbaugh, *op cit.,* p. 521.

3. 295 U.S. 555 (1935).

4. 301 U.S. 103 (1937).

5. Swaine II, pp. 696-97.

6. Ronen Shamir, *Managing Legal Uncertainty* (Durham, NC: Duke University Press, 1995), p. 67.

7. William H. Harbaugh, *op. cit.*, pp. 367–70.

8. Stephen Kinzer, *The Brothers* (New York: St. Martin's Griffin, 2013), p. 55.

9. Swaine II, pp. 326–30, 449–50; Kennedy, *What the New Deal Did* (2009).

10. Swaine II, pp. 326–30.

11. Eugene V. Rostow, Bituminous Coal and the Public Interest, 50 *Yale Law Journal* 543 (1941), p. 94.

12. Robert E. Cushman, Constitutional Law in 1934–35: The Constitutional Decisions of the Supreme Court of the United States in the October Term, 1934, *The American Political Science Review*, Vol. 30, No. 1 (February 1936), pp. 59–60; Robert L. Stern, The Commerce Clause and the National Economy, 1933–1946, *Harvard Law Review*, Vol. 59, No. 5 (May 1946), pp. 653–54; Eugene V. Rostow, Bituminous Coal and the Public Interest, *Yale Law Journal,* Vol. 50, No. 4 (February 1941), p. 561.

13. See following note.

14. Arthur M. Schlesinger, *The Politics of Upheaval* (New York: Houghton Mifflin Company, 1960), p. 277.

15. Philip Dray, *There Is Power in a Union* (New York: Anchor Books, 2011), pp. 447–48; H. Peter Irons, *The New Deal Lawyers* (Princeton, NJ: Princeton University Press, 1993), pp. 90–100; Arthur M. Schlesinger Jr., *op. cit.*, pp. 283–85, 518.

16. Arthur M. Schlesinger Jr., *op. cit.*, 277–87, 518; Michael Hiltzik, *op. cit.*, pp. 283–84.

17. Robert L. Stern, The Commerce Clause and the National Economy, 1933–1946, *Harvard Law Review*, Vol. 59, No. 5 (May 1946), pp. 664–67; Swaine II, pp. 564–65.

18. See following note.

19. Swaine II, pp. 564–65; Robert L. Stern, *op. cit.*, pp. 669–70.

20. *United States v. Darby Lumber Co.*, 312 U.S. 100 (1941); *United States v. Wrightwood Dairy Co.*, 315 U.S. 110 (1942); *Wickard v. Filburn*, 317 U.S. 111 (1942).

21. Ronen Shamir, *Managing Legal Uncertainty* (Durham, NC: Duke University Press, 1995), pp. 92, 170; Swaine II, pp. 564–67.

22. John Hupper and Bruce Bromley, *Historical Society of the New York Courts, New York Legal History/Legal Luminaries* (1980); Marc Galanter, Lawyers in the Mist: The Golden Age of Legal Nostalgia, *Dickinson Law Review*, Vol. 122 (2007), pp. 273–74; Samantha Barbas, When Privacy Almost Won: Time, Inc. v. Hill, *University of Pennsylvania Journal of Constitutional Law*, Vol. 18 (2015), p. 528; David Margolick, The Law; At the Bar, *The New York Times,* May 20, 1988; Bruce Bromley, Judicial Control of Antitrust Cases, *Proceedings of the Seminar on Protracted Cases for United States Judges*, 23 F.R.D. (1958), pp. 417–18; Swaine II, pp. 611–14.

23. John Hupper, *op. cit.*; Samantha Barbas, The Esquire Case: A Lost Free Speech Landmark, *William & Mary Bill of Rights Journal,* Vol. 27 (2018), pp. 321–25, 351; Swaine II, pp. 615–16.

24. John Hupper, *op. cit.*; *Dorsey v. Stuyvesant Town Corp.,* 299 N.Y. 512 (N.Y. 1949).

CHAPTER 16

1. Arthur H. Dean, *op. cit.*, p. 75.

2. Burton Hersh, *op. cit.*, pp. 48–50; James Srodes, *op. cit.*, pp. 180–87; Stephen Kinzer, *op. cit.*, pp. 57–60; Daniel J. Linke, Hamilton Fish Armstrong: The Diplomatic Editor and Anti-Nazism in the 1930s, *The Princeton University Library Chronicle*, vol. 61, no. 2 (Winter 2000), pp. 145–69; Arthur H. Dean, *op. cit.*, p. 75; Ira Katznelson, *Fear Itself* (New York: Liveright Publishing Corporation, 2013), p. 319; Leonard Mosley, *op. cit.*, p. 108.

3. Martin Erdman, *Building the Kingdom of God on Earth* (Eugene OR: Wipf & Stock Publishers, 2005), p. 89.

4. John Foster Dulles, *War, Peace and Change* (New York: Harper, 1939).

5. Leonard Mosley, *Dulles* (New York: The Dial Press, 1978), pp. 95–100; Townsend Hoopes, *op. cit.*, pp. 46–52; Ronald W. Pruessen, *op. cit.*, pp. 154–61, 183; L & L, pp. 136–41; Peter Grose, *op. cit.*, pp. 131–33; Stephen Kinzer, *op. cit.*, p. 58.

6. Stephen Kinzer, *The Brothers* (New York: St. Martin's Griffin, 2013), p. 77.

7. Michael A. Davis, *Politics as Usual: Franklin Roosevelt, Thomas Dewey and the Wartime Presidential Campaign of 1944*, PhD thesis, University of Arkansas (2005), p. 104; Townsend Hoopes, *op. cit.*, pp. 53–61; Richard H. Immerman, *op. cit.*, pp. 20–26; Stephen Kinzer, *op. cit.*, pp. 58; L & L, p. 227.

8. Burton Hersh, *The American Elite and the Origin of the CIA*, (New York: Scribners, 1992), p. 90.

9. Stephen Kinzer, *op. cit.*, pp. 60–68; Burton Hersh, *op. cit.*, p. 77; Peter Grose, *op. cit.*, pp. 139–52; James Srodes, *op. cit.*, pp. 201–8; Leonard Mosley, *op. cit.*, pp. 104–15; David Talbot, *op. cit.*, p. 21.

10. *Beyond Rosie: A Documentary History of Women and World War II* (Fayetteville: University of Arkansas Press, 2015), p. xx.

11. L & L, pp. 144–45; Arthur H. Dean, *op. cit.*, pp. 50–51; Cynthia Grant Bowman, Women in the Legal Profession from the 1920s to the 1970s: What Can We Learn From their Experience About Law and Social Change? *Maine Law Review*, Vol. 61 (2009), pp. 6–7.

12. David Halberstam, The New Establishment: The Decline and Fall of the Eastern Empire, *Vanity Fair* (October 1994).

13. David Halberstam, The New Establishment: The Decline and Fall of the Eastern Empire, *Vanity Fair*, April 4, 2011; Progressive Hypocrisy at the Highest Levels: The Cast of Paul Weiss, *Manhattan Contrarian*, December 20, 2018.

14. Richard D. Challener, John Foster Dulles: The Princeton Connection, *The Princeton University Library Chronicle*, Vol. 50, No. 1 (Autumn 1988), pp. 21–23; Mark G. Toulouse, The Development of a Cold Warrior: John Foster Dulles and the Soviet Union, 1945–1952, *American Presbyterian*, Vol. 63, No. 3 (Fall 1985), p. 309; Ronald. W. Pruessen, Woodrow Wilson to John Foster Dulles: A Legacy, *The Princeton University Library Chronicle*, vol. 34, no. 2 (Winter 1973), p. 125; Anna Kasten Nelson, John Foster Dulles and the Bipartisan Congress, *Political Science Quarterly*, Vol. 103, No. 1 (Spring 1987), p. 45; L & L, p. 163; Richard H. Immerman, *op. cit.*, pp. 28–33; Townsend Hoopes, *op. cit.*, pp. 62–88; Leonard Mosley, *op. cit.*, pp. 214–21; David Talbot, *op. cit.*, pp. 168–71, 198; Stephen Kinzer, *op. cit.*, p. 95.

15. David Talbot, *op. cit.*, pp. 144–47, 166–71, 198; Burton Hersh, *op. cit.*, pp. 160, 217–19, 254–55, 264–66, 283–84, 292; James Srodes, *op. cit.*, pp. 355, 388–89, 397, 430–33; Stephen Kinzer, *op. cit.*, pp. 86–90, 97, 108; David F. Rudgers, The Origins of Covert Action, *Journal of Contemporary History*, Vol. 35, No. 2 (April 2000), p. 259.

16. L & L, pp. 161–62; Arthur Dean, *op. cit.*, p. 148.

CHAPTER 17

1. William H. Harbaugh, *op. cit.*, p. 425.
2. Russian War Relief Shift, *The New York Times*, January 8, 1942, p. 12.
3. Ralph Carson, *op. cit.*, p. 83.
4. *Ibid.*, p. 84.

5. Sam Pryor III, *Make it Happen: The Fascinating Life of Sam Pryor Jr.* (privately published, 2008), p. 121; *Davis Polk Wardwell Sunderland & Kiendl Firm Biographical Directory* (privately published, 1954) ("*DPWSK Biographical Directory*").

6. Ralph Carson, *op. cit.*, p. 83; *DPWSK Biographical Directory*, pp. 15–16.

7. Ibid., 14–15.

8. Ralph Carson, *op. cit.*, pp. 83–84n97.

9. Historical Society of the New York Courts, Oral History Program, Interview of Robert B. Fiske, Jr., p. 21 (December. 1, 2015).

10. Samuel F. Pryor, III, *op. cit.*, p. 48.

11. *Ibid.*, p. 46.

12. *Ibid.*

13. The job of receptionist at a downtown law firm had, by now, also changed. Attractive young women from established families and often the daughters of clients or prominent lawyers from other firms, now filled the position. There were any number of romances, if not marriages, between young lawyers and receptionists.

14. Samuel F. Pryor, III, *op. cit.*, pp. 47–48.

15. 343 U.S. 579 (1952).

16. William H. Harbaugh, *op. cit.*, p. 482.

17. 347 U.S. 483 (1954).

18. William H. Harbaugh, *op. cit.*, pp. 487–88, 501.

19. *Ibid.*, p. 484.

20. *Ibid.*, pp. 483, 494–95.

21. *Ibid.*, p. 507.

22. Samuel F. Pryor, *op. cit.*, p. 48.

23. 163 U.S. 537 (1896).

24. William H. Harbaugh, *op. cit.*, p. 487–88.

25. *Ibid.*, p. 484–87.

26. 347 U.S. at 486 n.1.

27. 28 U.S.C. § 2281 (1948).

28. 28 U.S.C. § 1253.

29. Byrnes is the only person to have served as a U.S. Congressman, Senator, Cabinet officer (Secretary of State, 1945–1947), Justice of the United States Supreme Court, and Governor of a state. He also was a close aide to Franklin Roosevelt, who relied upon Byrnes so extensively that the press called Byrnes the "Assistant President."

30. William H. Harbaugh, *op. cit.*, pp. 487–88.

31. *Ibid.*, p. 491.

32. *Ibid.*, pp. 483–84.

33. 342 U.S. 350 (1952).

34. 47 U.S. at pp. 486–7, n. 1.

35. 163 U.S. at pp. 552; William H. Harbaugh, *op. cit.*, 492n14.

36. *Ibid.*, p. 507.

37. 345 U.S. 972.

38. William H. Harbaugh, *op. cit.*, p. 516.

39. 347 U.S. at 495.

40. William H. Harbaugh, *op. cit.*, p. 518.

41. Samuel F. Pryor, III, *op. cit.*, p. 55.

42. Louis Auchincloss, *The Great World and Timothy Colt, passim.*

43. Lawrence E. Walsh, *op. cit.*, p. 194.

44. His twin brother was Paul Bator, an expert on federal courts and procedure who taught for many years at Harvard Law School. The brothers graduated from Harvard Law School two years apart. It was said that they agreed between themselves that they would enter in different Law School classes so that each of them could be first in the class.

45. Ralph Carson, *op. cit.*, p. 99.

46. *Yearbook for Samuel J. Tilden High School*, 1945, p. 58.

47. Ralph Carson, *op. cit.*, p. 100.

48. Meanwhile, associates who had been passed over for partnership resided on the east side of the 43rd floor, which came to be called "the Departure Lounge."

49. Lawrence E. Walsh, *op. cit.*, p. 194.

CHAPTER 18

1. See following note.

2. Connie Bruck and Alan Dershowitz, Advocate, *The New Yorker*, July 29, 2019.

3. Milton S. Gould, Looking Back on the New York Bar, *Litigation*, Vol. 14, No. 1, Examining Witnesses (Fall 1987), pp. 43–44, 60–61; Robert W. Merry, America's First Elites, *The American Conservative*, November 25, 2018; E. Digby Baltzell, *The Protestant Establishment: Aristocracy and Caste in America* (1964). Although Gould recalls events fifty years before publication, his description is also true of the 1940s, 1950s, and beyond.

4. John Weir Close, The Lucky Sperm Club: Jews, M & A and the Unlocking of Corporate America, *PBS News Hour*, January 2, 2014.

5. See following note.

6. Eli Wald, The Rise and Fall of the WASP and Jewish Law Firms, *Stanford Law Review,* Vol. 60, Issue 6 (2008), pp. 1803–66; Jerold S. Auerbach, From Rags to Riches: The Legal Profession, Social Mobility and the American Jewish Experience, *American Jewish Historical Quarterly,* Vol. 66, No. 2 (December 1976), pp. 261–62; Larissa McFarquhar, East Side Story, *The New Yorker,* February 12, 2008.

7. *Ibid.*

8. *Ibid.*

9. *Ibid.*

10. Eli Wald, The Rise and Fall of the WASP and Jewish Law Firms, 60 *Stanford Law Review* (2010), p. 1803 et seq.

11. *Ibid.*

12. Francis Menton, Is Lack of "Diversity" at Big Law Firms a Crisis, *Manhattan Contrarian,* June 5, 2014.

13. See following note.

14. Tomiko Brown-Nagin, Identity Matters: The Case of Constance Baker Motley, *Columbia Law Review,* Vol. 117, No. 7 (November 2017), pp. 1707–12; Cynthia Grant Bowman, Women in the Legal Profession from the 1920s the 1970s: What Can We Learn from Their Experience About Law and Social Change, *Maine Law Review,* vol. 61 (2009), p. 9; Eli Wald, The Changing Professional Landscape of Large Law Firms, Glass Ceilings and Dead Ends: Professional Ideologies, Gender Stereotypes, and the Future of Women Lawyers at Large Law Firms, *Fordham Law Review,* vol. 78 (2010), pp. 2245–88.

15. See following note.

16. Cynthia Grant Bowman, *op. cit.*, p. 15; Elizabeth Olson, A Bleak Picture for Women Trying to Rise at Law Firms, *The New York Times,* July 24, 2017.

17. See following note.

18. David B. Wilkins, From Separate Is Inherently Unequal to Diversity Is Good for Business: The Rise of Market-Based Diversity Arguments and the Fate of the Black Corporate Bar, *Harvard Law Review*, vol. 117, no. 5 (March 2004), pp. 1548–1615.

19. See following note.

20. Elizabeth Olson, Many Black Lawyers Navigate a Rocky, Lonely Road to Partner, *The New York Times,* August 12, 2015; Elizabeth H. Gorman and Fiona M. Kay, Racial and Ethnic Minority Representation in Large U.S. Law Firms in *Law Firms, Legal Culture, and Legal Practice,* Austin Sarat, ed. (Bingley, UK: Emerald Group Publishing Ltd., 2010), p. 215; J. Cunyon Gordon, Painting by Numbers "And, Um, Let's Have a Black Lawyer Sit At Our Table," *Fordham Law Review*, Vol. 71, Issue 4 (2003), p. 1257 *et seq.*; Renwei Chung, High Minority Attrition Rates Continue to Plague Large Law Firms, *Above the Law,* March 11, 2016; Andrew Bruck and Andrew Canter, Supply, Demand and the Changing Economics of Large Law Firms, *Stanford Law Review*, Vol. 60, No. 6 (April 2008), p. 2090.

21. Sara Randazzo, The Flip Side of Making Partner, *The Wall Street Journal,* August 10, 2019, p. B1.

22. Marc Galantner and Thomas Palay, *op cit.*, p. 136; James Stewart, *The Partners* (New York: Warner Books, 1984), pp. 53–113; Eli Wald, The Changing Professional Landscape of Large Law Firms, Glass Ceilings and Dead Ends: Professional Ideologies, Gender Stereotypes, and the Future of Women Lawyers at Large Firms, *Fordham Law Review,* Vol. 78, Issue 5 (2010), pp. 2272–73; Adam Liptak, Thomas Barr, Top Lawyer in I. B. M. Case Dies at 77, *The New York Times,* January 30, 2008.

23. Robert Armstrong, New York, Once the City of Dreamers, is Now Dangerously Dull, *Financial Times,* Life & Arts, p. 4, June 29–30, 2019.

Bibliography

Aalders, Gerhard, and Cees Wiebes, Stockholm's Enskilda Bank, German Bosch and I.G. Farben. A Short History of Cloaking, *Scandinavian Economic History*, vol. 33, no. 1 (1985), pp. 33–34.

Acheson, Dean, *Fragments of My Fleece* (George J. McLeod Ltd., 1971).

Ahamed, Liaquat, *Lords of Finance* (New York: The Penguin Press, 2009).

The Albany Journal, September 16, 1887.

Alger, George W., Review of the Cravath Firm and Its Predecessors: 1819–1947, *American Bar Association Journal*, vol. 1, no. 5 (May 1947).

Alger, George W., The Cravath Firm and Its Predecessors, *American Bar Association Journal*, vol. 31, no. 5 (May 1947), pp. 480–82.

Alvey, Lori J., *The War of the Currents: Examining the History Behind The Last Days of Night*, Kentucky Bar Association (June 14, 2018).

America's Devious Dream: Roosevelt and the Panama Canal, *BBC History Magazine*, November 2006.

Ameringer, Charles D., The Panama Canal Lobby of Philippe Bunau-Varilla and William Nelson Cromwell, *The American Historical Review*, vol. 68, no. 2 (January 1963), pp. 346–46.

Armstrong, Robert, New York, Once the City of Dreamers, is Now Dangerously Dull, *Financial Times*, Life & Arts, p. 4, June 29–30, 2019.

Arnold, Thurman, *The Folklore of Capitalism* (New Haven, CT: Yale University Press, 1937).

Auerbach, Jerold S., From Rags to Riches: The Legal Profession, Social Mobility and the American Jewish Experience, *American Jewish Historical Quarterly*, vol. 66, no. 2 (December 1976), pp. 261–62.

Auerbach, Joseph, *The Bar of Other Days* (New York: Harper & Brothers, 1940).

Auchincloss, Louis S., *A Voice from Old New York* (Boston: Houghton Mifflin, 2010).

Auchincloss, Louis, *The Great World and Timothy Colt* (Boston: Houghton Mifflin, 1957).

Baird, Douglas G., and Robert K. Rasmussen, Boyd's Legacy and Blackstone's Ghost, Sup. Ct. Rev. (1999), pp. 393, 401–8.

Baltzell, E. Digby, *The Protestant Establishment: Aristocracy and Caste in America* (1964).

Bangs, Francis S., Leading Lawyer, Dies, *New York Times*, March 3, 1920, p. 11.

Barbas, Samantha, When Privacy Almost Won: *Time, Inc. v. Hill*, *University of Pennsylvania Journal of Constitutional Law*, vol. 18 (2015), p. 528.

Barbas, Samantha, The Esquire Case: A Lost Free Speech Landmark, *William & Mary Bill of Rights Journal*, vol. 27 (2018), pp. 321–25, 351.

Berfield, Susan, *The Hour of Fate: Theodore Roosevelt, J. P. Morgan and the Battle to Transform American Capitalism* (Bloomsbury, NY: Tin House Books, 2020).

Berle, Review of Beryl Harold Levy's Corporation Lawyer . . . Saint or Sinner? The New Role of the Lawyer in Modern Society, *Harvard Law Review*, vol. 76, 432 (1962).

Bird, Kai, *The Chairman* (New York: Simon & Schuster, 1992).

Borkin, Joseph, *The Corrupt Judge* (Clarkson N. Porter, Inc., 1962).

Bowman, Cynthia Grant, Women in the Legal Profession from the 1920s to the 1970s: What Can We Learn From their Experience About Law and Social Change? *Maine Law Review*, vol. 61 (2009), pp. 6–7.

Bradley, Robert L Jr., *Edison to Enron* (Beverly, MA: Scrivener Publishing, 2011).

Brandeis, Louis D., *Other People's Money* (New York: Frederick A. Stokes Co., 1914).

Bratton, William W., and David A. Skeel Jr., Bankruptcy's New and Old Frontiers, 166 *University of Pennsylvania Law Review*, vol. 166, no. 7 (June 2008), pp. 1576–79.

Brian, Denis, *Pulitzer: A Life* (New York: Wiley, 2007).

Bromley, Bruce, Judicial Control of Antitrust Cases, *Proceedings of the Seminar on Protracted Cases for United States Judges*, 23 F.R.D. (1958), pp. 417–18.

Brown, Henry Collins, *Glimpses of Old New-York* (New York: Lent & Graff, 1917).

Brown-Nagin, Tomiko, Identity Matters: The Case of Constance Baker Motley, *Columbia Law Review*, vol. 117, no. 7 (November 2017), pp. 1707–12.

Bruck, Andrew, and Andrew Canter, Supply, Demand and the Changing Economics of Large Law Firms, *Stanford Law Review*, vol. 60, no. 6 (April 2008), p. 2090.

Bruck, Connie, and Alan Dershowitz, Advocate, *The New Yorker*, July 29, 2019.

Burrows, Edward G., and Mike Wallace, *Gotham* (Oxford, UK: Oxford University Press, 1999).

Carlisle, J. M., *The Cowboy and the Canal* (London: Tangent Publishers, 2014).

Carosso, Vincent P., *The Morgans* (Cambridge, MA: Harvard University Press, 1987).

Carosso, Vincent P., A Financial Elite: New York's German-Jewish Investment Bankers, *American Jewish History Quarterly*, vol. 66, no. 1 (September 1976), p. 85.

Carson, Ralph, *Davis Polk Wardwell Sunderland & Kiendl, A Background with Figures*, (Privately published, n.d.).

Castigliola, Frank C., Anglo-American Rivalry in the 1920s, *The Journal of Economic History*, vol. 37, no. 4 (December 1977), p. 914.

Castigliola, Frank, The United States and the Reconstruction of Germany in the 1920s, *The Business History Review*, vol. 50, no. 4 (Winter, 1976), p. 476.

Challener, Richard D., John Foster Dulles: The Princeton Connection, *The Princeton University Library Chronicle*, vol. 50, no. 1 (Autumn 1988), pp. 21–23.

Chernow, Ron, *The House of Morgan* (New York: Grove Press, 1990).

Chetverikova, Olga, *Oriental Review*, April 13, 2010.

Chung, Renwei, High Minority Attrition Rates Continue to Plague Large Law Firms, *Above the Law*, March 11, 2016.

Close, John Weir, The Lucky Sperm Club: Jews, M & A and the Unlocking of Corporate America, PBS News Hour, January 2, 2014.

The Commercial & Financial Chronicle, vol. 74 (William B. Dana Company, 1902).

Crane, Daniel, The Dissociation of Incorporation and Regulation in the Progressive Era and the New Deal," in *Corporations and American Democracy*, Naomi Lamoreaux and William J. Novak, eds. (Cambridge, MA: Harvard University Press, 2017).

Cushman, Robert E., Constitutional Law in 1934–35: The Constitutional Decisions of the Supreme Court of the United States in the October Term, 1934, *The American Political Science Review*, vol. 30, no. 1 (February 1936), pp. 59–60.

Daggett, Stuart, Railroad Reorganization, *Harvard Economic Studies*, Vol. IV (New York: Houghton, Mifflin & Co., 1908).

Davis, Michael A., Politics as Usual: Franklin Roosevelt, Thomas Dewey and the Wartime Presidential Campaign of 1944, PhD thesis, University of Arkansas (2005).

Dean, Arthur, *John Foster Dulles, An Appreciation* (Publisher unknown, 1959).

Dean, Arthur H., *William Nelson Cromwell, 1854–1948* (New York: Ad Press, 1957).

Despino, Ovidio Diaz, *How Wall Street Created a Nation* (New York: Four Walls Eight Windows, 2001).

The Diamond of Psi Upsilon, vol. 24, issue 2, New York Psi Upsilon Fraternity (1938), p. 100.

"Dog Eat Dog: The Laws of War in American History," https://erenow.com/ww/lincolns code the laws of war in American history.

Dolan, John A., Hale and Dorr: Background & Styles (Boston: Hale and Dorr, 1993).

Dray, Philip, *There Is Power in a Union* (New York: Anchor Books, 2011).

Dulles, John F., Our Foreign Loan Policy, *Foreign Affairs,* October 1926.

Edwards, George, Commentary on Judicial Ethics, *Fordham Law Review*, vol. 38, issue 2 (1969), pp. 269–70.

Ehrman, Martin, Building the Kingdom of God on Earth: The Churches' Contribution to Marshall Public Support for World Order and Peace, 1919–1945 (Eugene, OR: Wipf and Stock, Publishers, 2005).

Fleischer, Matt, "*Sullivan & Cromwell v. Cravath*: There Was That 1861 Case . . . ," *The Observer*, April 26, 1999.

Freedland, Fred, History of Holding Company Legislation in New York State: Some Doubts as to the "New Jersey First" Tradition, *Fordham Law Review*, vol. 4, 369, 401 (1955).

Frye, Brian L., The Ballad of Harry James Tompkins, *Akron Law Review*, vol. 52, 355 (2019).

Galanter, Marc, Lawyers in the Mist: The Golden Age of Legal Nostalgia, *Dickinson Law Review*, vol. 122 (2007), pp. 273–74.

Galanter, Marc, and Thomas Palay, *Tournament of Lawyers* (Chicago: University of Chicago, 1991).

Gelderman, Carol, and Louis Auchincloss, *A Writer's Life* (New York: Random House, 1993).

Gordon, Cunyon, Painting by Numbers "And, Um, Let's Have a Black Lawyer Sit At Our Table," *Fordham Law Review*, vol. 71, issue 4 (2003), p. 1257.

Gordon, Gordon W., Money! Power! Ambition! *Legal Affairs*, March/April 2006.

Gorman, Elizabeth H., and Fiona M. Kay, Racial and Ethnic Minority Representation in Large U.S. Law Firms in *Law Firms, Legal Culture, and Legal Practice,* Austin Sarat, ed. (Bingley, UK: Emerald Group Publishing Ltd., 2010).

Gould, Milton S., Looking Back on the New York Bar, *Litigation*, vol. 14, no. 1, Examining Witnesses (Fall 1987), pp. 43–44, 60–61.

Gould-Adams, Richard *John Foster Dulles: A Reappraisal* (New York: Appleton-Century-Crofts, 1962).

Grose, Peter, *Gentleman Spy* (Boston: Houghton Mifflin, 1994).

Halberstam, David, The New Establishment: The Decline and Fall of the Eastern Empire, *Vanity Fair*, April 4, 2011.

Harbaugh, William H., *The Life of John W. Davis* (Oxford, UK: Oxford University, Press, 1973).

Harbaugh, William H., *Lawyer's Lawyer: The Life of John W. Davis* (Oxford, UK: Oxford University Press, 1973).

Hazard, Geoffrey C. Jr., and Angelo Dondi, *Legal Ethics: A Comparative Study* (Stanford, CA: Stanford University Press, 2004), p. 158.

Hearings Before the Senate Committee on Banking & Currency on S. Res 84 and S. Res. 56, United States Senate, 73rd Cong., 1st Sess., Part 1, p. 25 (May 23, 1933).

Helferich, Gerard, *An Unlikely Trust: Teddy Roosevelt. J. P. Morgan, and the Improbable Partnership that Remade American Business* (Lanham, MD: Rowman & Littlefield, 2015).

Hersh, Burton, *The Old Boys: The American Elite and the Origins of the CIA* (Online: Tree Farm Books, 1992).

Hershey, Amos S., German Reparations, *The American Journal of International Law*, vol. 15, no 3 (July 1921), p. 412.

Hiltzik, Michael, *The New Deal* (New York: The Free Press, 2011).

Hobson, Wayne K, *The American Legal Profession and the Organizational Society, 1900–1930* (New York: Garland Publishing, 1986).

Hoffman, Jan, Oldest Law Firm Is Courtly, Loyal and Defunct, *New York Times,* October 2, 1994, p. 33.

Holland, Max, Review of Citizen McCloy, *The Wilson Quarterly* (1976), vol. 15, no. 4 (Autumn, 1991), pp. 22–42.

Hoopes, Townsend, *The Devil and John Foster Dulles* (New York: Atlantic-Little Brown, 1973),

Hubbell's Legal Directory for Lawyers & Business Men (New York, 1883).

Hoopes, Townsend, God and John Foster Dulles, *Foreign Policy*, no. 13 (Winter 1973–74), p. 162.

Hupper, John, and Bruce Bromley, *Historical Society of the New York Courts, New York Legal History/Legal Luminaries* (1980).

I.F. Stone Weekly, April 22, 1957.

Immerman, Richard H., *John Foster Dulles* (Wilmington, DE: Scholarly Resources, Inc., 1999).

Indianapolis Star, Shows Cruelty of Bolsheviki; Newspaper Correspondent Imprisoned and Suffers Tortures with Thousands of Others, November 24, 1918, p. 24.

Irons, Peter, The New Deal Lawyers (Princeton, NJ: Princeton University Press, 1993).

Isaacson, Walter, and Evan Thomas, *The Wise Men* (New York: Simon & Schuster, 1997).

James, Harold, The Causes of the German Banking Crisis of 1931, *The Economic History Review*, vol. 37, no. 1 (February 1984), p. 69.

Jones, Kenneth Paul, Discord and Collaboration: Choosing an Agent General for Reparations, *Diplomatic History*, vol. 1, no. 2 (Spring 1977), pp. 118–39.

Jonnes, Jill, *Empires of Light* (New York: Random House, 2003).

Kennan, George F., *The Decision to Intervene* (Princeton, NJ: Princeton University Press, 1958).

Kennan, George F., *Memoirs 1925–1963* (New York: Pantheon Books, 1972).

Kennedy, David M., What the New Deal Did, *Political Science Quarterly*, vol. 124, no. 2 (Summer 2009), pp. 261–62.

Kindelberger, Charles, *The World in Depression* (Berkeley: University of California Press, 1986).

Kinzer, Stephen, *The Brothers* (New York: St. Martin's-Griffin, 2013).

Klein, Maury, *Union Pacific: 1894–1969* (Minneapolis: University of Minnesota Press, 2006).

Koegel, Otto E., *Walter S. Carter* (New York: Round Table Press, 1953).

Kramer, Victor A., The Trial of the Investment Banking *Case, Litigation,* vol. 14, no. 4 (Summer 1985), pp. 43–46, 59–60.

Lambert, *The Power Brokers* (Cambridge, MA: MIT Press, 2015).

Lebor, Adam, Tower of Basel: The Shadowy History of the Bank that Rules the World (New York: Hachette, 2013).

Leffingwell, Russell C., Prices, Wages and Inflation, *Proceedings of the Academy of Political Science,* vol. 23, no. 1 (May 1948), pp. 65–68.

Levy, Beryl H., Corporation Lawyer—Saint or Sinner? The New Role of the Lawyer in Modern Society, *Chilton* 1961.

Linke, Daniel J., Hamilton Fish Armstrong: The Diplomatic Editor and Anti-Nazism in the 1930s, *The Princeton University Library Chronicle*, vol. 61, no. 2 (Winter 2000), pp. 145–69.

Liptak, Adam, Thomas Barr, Top Lawyer in I. B. M. Case Dies at 77, *New York Times,* January 30, 2008.

Lisagor, Nancy, and Frank Lipsius, *A Law Unto Itself: The Untold Story of the Law Firm Sullivan and Cromwell* (St. Paul, MN: Paragon House, 1988).

Lockhart, R. H. Bruce, *Memoirs of a British Agent* (Chicago: Frontline Books, 1932).

Lundberg, Ferdinand, The Law Factories, *Harpers Magazine* (July 1939).

MacFarquhar, Larissa, East Side Story, *The New Yorker,* February 25, 2008.

Mackaye, Milton, Public Man, *New Yorker*, January 2, 1932, p. 23.

Margolick, David, The Law; At the Bar, *New York Times,* May 20, 1988.

Martin, George, *CCB: The Life and Century of Charles C. Burlingham, New York's First Citizen, 1858–1969* (New York: Hill & Wang, 2005).

McCraw, Thomas K., *Prophets of Regulation* (Cambridge, MA: Belknap Press, 1984).

McCraw, Thomas K., *American Business 1920–2000: How It Worked* (Wheeling, IL: Harlan-Davidson, Inc., 2000).

McCullough, David, *The Path Between the Seas* (New York: Simon & Schuster, 1977).

McFarquhar, Larissa, East Side Story, *The New Yorker,* February 12, 2008.

McGuire, Patrick, Money and Power; Financiers and the Electric Manufacturing Industry, 1876–1896, *Social Science Quarterly*, vol. 71, no. 3 (September 1990), pp. 510–30.

McKenzie, Troy A., Bankruptcy and the Future of Aggregate Litigation: The Past as Prologue, *Washington University Law Review* (2013), vol. 90.

McNichol, Tom, *AC/DC: The Savage Tale of the First Standards War* (San Francisco: Jossey Bass, 2006).

Means, Gardiner, Review of The Investor Pays, *New York Times*, June 25, 1933.

Mehrotra, Ajay K., Lawyers, Guns and Public Monies: the U.S. Treasury, World War I and the Administration of the Modern State, *Law and History Review*, vol. 28, no. 1 (February 2010), pp. 173–225.

Menton, Francis, Is Lack of "Diversity" at Big Law Firms a Crisis, *Manhattan Contrarian,* June 5, 2014.

Merry, Robert W., America's First Elites, *The American Conservative*, November 25, 2018.

Meyer, Balthasar Henry, *A History of the* Northern Securities *Case* (Madison, WI: 1906).

Moody, John, *The Truth About Trusts: A Description and Analysis of the Trust Movement* (Chicago: Moody Publishing Company, 1904).

Moore, Graham, *The Last Days of Night* (New York: Random House (2016).

Mosley, Leonard, *A Biography of Eleanor, Allen and John Foster Dulles and Their Family Network* (New York: The Dial Press, 1978).

Mosley, Leonard, *Dulles* (New York: The Dial Press, 1978).

National Railway Publication Company, The Official Railway Guide: North American Freight Service Edition (New York, 1889).

Nelson, Anna Kasten, John Foster Dulles and the Bipartisan Congress, *Political Science Quarterly*, vol. 103, no. 1 (Spring 1987), p. 45.

New York Times, November 28, 1893, p. 8.

New York Times, "Amendments to the Pacific Roads Indebtedness Bill Considered," January 17, 1895, p. 15.

New York Times, "Northern Pacific: Two Receivers Resign," January 10, 1896, p. 15.

Noonon, John T., The Lawyer Who Overidentifies with His Client, *Notre Dame Law Review*, vol. 76, April 1, 2001, pp. 834–42.

Obituary Record of the Society of Alumni, Williams College 1919–1920 (Williamstown, MA. April 1920).

Ode to a Scapegoat, *The Wall Street Journal*, October 26, 1999.

Oller, John, *White Shoe* (New York: Dutton, 2019).

Olson, Elizabeth, A Bleak Picture for Women Trying to Rise at Law Firms, *New York Times*, July 24, 2017.

Olson, Elizabeth, Many Black Lawyers Navigate a Rocky, Lonely Road to Partner, *New York Times*, August 12, 2015.

Olsson, Olf, Stockholm's Enskilda Bank and the Bosch Group, 1939–50, *Banking and Enterprise*, no. 1, Stockholm (1998).

Parker, Matthew, *Panama Forever: The Epic Story of the Building of the Panama Canal* (London: Palgrave MacMillan, 2009).

Pawoski, Ronald E., *American Presidential Statecraft: From Isolationism to Internationalism* (London: Palgrave McMillan, (2017).

Perino, Michael, *The Hellhound of Wall Street: How Ferdinand Pecora's Investigation of the Great Crash Forever Changed American Finance* (London: Penguin Press, 2010). H.V. and H.W. Poor, *Manual of the Railroads of the United States*, vol 22, p. 342, 363 (1889).

Preparata, Guido G., *Conjuring Hitler* (London: Pluto Press, 2005).

Progressive Hypocrisy at the Highest Levels: The Cast of Paul Weiss, *Manhattan Contrarian*, December 20, 2018.

Pruessen, Ronald W., *John Foster Dulles, The Road to Power* (New York: The Free Press, 1982).

Pruessen, Ronald W., Woodrow Wilson to John Foster Dulles: A Legacy, *The Princeton University Library Chronicle*, vol. 34, no. 2 (Winter 1973), p. 125.

Pryor, Samuel F. III, *My Interesting Life* (self-published, 2014).

Randazzo, Sara, The Flip Side of Making Partner, *The Wall Street Journal*, August 10, 2019, p. B1.

Rasmussen, Robert K., and Douglas Baird, Boyd's Legacy and Blackstone's Ghost, *Vanderbilt University Law School Joe C. Davis Working Paper Series*, Working Paper Number 99–8, December 15, 1999, pp. 22–23, 24, 32.

Rice, Raymond, and Albert J. Harno, Shares with No Par Value, *Minnesota Law Review* 2149 (1921).

Rice, W. G., and F. L. Stetson, Was New York's Vote Stolen? *North American Review* vol. 79, no. 84 (January 1914).

Roberts, Priscilla, The Anglo-American Theme: American Visions of an Atlantic Alliance, *Diplomatic History*, vol. 21, no. 3 (Summer 1997), p. 356.

Roberts, Priscilla, and Paul D. Cravath, The First World War and the Anglophile Internationalist Tradition, *Australian Journal of Politics and History*, vol. 5 (June 2005).

Rostow, Eugene V., Bituminous Coal and the Public Interest, *Yale Law Journal,* vol. 50, no. 4 (February 1941), p. 561.

Russell, Charles Howland, *Charles Howland Russell 1851–1921* (New York, 1935).

Rudgers, David F., The Origins of Covert Action, *Journal of Contemporary History*, vol. 35, no. 2 (April 2000), p. 259.

Safire, William, On Language: Gimme the Ol' White Shoe, *New York Times*, November 9, 1997, Section 6, p. 28.

Satterlee, Herbert L., *J. Pierpont Morgan: An Intimate Portrait 1837–1913* (New York: MacMillan & Co., 1939).

Schlesinger, Arthur M. Jr., *The Crisis of the Old Order* (Boston: Houghton-Mifflin, 2002).

Schlesinger, Arthur M. Jr., *The Politics of Upheaval* (Boston: Houghton Mifflin Co., 1960).

Schuker, Stephen A., Review of Selected Letters of R. C. Leffingwell by R. C. Leffingwell and Edward Pulling, *The Business and History Review*, vol. 54, no. 2 (summer 1980), pp. 260–62.

Securities and Exchange Commission, Report on the Study and Investigation of the Work, Activities, Personnel and Functions of Protective and Reorganization Committees, Part I-VIII (1937–1940) (written under the direction of William 0. Douglas).

Shamir, Ronen, *Managing Legal Uncertainty* (Durham, NC: Duke University Press, 1995).

Shaw, Albert, ed., *The American Review of Reviews*, vol. 43, p. 162 (1911). New York.

Simmons, Beth A., Why Innovate? Funding the Bank for International Settlements, *World Politics*, vol. 45, no. 3 (April 1993), p. 359.

Simpson, Christopher, *Splendid Blond Beast* (London: Grove Press, 1993).

Skeel, David A. Jr., *Debt's Dominion* (Princeton, NJ Princeton University Press, 2001), p.

Skeel, David A. Jr., Competing Narratives in Corporate Bankruptcy. *Michigan State Law Review* (2009), pp. 1190–93.

Smith, Gaddis, Reconsideration of the Cold War: Shadow of John Foster Dulles, *Foreign Affairs*, January 1974.

Srodes, James, *Allen Dulles Master of Spies* (Washington, DC: Regnery Publishing, 1999).

Steiner, Zara, *The Lights That Failed* (Oxford, UK: Oxford University Press, 2005).

Stern, Robert L., The Commerce Clause and the National Economy, 1933–1946, *Harvard Law Review*, vol. 59, no. 5 (May 1946), pp. 653–54.

Stewart, James, *The Partners* (New York: Warner Books, 1984).

Stewart, James B., A Law Firm Where Money Seemed Secondary, *New York Times,* September 24, 2012.

Stetson, F. L., Samuel J. Tilden, The Great Democrat, p. 7. Address delivered to the Tilden Centennial Committee, February 10, 1914.

Stetson, F. L., Some Legal Phases of Corporate Financing, Reorganization, and Regulation (New York: The MacMillan Co., 1917).

Strong, Theron George, *Landmarks of a Lawyer's Lifetime* (New York: Dodd, Mead, 1914).

Strouse, Jean, *Morgan: American Financier* (New York: Harper Perennial, (2000).

Sutton, Antony C., *Wall Street and the Rise of Hitler* (San Pedro, CA: GSG & Associates, 2002).

Swaine, Robert T., Corporate Reorganization—An Amendment to the Bankruptcy Act—A Symposium, *Virginia Law Review*, vol. 19, 317 (1933).

Swaine, Robert T., Reorganization of Corporations: Certain Developments of the Last Decade, *Columbia Law Review*, vol. 27, 901, 912–13 (1927).

Swaine, Robert T., Reorganization—The Next Step: A Reply to Mr. James N. Rosenberg, *Columbia Law Review*, vol. 22, no. 2 (February 1922), p. 131.

Talbot, David, *The Devil's Chessboard* (New York: Harper-Collins, 2015).

Time Magazine, July 8, 1940, p. 58.

Toulouse, Mark G., The Development of a Cold Warrior: John Foster Dulles and the Soviet Union, 1945–1952, *American Presbyterian*, vol. 63, no. 3 (Fall 1985), p. 309.

The Trow City Directory Company's Directory of New York City (New York, 1889).

Tugwell, Rexford Guy, *Grover Cleveland* (New York: Macmillan, 1968).

United States House of Representatives, The Paper Trust, 58th Congress, 2d Sess., Hearings Before the Committee on the Judiciary (April 5, 1904), pp. 65-68.

Usselman, Steven W., From Novelty to Utility: George Westinghouse and the Business of Innovation During the Age of Edison, *The Business History Review*, vol. 66, no. 2 (Summer 1993), pp. 251–304.

Wald, Eli, The Rise and Fall of the WASP and Jewish Law Firms, *Stanford Law Review*, vol. 60 (2008).

Wald, Eli, The Changing Professional Landscape of Large Law Firms, Glass Ceilings and Dead Ends: Professional Ideologies, Gender Stereotypes, and the Future of Women Lawyers at Large Firms, *Fordham Law Review*, vol. 78, issue 5 (2010), pp. 2272–73.

Walsh, Lawrence E., *The Gift of Insecurity: A Lawyer's Life* (Washington, DC: American Bar Association, 2003).

Wardwell, Allen, Memorial of Francis Lynde Stetson, *New York County Lawyers' Association, Year Book 1921* (New York: J. Little & Ives Company, 1921), p. 226.

Weisberger, Bernard A., The Strange Affair of the Taking of the Panama Canal Zone, *American Heritage*, vol. 27, issue 6, October 1976.

Wertz, William F. Jr., The Plot Against FDR: A Model for Bush's Pinochet Plan Today, *EIR History*, vol. 32, no. 3 (January 21, 2005), pp. 21–22.

Whitney, William D., The Investment Bankers' Case Including a Reply to Professor Steffen, *Yale Law Journal*, vol. 64, issue 3, pp. 319–44.

Wildman, Edwin, Romance of Success, William Nelson Cromwell, the Man Behind the Panama Canal, *The Omaha Sunday Bee*, December 13, 1908.

Wilkins, David B., From "Separate Is Inherently Unequal" to Diversity Is Good for Business: The Rise of Market-Based Diversity Arguments and the Fate of the Black Corporate Bar, *Harvard Law Review*, vol. 117, no. 5 (March 2004), pp. 1548–1615.

William Nelson Cromwell to Henry Villard, November 15, 1885, Henry Villard Papers, Box 23, Folder 198, Harvard Business School, Baker Library Historical Collections.

Wilmarth, Arthur E. Jr., Prelude to Glass-Steagall: Abusive Securities Practices by National City Bank and Chase National Bank in the Roaring Twenties, *Tulane Law Review*, vol. 90 (2016), pp. 1285, 1306–19.

Winks, Robin, The Wise Man of Intelligence: Uncovering the Life of Allen Dulles, *Foreign Affairs*, vol. 73, no. 6 (November-December, 1994), p. 147.

Wright, Charles Alan, Review of A Brief History of the Reorganization of the New York, New Haven & Hartford Railroad Company, *Yale Law Journal*, vol. 59, 1192 (1950).
Yeadon, Glen, *The Nazi Hydra in America* (York, PA: Progressive, 2008).
Yeadon, Glen, and John Hawkins, *The Nazi Hydra in America* (West Bengal, India: Progressive, 2008).

Index